# LAUBACH WAY TO
# ENGLISH

**TEACHER'S MANUAL**

**FOR SKILL BOOK** **1**

**LAUBACH WAY TO READING**

Jeanette D. Macero
Martha A. Lane

New Readers Press
Publishing Division of
Laubach Literacy International

Materials needed for this level of the Laubach Way to English series:

For the teacher

- Laubach Way to English: *ESL Teacher's Manual for Skill Book 1*

- Laubach Way to English: *ESL Illustrations for Skill Book 1*

For the student

- Laubach Way to Reading: *Skill Book 1 Sounds and Names of Letters*

- Laubach Way to Reading: *In the Valley*

- Laubach Way to Reading: *Checkups for Skill Book 1*

EACH ONE TEACH ONE

ISBN 0-88336-391-7

© 1976, revised 1981, 1991

New Readers Press
Publishing Division of
Laubach Literacy International
Box 131, Syracuse, New York 13210

Printed in the United States of America

Designed by Caris Lester, Kay Koschnick, Jeanne Oates

20   19   18   17   16   15   14   13   12   11
10    9    8    7    6    5    4    3

# Table of Contents

# Acknowledgments

The authors wish to acknowledge with gratitude the help of the following persons:

— Volunteer tutors in the National Affiliation for Literacy Advance (NALA), a membership organization of Laubach Literacy International. Their pioneering efforts in ESOL-literacy tutoring led to the development of *The Laubach Way to English* and their experience has contributed to its content.

— Riorita Ceniza, an educational technologist, who provided a content analysis of the original manuscript and behavioral objectives for an ESOL program.

— Muriel Pierson, Jan Rose Sabey, tutors in California and Illinois, especially those at Lake View Presbyterian Church in Chicago, and countless students. Their encouragement and patient testing of ideas made this series of manuals possible.

— Daniel, Diana, and Peter Macero for their unfailing support and encouragement.

— The staff of New Readers Press and Laubach Literacy for their cooperation, especially Dr. Robert S. Laubach, Caroline Blakely, Priscilla Gipson, and the editor, Kay Koschnick, for her painstaking efforts, patience, and advice at every stage of the work.

# About the Authors

## Jeanette D. Macero

Jeanette D. Macero, associate professor of English at Syracuse University, has been involved with teaching ESOL at all levels for 20 years. She began her work at the English Language Institute at the University of Michigan, studying and working with Charles Fries and Robert Lado.

Mrs. Macero has organized and administered programs in ESOL, citizenship, and basic education for schools and community groups and has been consultant to several adult education departments in both universities and public school systems. She has trained ESOL teachers for the Peace Corps and has taught ESOL methodology to many native-speaking and non-native-speaking teachers. In addition, she was linguistic consultant and quiz writer for the easy English newspaper *News for You* at its inception.

Mrs. Macero is on the executive board of the New York State ESOL-Bilingual Educators Association and is a review editor for its publication *Idiom*. She is on the advisory panel of the National Affiliation for Literacy Advance (NALA) and is a member of Teachers of English to Speakers of Other Languages (TESOL), the National Association for Foreign Student Affairs (NAFSA), and the American Council on the Teaching of Foreign Languages (ACTFL).

## Martha A. Lane

Martha A. Lane, as coordinator of Volunteer Reading Aides for Lutheran Church Women, helps communities to organize adult literacy and ESOL-literacy tutoring programs, in cooperation with other denominations and organizations, and conducts training workshops for tutors and tutor trainers.

Miss Lane has been tutoring students and training other tutors since 1968. She is certified as a Master Tutor Trainer by the National Affiliation for Literacy Advance (NALA) and serves on that organization's TESL committee.

She has a master's degree in magazine journalism from Northwestern University and was associate editor of *Together* magazine for six years. She is the author of *A Teacher's Guide to Teaching English as a Second Language with the New Streamlined English Series*, the predecessor to *The Laubach Way to English.*

Miss Lane is a member of Teachers of English to Speakers of Other Languages (TESOL), the National Association for Public Continuing and Adult Education (NAPCAE), the National School Volunteer Program, and the International Reading Association.

# Introduction: What Is the 'Laubach Way to English'?

The Laubach Way to English is a series of manuals especially designed for teaching English to speakers of other languages (ESOL), particularly to functionally illiterate adults. These teacher's manuals provide a comprehensive beginning English program in listening, speaking, reading, and writing skills.

Each teacher's manual is correlated to a skill book in the Laubach Way to Reading series. The skill book is the student's text-workbook in reading and writing.

## The Laubach Way to Reading series

The Laubach Way to Reading series is a systematic program of teaching more than 260 carefully articulated, sequential, reading and writing skills, beginning at the zero level of literacy. The learner progresses from the sounds and regular spellings of the basic consonants to those of the short vowels, the long vowels, and finally to irregular spellings and more difficult reading and writing skills.

> **The Laubach Way to Reading series**
>
> Skill Book 1: Sounds and Names of Letters
> Skill Book 2: Short Vowel Sounds
> Skill Book 3: Long Vowel Sounds
> Skill Book 4: Other Vowel Sounds
> and Consonant Spellings

## The "Laubach method"

The Laubach Way to Reading is a revision of the New Streamlined English series, which grew out of the work of the late Dr. Frank C. Laubach. Dr. Laubach spent more than 40 years of pioneering work in literacy education in 103 countries.

The "Laubach method" he developed starts with the known—the spoken word—and moves to the unknown—the written word—in easy steps that elicit the correct response from the student and reinforce it immediately. The emphasis is on learning by association rather than by rote memory. In the first five skill book lessons, sound-symbol relationships are taught with key words and pictures superimposed with letters. These pictorial memory association cues are phased out as the student attains independence in word attack skills. Lessons stress reading for meaning from the very beginning. Writing skills—beginning with the formation of letters—reinforce reading skills.

## Meeting the needs of ESOL students

The skill books were originally written for adult native speakers of English with no reading skill. For many years, however, large numbers of volunteer tutors affiliated with Laubach Literacy International have been asked to teach ESOL students as well.

To improve its services to ESOL students, particularly the functionally illiterate, Laubach Literacy commissioned this series of manuals, the Laubach Way to English, to provide a comprehensive ESOL program.

Developing these manuals involved adapting the methods of teaching the reading and writing lessons to the easy wording a beginning ESOL student could understand. It also involved adding methods of teaching conversation skills.

Laubach Literacy selected as authors for the *ESOL Teacher's Manual for Skill Book 1* Martha A. Lane and Jeanette D. Macero. Together, they brought to the project both grass-roots experience with ESOL-literacy tutoring and expertise in teaching ESOL methodology.

## The Laubach Way to English: A comprehensive ESOL program

The teacher's manual these authors developed provides comprehensive instructions for teaching listening, speaking, reading, and writing skills. Practice in the listening-and-speaking conversation skills includes dialogs, vocabulary, structures, pronunciation, and intonation. These skills are sequenced systematically so that the student has thorough aural-oral practice with vocabulary and structures before meeting them in the reading. Additional vocabulary and structures, not found in the reading, are provided for their usefulness in everyday life.

This manual begins with six introductory units in conversation skills that prepare the student for entry into *Skill Book 1.*

*ESOL Illustrations for Skill Book 1*, a teacher's picture book, must be used in conjunction with this manual. The pictures can be used to show the student the meaning of new vocabulary in the introductory units and in the conversation skills section of the lessons that follow.

In addition to conversation skills, the manual provides instructions for teaching the skill book lessons in reading and writing, as well as additional practice in word attack skills.

Throughout the lessons, the teacher's demonstrations and verbal instructions to the student are in a simple form for easy comprehension by the ESOL student.

Although designed specifically for teaching adults who are illiterate in their native language as well as in English, the Laubach Way to English can be used successfully with many other ESOL students. In particular, literate students whose native languages have writing systems other than the Roman alphabet should find the practice in basic reading and writing skills beneficial.

## Each One Teach One, and classrooms too

Among other things, the "Laubach method" has traditionally meant "Each One Teach One," a volunteer tutor and a student, teaching and learning in an atmosphere of caring and compassion.

Accordingly, the methods described in the Laubach Way to English apply to a one-to-one teaching situation, but suggestions are offered for adapting the methods for classroom use, where necessary. Thus, the series is useful for ESOL-ABE classes in public schools as well as for tutoring programs.

## For volunteer tutors and beginning teachers

The detailed step-by-step-instructions in the Laubach Way to English make it possible for both volunteer tutors and beginning ESOL teachers to use the manuals with ease and confidence.

**Notes on typography and style:**

● Slash marks around a letter or letters indicate the sound for which they stand. Thus, you say /g/ like the beginning consonant sound in *girl,* and /j/ like the beginning consonant sound in *jumping.*

Letters in italics are read by their letter names, as: *a, b, c.*

● Although the authors recognize that there are teachers and students of both sexes, they have chosen, for the sake of clarity, to use the pronoun *she* to refer to the teacher and *he,* to the student.

Conversation skills practices and their corresponding illustrations show both sexes in a variety of roles and activities.

# Introductory Units: General Procedures

The first units are very important ones. In them, you begin to establish rapport with the student and, at the same time, introduce him to the procedures and techniques your learning sessions will follow.

These introductory units are designed to be used before *Skill Book 1* itself is introduced. It is advisable, however, to bring the skill book to the lesson to make sure the student understands that he will be using it.

Do not omit any parts of these introductory units. If they are easy for your student, go through them quickly. On the other hand, for the beginner, repetition and practice are essential.

The instructions presented in this teacher's manual are very important. Even if you have had experience in teaching English as a second language with The New Streamlined English Series, it is a good idea to review the steps for each lesson before you meet with your student. The material is arranged in increasing order of difficulty for your student—from imitation to practice to production without assistance. Therefore, do not skip any of the steps or rearrange them.

The material in the lefthand column is for your information. Do not read it to your student or explain it to him. The material in the righthand column is what you are to say and do as you are teaching. Practice your part of the lesson so that you are familiar with your lines and cues. When you know exactly what to say and do, the lesson will proceed at a lively pace and will not falter. Every minute will thus be used in a positive way.

The introductory units are each divided into several parts. Each unit begins with a list of objectives which tell you what the student should be able to do at the completion of that unit. Then there is a simple dialog, which the student will find useful in both the learning situation and his daily life. This is followed by the vocabulary items to be taught and the structural patterns in which the words are to be used. Next, there is pronunciation practice to help the student gain some flexibility in making the sounds of English. This is followed by reading and writing sections, which are kept to a minimum in the introductory units. Last, there is an oral evaluation, or review, of what has been presented.

The ideal situation is for you to speak less than a fourth of the time, thus giving your student ample time for imitation and practice. Although this may be difficult to do in the early lessons, it is a goal you should strive toward. Let the student do the work. Do not be too quick to supply the answer if the student hesitates. Give him the opportunity to think in English. If his response is less than perfect, you say it and have the student repeat after you. Always praise and encourage him, using words like *good, better,* and *fine* often.

In order to achieve a learning situation in which the student is doing most of the talking, you should become familiar with the gestures indicated throughout this manual; use them instead of words whenever possible. To keep the student's interest and attention, maintain eye contact with your student, smile, and be encouraging. Never scold or become impatient or show discouragement. Learning a language is a slow and steady process, not one in which dramatic leaps take place. You and your student will both feel a sense of achievement if the student can learn something new at each session.

You are embarking on a rewarding and challenging adventure. It is our hope that this manual aids you on your way.

# Introductory Unit A

## OBJECTIVES

When a student completes this unit, he should be able to:

1. Greet others and say good-bye.
2. Understand classroom directions—both words and gestures.
3. Identify classroom objects in the frame "This is a _____."
4. Say sentences with *be* plus the subject pronouns *I, you, it*.
5. Do all of the above with acceptable (that is, understandable) pronunciation, rhythm, and intonation.
6. Read and write his name.

## VISUAL AIDS

1. Prepare a nametag for yourself and one for your student(s).
2. Accompanying *ESOL Illustrations for Skill Book 1*, pp. 2-5.
3. A picture is only a good substitute for the object itself. If at all possible, have the following in the classroom:

| | | |
|---|---|---|
| pen | book | desk |
| pencil | table | chair |

## DIALOG

> Teacher: Hello. How are you?
> Student: Fine, thank you. How are you?
>
> Teacher: Fine, thanks.
>   My name's Mrs. _____.
>   What's your name?
> Student: My name's Bob Samson.

### Instructions to the teacher

1. Teacher models entire dialog—both the role of the Teacher and the role of the Student—two or three times while the student listens.

   Notice that you do not say the words *Teacher* and *Student* when modeling the dialog.

   To indicate change of roles, shift your weight from one foot to the other and turn your body slightly.

   Use your own name and the title you prefer, if any, where the teacher says her name in the dialog.

   **Class:** Use the name Bob Samson for choral repetition.

   **One-to-one:** Use your student's name instead of Bob Samson.

2. Teacher models one line of the dialog and asks the student to repeat.

   **Class:** In a class situation, first have the class repeat in unison. Then divide the class into groups and have each group repeat. With unison work of this kind, have the members of the class begin each line of the dialog exactly at the same moment, or there will be utter confusion.

### Script for teaching

[Put up your hand as in a Stop gesture to indicate that you want the student to listen, not repeat, at this time. Say "Listen."]

Hello. How are you?
Fine, thank you. How are you?
Fine, thanks.
My name's Mrs. _____.
What's your name?
My name's Bob Samson.

[Say "Repeat" and use a Beckoning gesture to indicate that you want the student to say each line after you.]

Teacher: Hello. How are you?
Student: Hello. How are you?

Teacher: Hello. How are you?
Student: Hello. How are you?

Teacher: [Praise student. Say "Good."]

Continue with each line of the dialog.

Teacher: Fine, thank you.
How are you?
Student: Fine, thank you.
How are you?

Teacher: Fine, thank you.
How are you?
Student: Fine, thank you.
How are you?

Teacher: Fine, thanks.
Student: Fine, thanks.

Teacher: Fine, thanks.
Student: Fine, thanks.

[Point to yourself.]
Teacher: My name's Mrs. _____.
What's your name?
Student: My name's Mrs. _____.
What's your name?

Teacher: My name's Mrs. _____.
What's your name?
Student: My name's Mrs. _____.
What's your name?

[Now indicate your student. Use his name.]
Teacher: My name's _____.
Student: My name's _____.

Teacher: My name's _____.
Student: My name's _____.

**Note:** If you are working with just one student and you feel uncomfortable about asking him to say your name, substitute his name here. Then, use your own name in the last part without asking the student to repeat.

**One-to-one:**

3. Teacher and student each take their own roles in the dialog.

4. Teacher and student reverse roles of the dialog.

**Class:**

3. In a class situation have the members of the class say the dialog in unison, then in pairs.

In larger classes, divide the class in half, with each half taking different roles of the dialog.

Then divide the class in quarters, ending with one-to-one practice.

At this stage, have each student use his own name. Keep the pace brisk.

[Say the first line of the dialog. If the student begins to repeat after you, use the Stop gesture to indicate that you want him to listen. If the student cannot give you the second line of the dialog, prompt him. Gesture and say "Listen" and then "Repeat."]

**Note:** If you have reason to believe that the whole dialog would be too much for your student, do only the last three lines at this time. (These lines may be easier because the student will recognize his name.) Do the first part of the dialog in Unit B.

## VOCABULARY: Classroom Objects

> This is a book.
>    pen.
>    pencil.
>    table.
>    desk.
>    chair.

1. Teacher picks up a book and models, "This is a book," saying it several times.

[Say "Listen" and use Stop gesture.]

2. Teacher models the sentence and asks student to repeat.

Teacher: This is a book.
Student: This is a book.

Teacher: This is a book.
Student: This is a book.

[Hold up the book and beckon to the student to say the sentence without your saying it again. Say "Good" if he does. If he cannot, continue repeating it and having him imitate you.]

3. Teacher holds up the book and asks, "What's this?"

Teacher: What's this? (This is a book.)
Student: This is a book.

**Note:** Use these three steps to teach the rest of the objects.

The question "What's this?" is used only for recognition at this point. Any time you use a new question form for recognition, you should model the response if the student cannot give the answer fairly quickly.

4. Teacher holds up a pen and says, "This is a pen," repeating it several times.

[Say "Listen" and use Stop gesture.]

5. Repeat steps 2 and 3 above with the new object.

Teacher: This is a pen.
Student: This is a pen.

Teacher: This is a pen.
Student: This is a pen.

Teacher: What's this?
Student: This is a pen.

6. Using steps 1-3, the teacher introduces *pencil, table, desk, chair.*

Before introducing each new object, review the previous objects by asking "What's this?"

**Class:** In a class situation, the teacher follows the above procedure, going from choral recitation to smaller groups to individual practice.

## VOCABULARY: Student/Teacher

> I'm a student.
> You're a teacher.

**Note:** Although these sentences that you are saying
are not true for you, the teacher, they are true sentences
for the student to practice and learn.

1. Teacher points to student and models,
   "I'm a student," several times.

   [Say "Listen" and point to the student.]

   Teacher: I'm a student.
            I'm a student.

2. Teacher models the sentence once and asks the
   student to repeat.

   [Say "Repeat" and use a Beckoning gesture.]

   Teacher: I'm a student.
   Student: I'm a student.

   Teacher: I'm a student.
   Student: I'm a student.

3. Teacher points to student and elicits the sentence
   from the student.

   [Gesture to student and beckon him to speak.
   Prompt him the first time if needed.]

   Student: I'm a student.

   [Say "Good" and gesture for more.]

   Student: I'm a student.

4. Teacher indicates herself and says,
   "You're a teacher," repeating it several times.

   [Say "Listen" and gesture to indicate the student.]

   Teacher: You're a teacher.
            You're a teacher.

5. Follow steps 2, 3, and 4 above.

6. Teacher reviews the two sentences. If you feel that
   your student is having difficulty understanding the
   meaning of these sentences, perhaps a picture of a
   student and teacher in a classroom would be helpful.
   Use the picture at the top of p. 5 in *ESOL Illustrations*.

   [Using gestures, say the two sentences. Then use the gestures
   alone, eliciting the sentences from the student.]

# DRILL: Substitution Drill with Vocal Cues

1. Teacher gives both the cue and the student response at first.

   **Note:** The first Substitution Drill must be done carefully and completely. Teacher should do both parts of the drill, being sure that the student does not repeat the cues. As the student begins to understand this type of drill, the teacher will give only one or two model sentences and then simply the cues. Substitution drills are useful both for practice and for checking up on how well the student has learned the vocabulary and structure being taught.

[Use gestures to indicate when the student is to listen and when he is to speak. Do not allow long pauses. If the student cannot produce the sentence, you say it and have him repeat it after you.]

| Teacher | Student |
|---|---|
| This is a pen. | |
| This is a pen. | |
| [Gesture to student to repeat.] | This is a pen. |
| pencil | |
| This is a pencil. | This is a pencil. |

[Shake your head if the student repeats the cue (pencil), as he probably will.]

| | |
|---|---|
| table | |
| This is a table. | This is a table. |
| chair | This is a chair. |
| student | This is a student. |
| book | This is a book. |
| pencil | This is a pencil. |
| pen | This is a pen. |

2. Repeat the substitution drill, giving the model sentence and the cues.

[Gesture for the student to repeat.
Use a Stop gesture if the student repeats the cues.]

| Teacher | Student |
|---|---|
| This is a pen. | This is a pen. |
| pencil | This is a pencil. |
| book | |
| chair | |
| table | |
| teacher | |
| student | |
| pen | |

# DRILL: Substitution Drill with Visual Cues

Teacher holds up or indicates the object and gives the expected student response until the student can do so unassisted.

[Hold up a pen. Say "Listen" and "Repeat."]

Teacher: This is a pen.
Student: This is a pen.

[Hold up a pen, and gesture for the student to speak. If the student cannot produce the sentence, you say it and have him repeat it.]

| Teacher indicates: | Student says: |
|---|---|
| book | This is a book. |
| table | This is a table. |
| desk | This is a desk. |
| chair | This is a chair. |
| teacher | This is a teacher. |
| student | This is a student. |

**STRUCTURE FOCUS:** Contractions of *be* with *I, You, It*

| | |
|---|---|
| I am Bob Samson. | I'm Bob Samson. |
| You are Mrs. _____ . | You're Mrs. _____ . |
| It is a pen. | It's a pen. |

Teacher models first the full form, then the contracted form, of each pair of sentences, having the student repeat each sentence after her. Use your student's name with *I* and your own name with *You*.

To introduce the contracted forms of *be* with the subject pronouns *I, You, It*, practice first the full form, then the contracted forms, which are more common in everyday usage.

Teacher: I am Bob Samson.
Student: I am Bob Samson.

Teacher: I'm Bob Samson.
Student: I'm Bob Samson.

[Continue the same way with the rest of the sentence pairs.]

[Say "Listen to *I am, I'm*." Use the student's name.]

Teacher: I am Bob Samson. I'm Bob Samson.
Student: I am Bob Samson. I'm Bob Samson.

Teacher: I'm Bob Samson.
Student: I'm Bob Samson.

[Say "Listen to *You are, You're*." Use your name.]

Teacher: You are Mrs. _____ . You're Mrs. _____ .
Student: You are Mrs. _____ . You're Mrs. _____ .

Teacher: You're Mrs. _____ .
Student: You're Mrs. _____ .

[Hold up a pen. Say "Listen to *It is, It's*."]

Teacher: It is a pen. It's a pen.
Student: It is a pen. It's a pen.

Teacher: It's a pen.
Student: It's a pen.

## DRILL: Substitution Drill with Vocal Cues

1. Teacher models the sentence and has the student repeat it.

2. Teacher gives the cues. Use contractions.

[Point to yourself as you say, "I'm Mrs._____."
Say "Please repeat." Gesture for the student to speak.]

| Teacher | Student |
|---------|---------|
| I'm Mrs._____. | I'm Mrs. _____. |
| You | You're Mrs. _____. |
| I | I'm Mrs. _____. |
| You | You're Mrs. _____. |

[If the student cannot make the responses, you give the responses and have him imitate you. Then do the drill from the beginning as directed.]

[In the next part of the drill, indicate the objects as you say the word.]

| Teacher | Student |
|---------|---------|
| It's a book. | It's a book. |
| pen | It's a pen. |
| pencil | |
| table | |
| desk | |
| pen | |
| chair | |
| pencil | |
| book | |

[If more practice is necessary because the student speaks haltingly, is slow to respond, or cannot respond, repeat this drill. This time, use *visual* cues, that is, indicate the object, but do not name it unless you have to.]

## PRONUNCIATION: Review

As review and for pronunciation drill, practice all the frames introduced so far (that is, all those items in the boxes). Now, however, the concentration will be focused on pronunciation, rhythm, and intonation.

Review:

1. Dialog of Unit A.
2. What's this? This is a pen.
3. What's this? It's a pen.
4. I'm _____.
5. You're Bob Samson.

[Turn back to the Dialog in this unit. Say the sentences of the dialog, having the student repeat after you.

As the student speaks, ask yourself:

1. Is each word understandable?

2. How well does the student pronounce the vowel sounds?

   a. The student should round his lips when saying the /oo/ in *book.* Does he?

   b. The student should spread his lips when saying the /ā/ in *table.* Does he?

3. The student should use the intonation curve that is ordinarily used for statements of fact. In English, the change of pitch on the last emphasized word is most important.

# READING AND WRITING: Student's Name in Manuscript

**One-to-one:**

Using previously prepared nametags, model the sentences.

[Point to the nametag and use the student's first and last name. Say "Repeat."]

Teacher: I'm_____ _____.
Student: I'm_____ _____.
Teacher: I'm_____ _____.
Student: I'm_____ _____.

[Take out a piece of paper and write the student's name exactly as you want him to do it. Use manuscript writing (printing) with capital and lowercase letters as shown in the Manuscript Charts at the end of this unit.]

[Say "Write your name."]

[If student has difficulty writing his name, practice it with him.]

**Class:**

1. Using the name Bob Samson, model the sentence.

[Write *Bob Samson* on the blackboard. Say "Repeat."]

Teacher: I'm Bob Samson.
Student: I'm Bob Samson.

Teacher: I'm Bob Samson.
Student: I'm Bob Samson.

[Write the name Bob Samson in manuscript on the blackboard. Have the students copy it. Circulate around the room as the students write. Help those having a lot of difficulty.]

2. Pass out individual nametags to each student. Be sure that each name is written in manuscript with capital and small letters.

[Say "Write your name."
Have each student write his name several times, as legibly as possible. Walk around the room, giving help where needed.]

# LEAVE-TAKING

1. Teacher models sentence indicating leave-taking. Use the time expression (tomorrow, next Monday, etc.) which indicates your next class meeting.

[Close your book, stand up, or in some way indicate that it is time to leave. Say "The class is over." The student does not repeat this.]

Teacher: Good-bye. I'll see you tomorrow.
Student: Good-bye. I'll see you tomorrow.

2. At a subsequent meeting, other appropriate expressions of greetings and leave-takings may be taught (e.g., Hi. See you later. So long.) Do not confuse the beginning student with alternate ways of saying things.

[Repeat until the student can say this with ease and in a pronunciation you understand.]

## To the Teacher: Manuscript Writing

Manuscript writing, commonly called printing, is easier for the new writer than cursive writing. It is similar to the printed letters in the student's reading book, so he does not have to learn two sets of letters. It is useful for everyday needs, such as filling out forms, writing addresses, and other writing that must be very legible.

### How to form the letters

As the teacher, you should always write the letters the same way as they are taught in the student's skill book. The manuscript charts on these two pages show you how.

As much as possible with the letter-forms taught in the reading, the letters are written without lifting the pencil until the letter is completed. This enables the student to feel the shape of the letter as a complete unit. The sequence of strokes resembles the sequence in cursive writing so that an easy transition will be possible later on.

The dot-and-arrow figure after each letter shows how to write the letter:

— Start at the dot, and follow the arrow. Do not lift your pencil.

— If there is more than one dot, start at the dot numbered 1 and follow the arrow as far as you can. Then lift your pencil and go to the dot numbered 2, and so on.

A re-trace stroke, such as in the *d*, is shown with lines that stand a little apart so you can see the different directions clearly. When you actually write the letter, of course, you will re-trace one line right on top of the other.

### Ways to help your student

Adults vary a great deal in their ability to write. Those who do fine work with their hands will usually learn to write easily. Others may need more help. You can help your student in these ways:

1. Be sure the student holds his pencil correctly between the thumb and middle finger. The first (index) finger rests lightly on top of the pencil to help guide it. For a right-handed person, the fingers should be about an inch from the pencil point (just above the place where the paint is sharpened away to bare wood). A left-handed person should hold the pencil a little higher and write with the paper slanted to the right.

2. In the beginning, it may help your student to write the letter in the air with an arm-and-shoulder motion. It may also help him to practice straight lines and curves.

3. Don't be overly fussy about making the student write his letters *exactly* like the samples. Minor variations are acceptable if the basic letter shape is clear and unmistakable. It is also all right if the student writes a little larger or smaller than the samples, so long as his tall lowercase letters and capitals are proportionate to his short lowercase letters.

4. Be patient and give a great deal of encouragement and praise.

### Lowercase letters

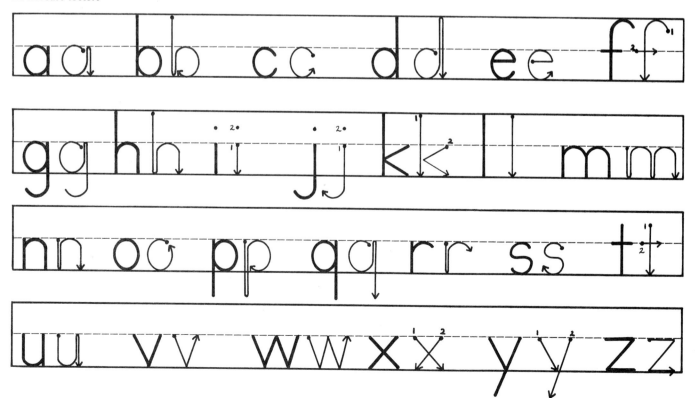

**Capital letters**

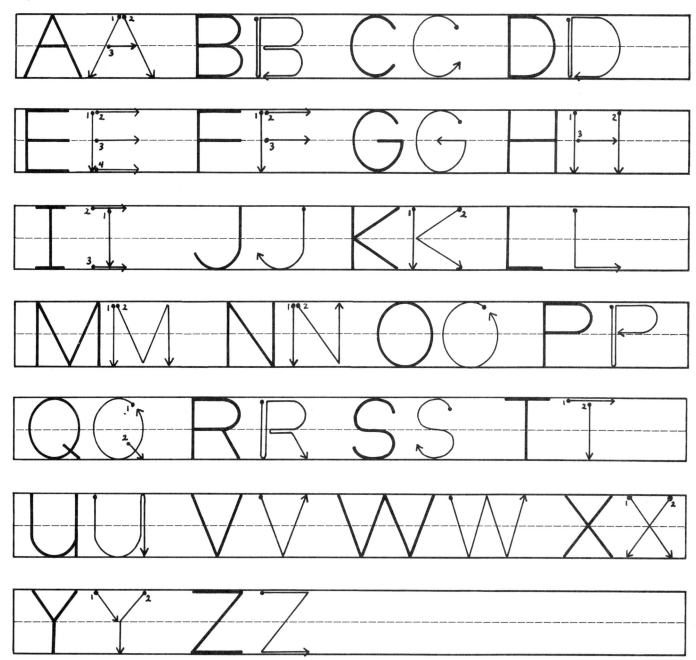

**Numbers**

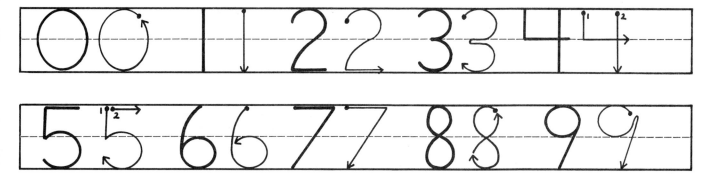

# Introductory Unit B

## OBJECTIVES

When a student completes this unit, he should be able to:

1. Say the dialog and vocabulary in Introductory Unit A.
2. Identify additional classroom objects in the frame, "This is a _____."
3. Identify the colors: white, black, red, yellow, blue, green, and brown.
4. Identify some objects by name and color (e.g., a red book).
5. Say sentences with full and contracted forms of *be* plus the subject pronouns: *he, she, it*.
6. Have some flexibility in pronouncing and discriminating among the various vowel sounds of English.
7. Say the numbers 1-10.
8. Read and write the numbers 1-10.

## VISUAL AIDS

1. Accompanying *ESOL Illustrations for Skill Book 1*, pp. 6, 7, top of 8, and 10.

2. For the colors, use the squares on p. 10 of *ESOL Illustrations*. Color them in ahead of time with red, brown, yellow, black, blue, and green. Leave one square blank for white.

   If you prefer, you may bring sheets of colored construction paper instead.

3. Have on hand some colored objects so the student can identify colors, for example, a white handkerchief or tissue, a black comb, red lipstick, a yellow pencil, a brown chair.

4. Have on hand some lined notebook paper for writing the numbers.

## REVIEW

It is important to spend the opening minutes of each session reviewing the previous work. For intermediate or more advanced students, this may not be necessary to such a great degree.

### Review of Dialog

Model the dialog of Unit A, asking the student to repeat.

Review steps 1-4, which tell how to teach the dialog in Unit A, if you need to.

### Review of Vocabulary

Review the words *book, pen, pencil, table, desk, chair, teacher, student*.

[Hold up a book, ask and answer the question. Use gestures as you say "Listen" and "Repeat."]

Teacher:  Listen. What's this?
         It's a book.

Teacher:  What's this?
         It's a book. Repeat. It's a book.
Student:  It's a book.

[Hold up a pen.]
Teacher:  What's this?
Student:  It's a pen.

[Continue with other vocabulary items.
If the student cannot respond, give vocal cues. Keep the pace lively.]

## VOCABULARY: Common Classroom Words

```
This is a blackboard.
        a clock.
        a boy.
        a girl.
        paper.
```

1. Teacher indicates the blackboard and models "This is a blackboard."

[Indicate the blackboard and say "Listen."]

Teacher: This is a blackboard.
Student: This is a blackboard.

[Gesture for student to answer.]

Teacher: What's this?
Student: This is a blackboard.

2. Continue with other new vocabulary items: *clock, boy, girl, paper.*

Use *ESOL Illustrations*, pp. 6, 7, and top of 8.

## DRILL: Substitution Drill with Vocal Cues

Drill the vocabulary items introduced above. Give the model sentence and then the cues.

[Say "Listen."]

| Teacher | Student |
|---|---|
| This is a boy. | |
| This is a boy. | |

[Say "Repeat."]

| Teacher | Student |
|---|---|
| This is a boy. | This is a boy. |
| clock | This is a clock. |
| blackboard | |
| paper | |
| boy | |
| girl | |
| pen | |
| pencil | |

## DRILL: Substitution Drill with Visual Cues

Teacher models the first question and answer.

Drill the vocabulary items, indicating the actual items or pictures in *ESOL Illustrations*, as visual cues.

[Holding up a book, ask and answer the question. Use gestures to indicate when the student is to listen and when he is to speak.]

| Teacher | Student |
|---|---|
| What's this? | |
| This is a book. | |
| What's this? | This is a book. |
| Indicate: blackboard | This is a blackboard. |
| clock | |
| paper | |
| boy | |
| girl | |

## VOCABULARY: Colors

```
This is red.
        brown.
        yellow.
        black.
        blue.
        green.
        white.
```

**Note:** Use sheets of colored construction paper or the squares on p. 10 of *ESOL Illustrations*, which you have already colored in, to show the colors.

1. Indicating red, model the sentence "This is red."

[Hold up the red construction paper or point to the red square. Say "Listen."]

Teacher: This is red.
           This is red.

[Say "Repeat" and gesture.]

Teacher: This is red.
Student: This is red.

2. Model sentences identifying the colors brown, yellow, black, blue, green, and white.

[Continue as above with the remaining colors.]

## DRILL: Substitution Drill with Vocal Cues

Model the key sentences, then give the cues.

[Indicate red.]

| Teacher | Student |
| --- | --- |
| This is red. | |
| This is red. | |
| [Beckon to student and say "Repeat."] | This is red. |
| [Indicate each color and say its name only.] | |
| black | This is black. |
| yellow | |
| blue | |
| green | |
| brown | |
| white | |
| red | |

## DRILL: Substitution Drill with Visual Cues

Model the key sentences, then do the rest of the practice by simply indicating the various colors. (Hold up a sheet of colored construction paper or point to a colored square on p. 10 of *ESOL Illustrations*.)

[Indicate yellow.]

| Teacher | Student |
|---|---|
| This is yellow. | |
| This is yellow. | |

[Say "Repeat " and gesture.]    This is yellow.

[Continue with the other colors.]

## IDENTIFICATION DRILL

1. Teacher indicates various objects in the room to elicit what colors they are. Do not teach the names of any new objects or colors.

[Point to white tissue and say, "This is white."]

Teacher:  This is white.
          What color is this?
          This is white.

[Point to other colored objects available, e.g. a green book, red lipstick, black comb, white wall.]

Teacher:  What color is this?
          This is red.

[Beckon to student to respond.]

**Further practice:**

2. Model the sentence while the student listens. Use objects that you have readily available but use only colors and objects already taught. The key sentence and cues are only examples.

[Hold up a yellow pencil. Say "Listen."]

Teacher:  This is a yellow pencil.
Teacher:  This is a yellow pencil.

[Gesture to student to repeat.]

| Teacher | Student |
|---|---|
| This is a yellow pencil. | |
| What's this? | This is a yellow pencil. |

[Hold up or indicate the following objects or whatever you have available of items already taught.]

brown chair
green book
white paper
blue pen
brown table
black book

## STRUCTURE FOCUS: Subject Pronouns *He, She, It*

> This is a <u>boy</u>. <u>He</u> is a boy.
>
> This is a <u>girl</u>. <u>She</u> is a girl.
>
> This is a <u>book</u>. <u>It</u> is a book.

Teacher models key sentences illustrating use of the pronouns *he, she, it*.

Use the pictures of a boy and a girl on p. 6 and of a book on p. 2 of *ESOL Illustrations*.

[Use the picture of the boy. Point to the boy as you use the pronoun *he*. Say "Listen."]

Teacher: This is a boy. He is a boy.

[Gesture to student to repeat.]

Teacher: This is a boy. He is a boy.
Student: This is a boy. He is a boy.

[Use the picture of the girl.]

Teacher: This is a girl. She is a girl.

[Gesture to student to repeat.]

Teacher: This is a girl. She is a girl.
Student: This is a girl. She is a girl.

[Using the picture of a book, introduce *it* as above.]

## DRILL: Substitution Drill with Vocal Cues

1. Teacher models the sentence and expected student response at first. Then give only the cues.

[Gesture and say "Listen."]

| Teacher | Student |
| --- | --- |
| This is a boy. | |
| He is a boy. | |
| [Gesture and say "Repeat."] | He is a boy. |
| This is a boy. | |
| He is a boy. | He is a boy. |
| This is a girl. | She is a girl. |
| This is a book. | |
| This is a boy. | |
| This is a girl. | |
| This is a book. | |

## DRILL: Substitution Drill with Visual Cues

1. Teacher models the expected student response once or twice, then shows the picture alone.

[Gesture and say "Listen" while pointing to the picture of a boy.]

| Teacher | Student |
| --- | --- |
| He is a boy. | |
| He is a boy. | He is a boy |
| [Point to the picture of a girl.] | She is a girl. |
| [Point to the picture of a book.] | It is a book. |
| [Repeat these three items.] | |

# STRUCTURE FOCUS: Contractions of *be* with Singular Pronouns

| | |
|---|---|
| I am a girl. | I'm a girl. |
| You are a girl. | You're a girl. |
| It is a book. | It's a book. |
| He is a boy. | He's a boy. |
| She is a girl. | She's a girl. |

Teacher models the sentences and has the student repeat, using the procedures (steps 1 and 2) introduced in Unit A, Structure Focus: Contractions of *be.*

# DRILL: Substitution Drill with Vocal Cues

1. Teacher models the key sentence of the drill and then gives only the cues.

| Teacher | Student |
|---|---|
| I'm a teacher. | |
| I'm a teacher. | I'm a teacher. |
| You | You're a teacher. |
| She | She's a teacher. |
| He | He's a teacher. |
| You | You're a teacher. |
| I | I'm a teacher. |

2. Teacher models the key sentence and then gives only the cues.

| Teacher | Student |
|---|---|
| It's a book. | |
| It's a book. | It's a book. |
| pen | It's a pen. |
| pencil | |
| table | |
| desk | |
| chair | |
| book | |

## PRONUNCIATION: Vowel Sounds

**Note:** As preparation for this pronunciation practice, teach the meaning of *same* and *different*, using concrete objects. Hold up two objects that are exactly the same in size, shape, and color—such as two pencils. Say "Same," and have the student repeat. Then hold up two objects that are very different, such as a pen and a book, say "Different," and have the student repeat. If necessary, continue with two other pairs of same and different objects.

Remember that the student is not learning *same* and *different* thoroughly as vocabulary items at this point. He is merely learning their meanings well enough to use them as responses in the type of pronunciation practice given here.

1. Teacher models the vowel sounds of English, having the student repeat.

   Do not stop to explain the meaning of words. They are not being introduced as vocabulary items, but simply as words which contain the distinctive vowel sounds of English.

   Say first the sound (as, /ē/) and then the word (as, *beat*), repeating both the sound and the word.

   If you are not sure how to make the vowel sound by itself, look at the word first as a help.

[Say "Listen to /ē/, /ē/, /ē/."
Gesture for the student to repeat.]

Teacher: /ē/, /ē/, /ē/
    beat, beat, beat
Student: /ē/, /ē/, /ē/
    beat, beat, beat

[Say "Listen to /i/, /i/, /i/."
Gesture to the student to repeat.]

Teacher: /i/, /i/, /i/
    bit, bit, bit
Student: /i/, /i/, /i/
    bit, bit, bit

[Continue with other words, e.g. /ā/, /ā/, /ā/, mate, mate, mate.]

| mate | cat | boot | sock | buy |
|------|------|------|------|------|
| met | cut | book | suck | bough |
| mat | coat | | | boy |
| | caught | | | |

2. Model the sounds in pairs to see if the student can distinguish between them.

[Say "Listen. Are these the Same or Different?"]

Teacher: beat, beat. [Say "Same."]

Teacher: beat, boot. [Say "Different."]

Teacher: beat, beat. [Say "Same."]

Teacher: boot, beat. [Say "Different."]

3. Continue with other pairs. Say one word of a pair twice to elicit "Same." Say both words of a pair to elicit "Different." Don't stick to the pattern same-different-same-different, or the student may guess without listening. Vary the order.

   **Note:** The student will not fully master the distinction between the vowel sounds at this early stage.

   Move along from one pair to the next as soon as the student has given enough correct answers to indicate that he hears some distinction between the two sounds. Try to end on a correct answer, but if a particular pair is too difficult, go on anyway.

[Continue with *coat/cat*.
Gesture for the student to say "Same" or "Different."]

[Continue with other pairs.]

| mate/met | coat/caught | sock/suck | buy/boy |
|----------|-------------|-----------|---------|
| cat/cut | book/buck | buy/bough | beat/bit |

## READING AND WRITING: Numbers 1-10

1. Teacher models the counting of the numbers 1-10.

[Say "Listen." As you count, hold up the appropriate number of fingers.]

Teacher: 1, 2, 3, 4, 5, 6, 7, 8, 9, 10.

2. Teacher models the numbers, having the student repeat.

[Hold up fingers to show the numbers. Say "Listen," then "Repeat."]

Teacher: 1
Student: 1

[Continue through 10.]

3. After student can say the numbers understandably, teacher sits next to student and writes the numbers 1-10 on lined notebook paper.

   **Note:** Write the numbers exactly as they are taught on p. 25 of this manual. Use the lines on the paper as guidelines. Write the numbers in a vertical column so that there is space for the student to copy each number beside your model several times.

   **Class:** Teacher writes the numbers on the blackboard. As students write the numbers on their own paper, walk around the room giving help where needed.

[As you write each number, both you and student say it. Then have the student copy the number beside your model.]

Teacher: This is 1. What's this?
Student: This is 1.

Teacher: Good. Write 1.
[Student writes 1.]

[Continue with 2-10.]

[When you have written all the numbers, have the student read 1-10 again.]

# ORAL EVALUATION

It is recommended that the teacher have a notebook for recording the student's progress. It is especially necessary to make notes about items that a student is having difficulty with.

1. Using the sentence frame "This is a _____," review the vocabulary items.

   Do not prompt your student until it becomes quite evident that he cannot name the item.

   If your student can identify 10 or more of these items fairly quickly, then you can consider that he has learned them. If he cannot, make a notation in your notebook to review these items at the beginning of your next session.

[Using *ESOL Illustrations*, pp. 2-8, point to the pictures of the items and ask, "What's this?"]

This is a book.
  boy.
  clock.
  blackboard.
  boy.
  girl.
  pen.
  pencil.
  table.
  desk.
  chair.
  student.
  teacher.
This is paper.

2. Using the sentence frame "This is _____," review the colors.

   If your student can name five or more colors fairly quickly, you do not have to review them since they are included in future drills. But make notes of any colors he is unsure of.

[Use *ESOL Illustrations*, p. 10, or sheets of colored construction paper. Indicate the color and say, "What's this? This is red."]

[Continue with the other colors.]

This is white.
  yellow.
  black.
  blue.
  green.
  brown.
  red.

3. Review the pronouns, using the frames:

   This is a boy. He is a _____.
       girl. She is a _____.
       book. It is a _____.

   It is important that your student know all three of these pronouns. If he does not, you must review the Structure Focus: Subject Pronouns and the two Drills following it.

[Point to the picture of the boy and say, "This is a boy. He is a boy."]

[Continue with *girl, book,* and *boy* again, giving only the vocal cue "This is a girl," and so on.]

4. Review contractions of *be.*

   It is important that your student know all these items.

[Do the Drill that follows the Structure Focus: Contractions of *be* with Singular Pronouns.]

5. Have your student count from 1 to 10. If he cannot, make a note in your notebook. Numbers will be reviewed again at the end of Unit C.

# Introductory Unit C

## OBJECTIVES

When a student completes this unit, he should be able to:

1. Say the new dialog (address and telephone number).
2. Identify vocabulary items from Units A and B and the new vocabulary: *window, door, eraser*.
3. Form the plural of nouns already taught.
4. Pronounce the *-s* forms of the plural.
5. Say the numbers 11-20.
6. Read and write the numbers 11-20.
7. Read and write his name, address, and telephone number.

## VISUAL AIDS

1. For new vocabulary, use *ESOL Illustrations for Skill Book 1*, bottom of p. 8 and p. 9; for plural nouns, use pictures illustrating the plural of nouns already taught, pp. 2-9.

2. Prepare a card with the student's name, address, and telephone number written on it. Be sure to use manuscript with capital and small letters. See the section on Manuscript Writing at the end of Unit A.

## REVIEW

Review any items that your student had difficulty with when doing the Oral Evaluation at the end of Unit B.

## DIALOG

> Teacher: What's your address?
> Student: My address is 920 Main Street.
>
> Teacher: What's your telephone number?
> Student: My telephone number is 445-1876.

Teacher models one line of the dialog and asks student to repeat. Continue with each line of the dialog.

Refer to Unit A for detailed instructions on practicing the dialog.

**One-to-one:** Use the student's own address and telephone number.

**Class:** Use a simple local address and typical local phone number.

[Say the street numbers as they are said in everyday speech. For example, for 920, say "nine twenty."]

[For telephone numbers, say each number. Group the numbers in the same way that they are written. For example, for 445-1876, say, "four, four, five," pause, "one, eight, seven, six."]

## VOCABULARY: More Classroom Objects

> This is a window.
>       a door.
>       an eraser.

Teacher models the sentence while the student listens. Then the student repeats.

[Say "Listen" and indicate the window.]

Teacher: This is a window.
         This is a window.

[Gesture for student to repeat after you.]

Teacher: This is a window.
Student: This is a window.

[Continue with *door* and *eraser*.]

## DRILL: Substitution Drill with Visual Cues

Teacher holds up or indicates the object and asks, "What's this?"

| Teacher | Student |
|---|---|
| [Indicate eraser.] | |
| What's this? | |
| This is an eraser. | This is an eraser. |
| [Indicate door.] | |
| What's this? | This is a door. |
| [Indicate window.] | |
| What's this? | This is a window. |
| [Indicate the following and ask, "What's this?"] | |
| blackboard | |
| eraser | |
| pen | |
| desk | |
| clock | |
| door | |
| window | |

## VOCABULARY: Plural Forms of Nouns Taught

| books | pens | tables |
|-------|------|--------|
|       | pencils | chairs |

Using the "plural" pictures on pp. 2-9 of *ESOL Illustrations,* teacher models the plural forms of nouns already introduced.

**Note:** Practicing the words as single items (not in sentences) gives the student the opportunity to hear the singular and plural forms and to practice them before using them in sentences.

[Point to the "book" picture, then to the "books" picture, saying, "Book. Books."]

[Say, "Repeat. Book. Books."
Gesture for the student to repeat after you, giving the singular and plural, as you point to the pictures.]

[Continue the same way with the singular and plural forms of nouns already taught.]

| pen | pens |
|-----|------|
| pencil | pencils |
| table | tables |
| desk | desks |
| chair | chairs |
| student | students |
| teacher | teachers |
| boy | boys |
| girl | girls |
| blackboard | blackboards |
| clock | clocks |
| window | windows |
| door | doors |
| eraser | erasers |

## DRILL: Visual Cues

Indicating the "plural" pictures of objects, the teacher asks the student to give the plural forms.

Use the pictures on pp. 2-9 of *ESOL Illustrations.*

[Point to the "singular" picture and say the singular form. Then point to the "plural" picture and gesture for the student to speak.]

[If the student cannot remember the word, prompt him.]

[Vary the order in which you give the words.]

**STRUCTURE FOCUS:** *These are* _____.

> These are books.
> These are pens.
> These are pencils.
> These are chairs.

1. Teacher models the sentences several times, using the plural forms. Have the student repeat.

2. Point out that plural verbs go with plural nouns. Be aware that the student may have difficulty with the pronunciation of the vowel in *these*, confusing it with the vowel in *this*.

   [Say, "With *books*, we say *These are*. These are books."]

3. Point out that plural nouns are used with numbers above one.

   [Say, "With the numbers 2, 3, 4, we say *books*—2 books, 3 books, 4 books.
   With the number 1, we say *book*—1 book."]

   [Say "Listen," then gesture for the student to repeat.]

   Teacher: 2 pens, 3 pens, 4 pens.
   Student: 2 pens, 3 pens, 4 pens.

   Teacher: 1 pen.
   Student: 1 pen.

**DRILL: Substitution Drill with Visual Cues**

Use "plural" pictures on pp. 2-9 of *ESOL Illustrations*.

[Point to the "plural" picture. Say "Listen." Gesture when you want the student to speak.]

| Teacher | Student |
|---|---|
| What are these? | |
| These are books. | |
| | |
| What are these? | |
| These are books. | These are books. |
| | |
| What are these? | |
| pens | These are pens. |
| clocks | |
| windows | |
| doors | |
| erasers | |
| pencils | |
| tables | |

## PRONUNCIATION: /s/ and /z/ Sounds of Plural Ending

**Note:** All the sounds of English can be divided into voiced and unvoiced sounds.
Voiced sounds are produced with vibration of the vocal cords.
Unvoiced sounds are produced without vibration of the vocal cords.
The unvoiced sounds are /f/, /h/, /k/, /p/, /s/, /t/, /ch/, /sh/, /wh/, and
/th/ as in *thank*.
All the rest are voiced, including /th/ as in *this*.

1. When the final *sound* of a noun is an unvoiced sound,
   we form the plural by adding the unvoiced sound /s/.

   Examples: books, desks, students, clocks.

2. When the final *sound* of a noun is a voiced sound,
   we form the plural by adding the voiced sound /z/.

   Examples: pens, pencils, tables, chairs, windows,
   doors, erasers, boys, girls.

3. When the final sound of a noun is a sibilant sound (/s/, /z/, /sh/, /ch/, /j/),
   we form the plural by adding a separate syllable, /uz/.

   Examples: nurses, watches, judges.

   (Nouns ending in sibilants have not occurred in the material at this point.
   They are introduced in Unit D.)

### Procedure:

1. Teacher models the pronunciation of the plural
   form of nouns, focusing on the unvoiced ending.
   The student repeats.

   [Say, "Listen to the /s/. Book<u>s</u>." Prolong the /s/ sound.]

   [Say each word twice, having the student repeat twice.]

   Teacher: books, books.
   Student: books, books.

   [Continue with *students, clocks, desks*.]

2. Teacher models the pronunciation of the plural form
   of nouns, focusing on the voiced ending.
   The student repeats.

   [Say, "Listen to the /z/. Pen<u>s</u>." Prolong the /z/ sound.]

   Teacher: pens, pens.
   Student: pens, pens.

   [Continue with *pencil, table, chair, boy, girl, window, door*.]

3. Teacher gives the singular form as a vocal cue. The
   student gives the plural.

   [Give the singular form of nouns already taught—ending in
   either a voiced or unvoiced sound. Ask the student for the
   plural.]

   [Listen carefully to the student's pronunciation of the final
   sound or combination of sounds. Correct him if necessary.]

## READING AND WRITING: Numbers 11-20

1. Teacher reviews the numbers 1-10, modeling the counting of these numbers and having the student repeat.

2. Teacher introduces the numbers 11-20. Follow the same procedure as in Unit B for saying, reading, and writing the numbers. You do not need to hold up fingers to show the numbers, however.

### One-to-one:

3. Using the previously prepared card containing the student's name, street address, and telephone number, model the sentences, and have the student repeat.

### Class:

3. Write a local address and phone number on the board and have the class repeat them after you, then copy them. Walk around the room, giving help to those who need it.

   Next, have each student write the information about himself.

[Say "Please repeat."]

Teacher: 1, 2, 3, 4, 5, 6, 7, 8, 9, 10.
Student: 1, 2, 3, 4, 5, 6, 7, 8, 9, 10.

[Say "Please listen." Point to the appropriate line on the card as you say each sentence.]

I'm _____ _____.
My address is _____.
My telephone number is_____.

[Have the student point to the lines as he says the above.]

[Have the student write his name, street address, and telephone number on lined notebook paper.]

## ORAL EVALUATION

1. Use the "singular" pictures on pp. 8-9 of *ESOL Illustrations*. Point to the picture as a visual cue. Follow the procedure in the Oral Evaluation of Unit B. Always test the vocabulary items in a sentence frame.

2. Using the "plural" pictures on pp. 2-9 of *ESOL Illustrations*, test the plural forms of nouns in a sentence frame.

   You will be reviewing both the ability to identify the item and the ability to form the plural.

   Your student should be able to name all these items and to give their plural forms.

This is a window.
       door.
       eraser.

These are books.
       pens.
       pencils.
       doors.
       chairs.
       boys.
       clocks.
       blackboards.
       girls.
       tables.
       desks.
       students.
       teachers.

3. Have the student count from 1 to 20.

Make notes of items your student hesitates over a great deal or cannot do at all. These items should be reviewed at the beginning of your next session.

# Introductory Unit D

## OBJECTIVES

When a student completes this unit, he should be able to:

1. Say and respond to some polite expressions.
2. Identify selected occupations.
3. Say the plural form of the occupations and all other nouns previously taught.
4. Identify *man, woman, child, housewife* and give their irregular plural forms.
5. Use the subject pronouns *we, you, they* with the verb *are*, full and contracted.
6. Pronounce the vowel sound in *man* and *men*.
7. Say the numbers 21-30.
8. Read and write the numbers 21-30.

## VISUAL AIDS

Accompanying *ESOL Illustrations for Skill Book 1*, pp. 11-15 for new vocabulary and p. 5 for review of *student/teacher*.

## REVIEW

Review any items that your student had difficulty with when doing the Oral Evaluation in Unit C.

## DIALOG

```
Teacher:  Is this your book?
Student:  Yes, it is. Thank you.

Teacher:  That's a (nice tie).
Student:  Thank you.
```

1. Teacher models the dialog two or three times while student listens.

   Before beginning, set up the situation by placing the student's book in some other part of the room away from him.

   In the dialog, use an item of apparel that the student is wearing. If not *dress* or *tie*, use *shirt, watch*, or some other easy word. Use only this one item at this point.

   The object of this dialog is to teach the student to say thank you when someone does him a favor or pays him a compliment.

2. Continue, using steps 2-4 of the Dialog in Unit A.

[Using the Stop gesture, say "Listen."]

Teacher:  Is this your book?
          Yes, it is. Thank you.

[Gesture to student's tie or dress.]

Teacher:  That's a nice tie (pretty dress).
          Thank you.

Teacher:  Is this your book?
          [Use a Stop gesture so the student won't repeat the question.]
          Yes, it is. Thank you.
          Repeat.
          Yes, it is. Thank you.
Student:  Yes, it is. Thank you.

3. Practice the dialog, substituting one other "found" object and one other item of apparel that the student is wearing.

Teacher: Is this your pen?
Student: Yes, it is. Thank you.

Teacher: That's a nice sweater.
Student: Thank you.

## VOCABULARY: Review

```
These are books.
        pens.
        tables.
        pencils.
```

Review the -s plural of nouns previously taught. Refer to steps 1 and 2 of Structure Focus:
*These are* _____ , in Unit C.

## VOCABULARY: Occupations

```
This is a doctor.
       nurse.
       waiter.
       waitress.
       factory worker.
       taxi driver.
       student.
       teacher.
```

Teacher models sentences introducing the new vocabulary. Have the student repeat.

Use *ESOL Illustrations*, pp. 11-13 and p. 5

[Point to the picture of a doctor. Say "Listen."]

Teacher: This is a doctor.
         This is a doctor.

[Gesture for the student to repeat after you.]

Teacher: This is a doctor.
Student: This is a doctor.

[Continue the same way with the other occupations shown in the box.]

## DRILL: Substitution Drill with Vocal Cues

1. Teacher gives the cue and the expected student response. As the student begins to understand the drill, the teacher stops giving the response.

[Indicating the picture of a doctor, say "Please repeat."]

| Teacher | Student |
|---------|---------|
| This is a doctor. | This is a doctor. |

[Indicate the picture of a nurse.]

nurse

| Teacher | Student |
|---------|---------|
| This is a nurse. | This is a nurse. |

[Continue with the words below, pointing to the picture and saying the word as a cue.]

| waiter | factory worker | student |
|--------|----------------|---------|
| waitress | taxi driver | teacher |

2. Repeat this drill if the student hesitates a great deal.

## DRILL: Substitution Drill with Visual Cues

1. Teacher points to the picture and models one sentence.

[Point to the picture of a nurse and say "Please repeat."]

| Teacher | Student |
|---------|---------|
| This is a nurse. | This is a nurse. |

2. Continue the drill by simply pointing to the pictures.

[Continue pointing to various pictures of the occupations. Do not identify the picture unless the student cannot do so.]

3. Repeat the drill, varying the order of presentation.

## VOCABULARY: Plural Forms of Occupations

These are doctors.
    nurses.
    waiters.
    waitresses.
    factory workers.
    taxi drivers.
    students.
    teachers.

1. Using the "plural" pictures on p. 5 and pp. 11-13 of *ESOL Illustrations*, teacher models the plural forms of the occupations.

[Point to the "doctor" picture, then to the "doctors" picture, saying, "Doctor. Doctors."]

[Say, "Repeat. Doctor. Doctors."
Gesture for the student to repeat after you, giving the singular and the plural, as you point to the pictures.]

[Continue the same way with the singular and plural forms of the occupations.]

| | |
|---|---|
| waiter | waiters |
| waitress | waitresses |
| student | students |
| teacher | teachers |
| factory worker | factory workers |
| nurse | nurses |
| taxi driver | taxi drivers |

2. Teacher models sentences in the box containing plural forms, having the student repeat.

[Pointing to the appropriate "plural" picture, say "Listen," then "Repeat."]

Teacher: These are doctors.
Student: These are doctors.

[Continue with the other sentences in the box.]

## DRILL: Substitution Drill with Vocal Cues

1. Say the key sentence. Then say only the cues.

[Say "Listen," then Repeat."
Point to the appropriate picture as you give the cue.]

| Teacher | Student |
|---|---|
| These are doctors. | These are doctors. |
| nurses | These are nurses. |
| doctors | |
| taxi drivers | |
| factory workers | |
| waiters | |
| students | |
| teachers | |
| waitresses | |

## STRUCTURE FOCUS: Contrasting Singular and Plural Forms

Teacher models a singular and a plural sentence several times. Then the student repeats.

**Note:** This is a difficult pattern, for many students will have trouble with the pronunciation of *this* and *these*, and others will omit the *a* in the singular sentence.

[Holding up one finger for the singular and two for the plural, gesture and say "Please listen." Say "Repeat" when you want the student to speak.]

Teacher: This is a student.
　　　　　These are students.

Teacher: This is a student.
　　　　　These are students.

Student: This is a student.
　　　　　These are students.

[Continue with *doctor, nurse, waiter, waitress, taxi driver, factory worker, teacher.*]

## DRILL: Substitution Drill with Vocal Cues

Teacher models the key sentences, then says only the cues.

**Note:** This drill requires more of the student since he has to make several changes in the sentence to use the cue correctly, e.g.:

doctor    This is a doctor.

doctors    These are doctors.

[Say "Listen," then "Repeat."]

| Teacher | Student |
|---|---|
| This is a student. | This is a student. |
| students | |
| These are students. | These are students. |
| teachers | These are teachers. |
| teacher | This is a teacher. |
| doctor | |
| nurses | |
| taxi driver | |
| factory workers | |
| teachers | |
| students | |
| nurses | |
| nurse | |
| student | |
| waiter | |
| waitress | |

## STRUCTURE FOCUS: Irregular Plurals

| | |
|---|---|
| This is a <u>man.</u> | These are <u>men.</u> |
| This is a <u>woman.</u> | These are <u>women.</u> |
| This is a <u>child.</u> | These are <u>children.</u> |
| This is a <u>housewife.</u> | These are <u>housewives.</u> |

1. Using the pictures on pp. 14-15 of *ESOL Illustrations*, the teacher models the singular and plural forms of the nouns, having the student repeat.

   **Note:** The difficulty for students in learning the plural forms of *man, woman,* and *child* is that, unlike the majority of English nouns, these do not use an *-s* in the plural form. Furthermore, many students find the vowel changes in *man* to *men* and *woman* to *women* difficult to hear and to pronounce.

   The plural of *housewife* presents a twofold pronunciation problem: the student must pronounce a /v/ and add a /z/.

2. Repeat the drill, using only the pictures (singular and plural) as cues.

[Point to the "man" picture, then to the "men" picture, saying, "Man. Men."]

[Say, "Repeat. Man. Men."
Gesture for the student to repeat after you, giving the singular and plural, as you point to the pictures.]

[Continue the same way with the singular and plural forms.]

| | |
|---|---|
| woman | women |
| child | children |
| housewife | housewives |

## DRILL:  Substitution Drill with Vocal Cues

1. Teacher models the key sentence and the cues, then says only the cues.

| Teacher | Student |
|---|---|
| These are men. | These are men. |
| women | |
| These are women. | These are women. |
| children | These are children. |
| housewives | |
| men | |
| women | |

2. Teacher models the key sentence and the cues, then says only the cues.

   The cues include singular and plural forms, and regular and irregular plurals.

[Say "Listen" before you give the key sentence and the cues. Continue to give the sentence after the cue until the student can give the sentence himself.]

| Teacher | Student |
|---|---|
| This is a doctor. | This is a doctor. |
| doctors | |
| These are doctors. | These are doctors. |
| nurse | |
| This is a nurse. | This is a nurse. |
| student | This is a student. |
| teachers | |
| men | |
| waiters | |
| women | |
| factory workers | |
| housewife | |
| doctor | |
| children | |

## STRUCTURE FOCUS:  Plural Subject Pronouns

| | | | | | |
|---|---|---|---|---|---|
| I am a woman. | + | You are a woman. | = | We are women. |
| You are a woman. | + | You are a woman. | = | You are women. |
| He is a child. | + | She is a child. | = | They are children. |

Teacher models each set of sentences illustrating the use of *we, you* plural, and *they*. Have the student repeat the plural sentence in each set.

[Say, "Listen to *we*."]

Teacher: I am a woman.
You are a woman.
We are women.

Repeat.
We are women.

Student: We are women.

[Continue the same way with *you* plural and *they*.]

## DRILL: Substitution Drill with Vocal Cues

Teacher models the two singular sentences and the plural sentence that they "add up to."

Then the teacher gives only the two singular sentences as the cue and the student responds with the plural sentence.

| Teacher | Student |
|---|---|
| I am a woman. | |
| You are a woman. | |
| We are women. | We are women. |
| You are a woman. | |
| You are a woman. | You are women. |
| He is a child. | |
| She is a child. | They are children. |
| I am a housewife. | |
| You are a housewife. | We are housewives. |
| You are a student. | |
| You are a student. | You are students. |
| He is a doctor. | |
| She is a doctor. | They are doctors. |

## STRUCTURE FOCUS: Contractions of *be* with Plural Pronouns

| | |
|---|---|
| We are students. | We're students. |
| You are students. | You're students. |
| They are students. | They're students. |

Teacher models first the full form, then the contracted form, of each sentence. Have the student repeat the contracted form.

| Teacher | Student |
|---|---|
| We are students. | |
| We're students. | |
| Repeat. | |
| We're students. | We're students. |

[Continue the same way with *you're* and *they're*.]

## DRILL: Substitution Drill with Vocal Cues

Teacher models the key sentence of the drill and then gives only the cues.

| Teacher | Student |
|---|---|
| We're students. | |
| We're students. | We're students. |
| You | You're students. |
| They | They're students. |
| You | |
| We | |
| They | |
| We | |

# PRONUNCIATION: /a/ and /e/

1. Teacher models first the vowel sound in *man* and *add*, then the vowel sound in *men* and *Ed*.

   Do not explain the meaning of the words. This is simply pronunciation practice.

   **Note:** When making the vowel sound in *man,* the lips are spread. The tip of the tongue touches the lower teeth.

[Say, "Listen to /a/."
Repeat each word several times.]

| | | | |
|---|---|---|---|
| add | black | bad | and |
| man | pan | lamb | hat |

[Have the student repeat the words above after you.]

[Say, "Listen to /e/."
Repeat each word several times.]

| | | |
|---|---|---|
| Ed | pen | end |
| men | bed | send |

[Have the student repeat the words above after you.]

[Say, "Listen to *and, end.*"]

| Teacher: | and | end |
|---|---|---|
| | sand | send |
| | man | men |
| | add | Ed |

2. Teacher contrasts the two sounds, using minimal pairs, as *man/men*.

   **Note:** A minimal pair consists of two words, with different meanings, that sound exactly alike except for the two sounds being contrasted.

3. The student discriminates between the two sounds.

   Teacher tells the student that the vowel sound in *and* is "one" and that the vowel sound in *end* is "two."

   If the student makes a mistake, that is, if he says *and* is "two," the teacher repeats: "*And* is one, *end* is two." This will enable the student to hear the contrast again.

[Tell the student that *and, sand, man* are the first sound (one) and that *end, send, men* are the second sound (two). Test to see if he can identify them.

| Teacher | | Student |
|---|---|---|
| and | Say "one." | one |
| sand | Say "one." | one |
| end | Say "two." | two |

| Teacher | Student |
|---|---|
| men | two |
| sand | one |
| and | one |
| man | one |
| men | two |

[Continue until the student can identify without confusion.]

[Pointing to yourself, say "and." Indicating the student, say "end."]

| Teacher | Student |
|---|---|
| and | end |
| sand | send |
| add | Ed |
| and | end |
| man | men |

| Teacher | Student |
|---|---|
| end | and |
| send | sand |
| Ed | add |
| men | man |
| end | and |

4. Practice by saying one of the pair (*man*) and having the student say the other (*men*).

| Teacher | Student |
|---------|---------|
| and | end |
| send | sand |
| and | end |
| man | men |
| end | and |
| Ed | add |

5. Practice the sounds by using them in phrases and sentences. Do not explain vocabulary.

[Say, "Listen to *that black hat.* Repeat *that black hat.*"]

| Teacher | Student |
|---------|---------|
| that black hat | that black hat |
| that black pan | |
| a fat black cat | |
| in the afternoon | |
| That's a blackboard. | |

the black pen
Send the men.
That's Ed.
Get the pen.

[Practice the following question and answer for pronunciation drill.]

Is that Ed?
No, that's Dan.

## READING AND WRITING: Numbers 21-30

1. Teacher reviews the numbers 1-20, modeling the counting of these numbers and having the student repeat.

2. Teacher introduces the numbers 21-30, following the procedures in Unit B for saying, reading, and writing the numbers.

3. Teacher models the sentences from Unit C regarding the student's name, street address, and telephone number. The student repeats.

## ORAL EVALUATION

1. Review the occupations in the sentence frame "This is a _____."

[Using *ESOL Illustrations*, point to the "singular" pictures of the occupations. Do not prompt your student. Give him time to answer.]

This is a doctor.
      nurse.
      waiter.
      waitress.
      factory worker.
      taxi driver.
      student.
      teacher.

2. Review the occupations in the plural form in the sentence frame "These are _____."

If your student can name five of these occupations fairly quickly, you can proceed with the next section.

[Using *ESOL Illustrations*, point to the "plural" pictures.]

3. Review the irregular plurals in the sentence frame "These are _____."

If your student does not know all these items, be sure to make a note to review them.

[Review the Structure Focus: Irregular Plurals in this unit and do the Drill that follows it.]

These are men.
      women.
      children.
      housewives.

4. Review the subject pronouns *we, you* plural, and *they.*

Your student must know all these pronouns. If not, be sure to review them at the next session.

[Review the Structure Focus: Subject Pronouns in this unit and do the Drill that follows it.]

5. Have the student count from 1 to 30.

# Introductory Unit E

## OBJECTIVES

When a student completes this unit, he should be able to:

1. Say and respond to a new dialog.
2. Make Yes/No questions with *is*.
3. Give affirmative and negative short answers with *is*.
4. Say Yes/No questions and answers with the correct intonation.
5. Say the numbers 31-40.
6. Read and write the numbers 31-40.

## VISUAL AIDS

Accompanying *ESOL Illustrations for Skill Book 1*, pp. 2-15, illustrations of vocabulary already introduced, as needed.

## REVIEW

Review any items that your student had difficulty with when doing the Oral Evaluation in Unit D.

## DIALOG

| |
|---|
| Teacher: Are you a student? |
| Student: Yes, I am. |
| Teacher: Are you a doctor? |
| Student: No, I'm not. |
| I'm a student. |

1. Teacher models dialog two or three times while student listens.

2. Continue with steps 2-4 of the Dialog as in Unit A.

3. Practice the dialog, substituting occupations. This will serve as a vocabulary review.

Teacher: Are you a housewife?
Student: Yes, I am.

Teacher: Are you a nurse?
Student: No, I'm not.
I'm a housewife.

## STRUCTURE FOCUS: Questions with *is*

> This <u>is</u> a book.
> <u>Is</u> this  a book?
> Bob <u>is</u> a doctor.
> <u>Is</u> Bob  a doctor?

Teacher models statements and questions, having the student repeat the questions.

**Note:** When making questions with *is*, use the question word order, i.e., *is* comes before the subject word.

Questions such as "Is this a book?" and "Is Bob a doctor?" are called Yes/No questions because these are the usual answers to such questions. This is one of the basic question patterns in English. We use a rising intonation pattern with this kind of question.

[Say, "Listen to *is.*" Use a Stop gesture. Raise your eyebrows to indicate a question.]

Teacher:  This is a book.
          Is this a book?

[Gesture for student to repeat the question only.]

Student:  Is this a book?

Teacher:  This is a pen.
          Is this a pen?
Student:  Is this a pen?

[Continue with *pencil, clock,* and *book* again.]

## DRILL: Transformation Drill

1. Teacher gives a statement and indicates with examples that the student is to transform (change) the statement into a question.

| Teacher | Student |
|---|---|
| This is a blackboard. | |
| Is this a blackboard? | Is this a blackboard? |
| This is a door. | |
| Is this a door? | Is this a door? |
| This is a window. | Is this a window? |
| This is a door. | Is this a door? |
| This is a table. | |
| This is a desk. | |
| This is a chair. | |

2. Continue the transformation drill, adding colors. Model the statement and the question.

   The examples given are only suggestions. Use items readily available, but do not introduce new vocabulary.

| Teacher | Student |
|---|---|
| This is a red book. | |
| Is this a red book? | Is this a red book? |
| This is a yellow pen. | |
| Is this a yellow pen? | Is this a yellow pen? |
| This is a brown chair. | Is this a brown chair? |
| This is a blue book. | Is this a blue book? |
| This is a black pen. | |
| This is a green pencil. | |
| This is a brown desk. | |

3. Continue the drill, using the vocabulary on occupations already taught.

| Teacher | Student |
|---|---|
| He is a doctor. | |
| Is he a doctor? | Is he a doctor? |
| She is a nurse. | |
| Is she a nurse? | Is she a nurse? |

She is a housewife.          Is she a housewife?
She is a taxi driver.        Is she a taxi driver?

He is a child.
He is a student.
She is a waitress.
She is a nurse.
He is a teacher.
He is a waiter.

## STRUCTURE FOCUS: Affirmative Short Answers

```
Question:  Is this a book?
  Answer:  Yes, it is.
Question:  Is this a pen?
  Answer:  Yes, it is.
```

Teacher models questions and affirmative short answers, having the student repeat only the answers.

Do not use contractions in affirmative short answers. Use a falling intonation pattern.

**Note:** The verb *is,* used in the question, is also used in the affirmative short answer.

[Say, "Listen to *Yes, it is.*" Ask the question, indicating the item you are asking about. Use a Stop gesture.
Nod your head as you give the affirmative answer.
Gesture to your student when you want him to repeat.]

Teacher:  Is this a book?
          Yes, it is.
Teacher:  Is this a book?
          Yes, it is.
Student:  Yes, it is.

[Continue with *pencil, book* again, and *blackboard.*]

## STRUCTURE FOCUS: Negative Short Answers

```
Question:  Is this a book?
  Answer:  No, it isn't.
Question:  Is this a pen?
  Answer:  No, it isn't.
```

Teacher models questions and negative short answers, having the student repeat only the answers.

Do not use the full form *is not* since native speakers almost always use the contracted form *isn't.* Use a falling intonation pattern.

**Note:** The verb *is,* used in the question, is used in contraction with *not* (*isn't*) in negative short answers.

[Say, "Listen to *No, it isn't.*" Ask the question, indicating an item different from the one you are asking about; for example, hold up a pen when asking about a pencil. Use a Stop gesture.
Shake your head when you give the negative answer.
Gesture to your student when you want him to repeat.

Teacher:  Is this a pencil?
          No, it isn't.

Teacher:  Is this a pencil?
          No, it isn't.
Student:  No, it isn't.

[Continue with other items.]

## DRILL: Answering Questions

Teacher asks the student questions which will elicit negative and affirmative responses. Model both the question and the answer at first.

[Hold up a pen, ask and answer.]

Teacher: Is this a pen?
Yes, it is.

[Hold up a book, ask and answer.]
Teacher: Is this a pen?
No, it isn't.

[Hold up a pencil. Ask the question and gesture for the student to answer.]

Teacher: Is this a pencil?
Student: Yes, it is.

[Continue indicating various items which will elicit affirmative and negative answers.

Teacher: Is this a pen?
Is this a book?
Is this a desk?
Is this a clock?
Is this a pencil?
Is this a door?
Is this a window?

## DRILL: Asking Questions

The student asks questions.

If you have only one student, have him ask you questions.

With a class, students can ask one another questions and give short answers.

[Hold up a book, ask and answer.]

Teacher: Is this a book?
Yes, it is.

[Hold up a pen, and gesture to the student to ask a question. If he cannot, prompt him.]

Student: Is this a pen?
Teacher: Yes, it is.

## PRONUNCIATION: Intonation Practice

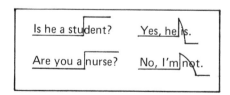

Note: It is necessary right from the beginning to train your student to use correct intonation. Correct intonation is vital. Minor errors in pronunciation will not be so noticeable if the student uses correct intonation. It is imperative, then, that the teacher herself use normal intonation and not distort it by speaking too slowly.

**Procedure:**

1. Practice the rising intonation in the questions.

   **Note:** In English, Yes/No questions are uttered with a rising intonation. The rising intonation indicates to the native speaker that a response is required.

[Use your hand to help the student realize when your voice is rising. As you say the words *Is he a,* draw an imaginary line in the air with your hand. As you say *student*, raise your hand higher to indicate the rise in intonation.]

[Have the student imitate your rising gestures as he repeats the questions. Listen carefully. It is entirely possible for the student to imitate your hand gestures faithfully while using incorrect intonation.]

[Practice Yes/No questions, using only vocabulary already introduced, such as the following.]

| | |
|---|---|
| Is this a desk? | Are you a nurse? |
| Is this a table? | Are you a housewife? |

2. Now practice the falling intonation used in the short answers.

[Use hand gestures, as above, to illustrate the falling intonation. Lower your hand to indicate the fall in intonation.]

Are you a doctor?    Yes, I am.
                     No, I'm not.

## READING AND WRITING: Numbers 31-40

Teacher reviews the numbers 1-30 and introduces the numbers 31-40, following the procedure described in Unit B.

## REVIEW: Questions with *is* and Numbers

1. Teacher combines numbers with a review of questions and answers with *is*.

[Write the number 1 on the board or on paper.]

Teacher:  Is this 1?
          Yes, it is.

[Write the number 6.]

Teacher:  Is this 2?
          No, it isn't.
          It's 6.

[Write the number 3.]

Teacher:  Is this 3? [Gesture for student to answer.]
Student:  Yes, it is.

[Write the number 5.]

Teacher:  Is this 5?
Student:  Yes, it is.

2. Teacher and student reverse roles. Have the student write the number and ask the question. Teacher answers.

[Say, "Write 7. Ask a question." If the student cannot, you ask the question and have him repeat it after you. Then try again with another number.]

Student:  Is this 7?
Teacher:  Yes, it is.

## ORAL EVALUATION

1. Test your student's ability to make questions with *is*. Listen for correct intonation.

   If your student can change statements to questions fairly quickly, proceed to the next item.

   If the student cannot make questions, make a note to review this pattern at the beginning of your next session. It is a basic sentence structure and a very important one.

   [Do the Transformation Drill in this unit.]

2. Test your student's ability to give short answers. Continue until your student can give short negative and affirmative answers fairly quickly.

   [Do the Drill: Answering Questions in this unit.]

3. Have your student count from 1 to 40.

# Introductory Unit F

## OBJECTIVES

When a student completes this unit, he should be able to:

1. Say and respond to a new dialog.
2. Make Yes/No questions with *are* and *am.*
3. Give affirmative and negative short answers with *am, is,* and *are.*
4. Say the names and nationalities of certain countries and national groups.
5. Distinguish aurally and orally between the *-teen* and *-ty* endings in numbers like 13 and 30.
6. Say the numbers 41-50.
7. Read and write the numbers 41-50.

## VISUAL AIDS

Accompanying *ESOL Illustrations for Skill Book 1*, world map on pp. 16-17, or a larger world map, or an atlas.

## REVIEW

Review any items that your student had difficulty with when doing the Oral Evaluation in Unit E.

## DIALOG

| | |
|---|---|
| Teacher: | Are you Chinese? |
| Student: | No, I'm not. I'm Korean. |
| | What are you? |
| Teacher: | I'm Spanish. |

1. Teacher models dialog two or three times while student listens.

2. Continue with steps 2-4 of the Dialog as in Unit A.

3. Vary the dialog by using the student's own nationality.

## VOCABULARY: Countries and Nationalities

| | |
|---|---|
| I'm from Spain. | I'm Spanish. |
| I'm from China. | I'm Chinese. |
| I'm from Korea. | I'm Korean. |
| I'm from Poland. | I'm Polish. |
| I'm from Germany. | I'm German. |
| I'm from the United States. | I'm American. |

1. Teacher models each pair of sentences—country and nationality—pointing to a map of the world to illustrate the meaning of the words.

   Be sure the student uses *the* with *United States* but not with the other countries given.

   Add your student's country and nationality if they are not already given.

[Say each sentence several times, pointing to the country on the map as you say its name. Use the map on pp. 16-17 of *ESOL Illustrations* or a large world map.]

2. Teacher models the sentences, having the student repeat.

[Point to Germany on the map and gesture for the student to repeat after you.]

Teacher: I'm from Germany. I'm German.
Student: I'm from Germany. I'm German.

[Continue with the other countries and nationalities.]

| | |
|---|---|
| Poland | Polish |
| Korea | Korean |
| China | Chinese |
| Spain | Spanish |
| the United States | American |

## DRILL: Substitution Drill with Visual Cues

Teacher points on the map to the various countries taught and elicits their names and nationalities from the student.

[Point to Germany on the map and say, "I'm from Germany. I'm German." Gesture for the student to respond as you point to the other countries.]

## STRUCTURE FOCUS: Questions with *am* and *are*

I am a teacher.
Am I a teacher?

You are a student.
Are you a student?

They are students.
Are they students?

Teacher models statements and questions, having the student repeat only the questions.

**Note:** In Unit E, we practiced Yes/No questions with *is*. This lesson expands the pattern to include *am* and *are*.

When making questions with *am* and *are,* use the question word order, i.e., *am* and *are* come before the subject word. Use a rising intonation pattern with these questions.

[Say, "Listen to *am* and *are*," and use a Stop gesture. Raise your eyebrows to indicate a question.]

Teacher: I am a teacher.
Am I a teacher?

[Gesture for the student to repeat the question.]

Teacher: I am a teacher.
Am I a teacher?
Student: Am I a teacher?

[Continue as above.]

Teacher: You are a student.
Are you a student?
Student: Are you a student?

Teacher: We are students.
Are we students?
Student: Are we students?

Teacher: They are students.
Are they students?
Student: Are they students?

## DRILL: Transformation Drill

1. Teacher gives a statement and illustrates by examples that the student is to transform (change) the statement into a question.

| Teacher | Student |
|---|---|
| I am a teacher. | |
| Am I a teacher? | Am I a teacher? |
| You are a student. | |
| Are you a student? | Are you a student? |
| I am a teacher. | Am I a teacher? |
| They are students. | |
| You are a student. | |
| We are students. | |

2. Continue the transformation drill using the nationalities already taught. Model the statement and the question.

| Teacher | Student |
|---|---|
| I am American. | |
| Am I American? | Am I American? |
| You are Chinese. | |
| Are you Chinese? | Are you Chinese? |
| They are German. | Are they German? |
| We are American. | |
| You are Polish. | |
| They are Spanish. | |
| They are Korean. | |

## REVIEW DRILL

Continue the transformation drill, adding the review item "Is he _____?" as in "Is he Chinese?"

| Teacher | Student |
|---|---|
| He is Chinese. | |
| Is he Chinese? | Is he Chinese? |

## STRUCTURE FOCUS: Affirmative Short Answers

| | |
|---|---|
| Are you a student? | Yes, I am. |
| Am I a teacher? | Yes, you are. |
| Are we students? | Yes, we are. |
| Are you students? | Yes, we are. |
| Are they students? | Yes, they are. |

1. Teacher models questions and answers, having the student repeat only the answers.

**Note:** The question with *am* is particularly difficult because of the switch in the pronouns *I* and *you*, which is required in ordinary conversation, e.g.: "Am *I* a teacher?" "Yes, *you* are." Teach this to the student, whose first inclination will be to answer, "Yes, I am." Consider the importance of this pattern in ordinary conversation. ("Am I late?" "Yes, you are.") Use a rising intonation pattern for these questions.

[Say, "Listen to *am* and *are*."
Ask the question. Nod your head as you give the affirmative answer.]

Teacher: Are you a student?
      Yes, I am.

Teacher: Are you a student?
      Yes, I am.
Student: Yes, I am.

[Continue with the other questions and answers.]

2. Teacher asks the question and the student answers.

[Say, "Listen" and use a Stop gesture before you ask the question.]

Teacher: Are you a student?
   Yes, I am.
   Repeat. Yes, I am.
Student: Yes, I am.

Teacher: Am I a teacher? [Gesture for student to answer.]
Student: Yes, you are.

[Continue with the other questions and answers.]

## STRUCTURE FOCUS: Negative Short Answers

| | |
|---|---|
| Are you a teacher? | No, I'm not. |
| Am I a student? | No, you aren't. |
| Are we doctors? | No, we aren't. |
| Are you students? | No, we aren't. |
| Are they teachers? | No, they aren't. |

1. Teacher models questions and answers, having the student repeat only the answers.

   **Note:** The verb **are**, used in the questions, is used in contracted form in negative short answers.

   Note again the switch in the pronouns *I* and *you*.

[Say, "Listen to *No, I'm not*." Ask the question. Shake your head as you give the negative answer.]

Teacher: Are you a teacher?
   No, I'm not.

Teacher: Are you a teacher?
   No, I'm not.
Student: No, I'm not.

[Continue with the other questions and answers.]

2. Teacher asks the questions and the student answers.

[Say, "Listen" and use a Stop gesture before you ask the question.]

Teacher: Are you a teacher?
   No, I'm not.
   Repeat. No, I'm not.
Student: No, I'm not.

Teacher: Am I a student? [Gesture for student to answer.]
Student: No, you're not.

[Continue with the other questions and answers.]

## DRILL: Answering Questions

Ask the student questions, indicating that you want negative answers. Frame questions to which the student can honestly give a negative answer. For example, to a Spanish student, say, "Are you Chinese?"

| Teacher | Student |
|---|---|
| Are you Chinese? | |
| No, I'm not. | |
| | |
| Are you German? | No, I'm not. |
| Are they waiters? | No, they aren't. |
| Am I a student? | |
| Are we doctors? | |

## READING AND WRITING: Numbers 41-50

Teacher reviews the numbers 1-40 and introduces the numbers 41-50, following the procedure described in Unit B.

## REVIEW: Questions with *is* and Numbers

Teacher combines numbers with a review of questions and answers with *is.*

[Write the number 41 on the board or on paper.]

Teacher: Is this 41?
Student: Yes, it is.

[Do the drill quickly and continue with it until the student can answer rapidly.]

## PRONUNCIATION: Number Endings *-teen* and *-ty*

> thirteen / thirty
> fourteen / forty
> fifteen / fifty

1. Teacher models the numbers, having the student repeat.

   **Note:** Be sure your student hears and pronounces the final /n/ sound in *thirteen, fourteen,* and *fifteen.*

   To help the student make the distinction between the *-teen* and *-ty* endings, stress the second syllable of *thirteen, fourteen,* and *fifteen*, but stress the first syllable of *thirty, forty,* and *fifty*. (In some contexts, the stress may be on the first syllable in the numbers *thirteen, fourteen*, and so on, but this is not important at this time.)

   With *thirteen* and *thirty*, the pronunciation problem is complicated by the difficulty almost all students have in pronouncing unvoiced /th/. Be sure that the student's tongue is between his teeth when he makes the unvoiced /th/ sound.

Teacher: thirteen, thirty
Student: thirteen, thirty

Teacher: fourteen, forty
Student: fourteen, forty

Teacher: fifteen, fifty
Student: fifteen, fifty

2. The student discriminates between the *-teen* and *-ty* numbers.

   [On paper or on the board, write: 13, 30, 14, 40, 15, 50. Say the numbers in random order, and have the student point to the number you say. Continue until the student can discriminate between the *-teen* and *-ty* numbers.]

3. The student pronounces the numbers, given visual cues.

   **Class:** Have the members of the class identify which number a fellow student is saying.

   [Using the numbers you have written, point to numbers in random order, and have the student pronounce them. Listen for correct pronunciation.]

## ORAL EVALUATION

1. Review countries and nationalities in a sentence frame.

   Student should be able to give his own country of origin and nationality with ease. He should be able to give four of the others fairly quickly. Make a note of any he needs to practice at the beginning of your next session.

   [Using a map of the world, point to the countries.]

   | I'm from Spain. | I'm Spanish. |
   |---|---|
   | China. | Chinese. |
   | Korea. | Korean. |
   | Poland. | Polish. |
   | Germany. | German. |
   | the United States | American. |

2. Test your student's ability to make questions with *am* and *are*.

   This is a basic structural pattern that needs to be mastered completely; it should be reviewed if the student has any difficulty.

   [Do the Transformation Drill in this unit.]

3. Test your student's ability to give affirmative and negative short answers.

   Note items that the student has difficulty with and review them at the beginning of your next session.

   [Do step 2 in Structure Focus: Affirmative Short Answers and in Structure Focus: Negative Short Answers. Then do the Drill: Answering Questions.]

4. Have your student count from 1 to 50.

# Lesson 1

## OBJECTIVES

When a student completes this unit, he should be able to:

1. Say the names of the days of the week.
2. Use new vocabulary, including the chart words.
3. Use *have/has* with subject pronouns.
4. Use the possessive pronouns *my, your, his, her*.
5. Use prepositional phrases with *in*.
6. Pronounce the sounds p/t/k contrasted with b/d/g.
7. Say, read, and write the numbers 51-60.
8. Say the sound for each of these letters: *b, c, d, f, g, h*.
9. Read the following new words:
   Chart words: *bird, cup, dish, fish, girl, hand*
   Story words: *this, the, a, is, has, her, in*.
10. Read a simple story, using the new chart and story words.
11. Write the letters *b, c, d, f, g, h*.

## VISUAL AIDS

1. A current calendar, showing the days of the week.
2. Accompanying *ESOL Illustrations for Skill Book 1*, pp. 18-21.

**Note:** The student begins *Skill Book 1* in this lesson. Have the skill book available for the Reading and Writing sections of this lesson.

## REVIEW

Review any items that your student had difficulty with when doing the Oral Evaluation in Unit F.

# I. Conversation Skills

### DIALOGUE

| |
|---|
| Teacher: What do you have in your hand? |
| Student: I have my English book in my hand. |

1. Teach the dialog, using the procedure outlined in Unit A.

2. Vary the dialog by using *a pen, a pencil,* and *an eraser*.

[Put a book in the student's hand.]

## VOCABULARY: Days of the Week

```
It's  Sunday.
      Monday.
      Tuesday.
      Wednesday.
      Thursday.
      Friday.
      Saturday.
```

Teacher models the sentences several times, having the student repeat.

**Note:** Spend a little extra time with "It's Tuesday" and "It's Thursday," for the pronunciation of these two proves especially troublesome.

For the /th/ sound in *Thursday,* the tip of the tongue must be between the teeth.

[Using a current calendar, point to each day of the week as you say the sentences.]

## VOCABULARY: Chart Words

```
This is a  bird.
           cup.
           dish.
           fish.
           girl.
           hand.
```

Teacher models the sentences several times, having the student repeat.

[As you say each sentence, point to the appropriate picture on p. 18 of *ESOL Illustrations*.]

## DRILL: Substitution Drill with Visual Cues

Teacher models the key sentence, then simply indicates the various pictures as cues.

[Indicating the picture, model key sentence.]

| Teacher | Student |
|---|---|
| What's this? It's a bird. | |
| Repeat. It's a bird. | It's a bird. |
| What's this? | It's a hand. |
| [Indicate pictures.] | It's a cup. |
| | It's a dish. |
| | It's a fish. |
| | It's a bird. |
| | It's a girl. |

## STRUCTURE FOCUS: *have/has*

> I <u>have</u> a cup.
> You <u>have</u> a cup.
> He <u>has</u> a cup.
> She <u>has</u> a cup.

Teacher models the sentences several times, having the student repeat.

[Say, "Listen to *have* and *has*."]

## DRILL: Substitution Drill with Vocal Cues

Teacher models the key sentence, then says only the cues.

| Teacher | Student |
|---|---|
| You have a cup. | You have a cup. |
| She | She has a cup. |
| I | |
| You | |
| He | |
| You | |

## STRUCTURE FOCUS: Subject Pronouns with *have/has*

> The <u>girl</u> has a cup.    <u>She</u> has a cup.
> The <u>boy</u> has a cup.    <u>He</u> has a cup.
> The <u>men</u> have cups.    <u>They</u> have cups.
> The <u>girls</u> have cups.    <u>They</u> have cups.

Teacher models each pair of sentences several times, having the student repeat.

[As you say each sentence, point to the appropriate picture on p. 19 of *ESOL Illustrations.*]

## DRILL: Replacement Drill

Teacher models the key sentence and the replacement.

| Teacher | Student |
|---|---|
| The girl has a cup. | |
| She has a cup. | She has a cup. |
| | |
| The boy has a dish. | He has a dish. |
| The men have cups. | They have cups. |
| The girl has a dish. | |
| The boy has a fish. | |
| The teacher has a book. | |
| The boys have a fish. | |
| The teachers have books. | |
| The man has a pen. | |

## STRUCTURE FOCUS: Possessive Pronouns *my*, *your*, *his*, *her*

> I have <u>my</u> book.
> <u>You</u> have <u>your</u> book.
> <u>Ann</u> has <u>her</u> book.
> <u>Bob</u> has <u>his</u> book.

Teacher models the sentences several times, having the student repeat.

Use the pictures at the top of pp. 20 and 21 in *ESOL Illustrations* to show Ann and Bob.

Stress that *I* correlates with *my, you* with *your, Ann (she)* with *her,* and *Bob (he)* with *his.*

[Before modeling the first sentence, say: "Listen to *I, my.*"]

[As you continue, say: "Listen to *you, your.*"
"Listen to *Ann, her.*"
"Listen to *Bob, his.*"]

## DRILL: Substitution Drill with Vocal Cues

1. Teacher models the key sentence, then says only the cue. Give the student response only until the student can do so on his own.

| Teacher | Student |
|---|---|
| I have my book. | I have my book. |
| You | |
| You have your book. | You have your book. |
| I | I have my book. |
| Ann | Ann has her book. |
| She | |
| You | |
| Bob | |
| He | |

2. Model another key sentence.

| Teacher | Student |
|---|---|
| I have my pen. | I have my pen. |
| You | |
| You have your pen. | You have your pen. |
| I | I have my pen. |
| He | He has his pen. |
| She | |
| Bob | |
| Ann | |
| I | |
| You | |

3. If the student has difficulty, model another key sentence.

| Teacher | Student |
|---|---|
| The girl has her pencil. | The girl has her pencil. |
| She | She has her pencil. |
| The boy | |
| Ann | |
| Bob | |
| He | |
| I | |
| You | |

## DRILL: Questions and Answers

1. Ask questions, placing the object in the student's hand first. Give the answer if necessary.

| Teacher | Student |
|---|---|
| What do you have? | I have my pencil. |
| | pen. |
| | book. |
| | pencil. |

2. Continue the drill, using the pictures on pp. 20 and 21 of *ESOL Illustrations*. Point to the object that you want the student to name in his answer.

| Teacher | Student |
|---|---|
| What does Ann have? | She has her cup. |
| | book. |
| | fish. |
| | bird. |
| What does Bob have? | He has his pencil. |
| | book. |
| | cup. |
| | dish. |

## STRUCTURE FOCUS: Prepositional Phrases with *in*

```
            I have a book  in my   hand.
You have a book  in your hand.
The girl has   a book  in her   hand.
The man has    a cup   in his   hand.
```

Teacher models the sentences several times, having the student repeat.

[Say, "Listen to *in*."]

Demonstrate the meaning of the first two sentences. For the last two, use the pictures on pp. 20 and 21 of *ESOL Illustrations*.

## DRILL: Questions and Answers

1. Teacher asks questions with *in* and the student answers.

[Put a book in your student's hand, and ask: "What do you have in your hand?" Use a Stop gesture so he will not repeat. Then say, "I have a book in my hand. Please repeat." Use a Beckoning gesture. "I have a book in my hand."]

[Continue with *pen, pencil, eraser, book*.]

2. Continue the drill, using the pictures on pp. 20 and 21 of *ESOL Illustrations*. Point to the object that you want the student to name in his answer.

[Pointing to the bird in the girl's hand, ask: "What does the girl have in her hand? The girl has a bird in her hand. Please repeat. The girl has a bird in her hand."]

[Continue asking questions.]

What does the girl have in her hand?
What does the man have in his hand?
What does the girl have in her hand?
What does the man have in his hand?

## PRONUNCIATION: p/t/k and b/d/g

| | | |
|---|---|---|
| people | table | cash |
| pound | toast | come |
| pie | taxi | cold |
| paper | team | car |

1. Teacher models the words that start with each sound several times, having the student repeat.

   If the student has difficulty with /p/, exaggerate the puff of air that occurs with /p/. Have the student hold up a sheet of paper in front of his face and say, "people, pie, pill." If /p/ is pronounced correctly, the puff of air will blow the paper.

   **Note:** The sounds /p/, /t/, and /k/ are unvoiced. When they occur at the beginning of a stressed syllable (*pie, people, table, cold*), there is aspiration (a puff of air). There is greater aspiration with /p/, less with /t/, and still less with /k/.

[Say, "Listen to /p/. People, pound, pie, paper. Please repeat."]

| Teacher | Student |
|---|---|
| people | people |
| pound | pound |
| pie | pie |
| paper | paper |

[Repeat with /t/ and then with /k/.]

| | | |
|---|---|---|
| bill | dill | gill |
| ban | die | gas |
| boy | doe | go |
| bean | dean | gun |

2. Teacher models the words that start with each sound several times, having the student repeat.

3. Contrast /b/ with /p/, /d/ with /t/, and /g/ with /k/, following the procedure used in the Pronunciation section of Unit D.

   **Note:** The sounds /b/, /d/, and /g/ are the voiced counterparts of /p/, /t/, and /k/.

   The sounds /b/ and /p/ are made with both lips.

   The sounds /d/ and /t/ are made with the tongue behind—not touching—the teeth.

   The sounds /g/ and /k/ are made with the tongue at the back of the mouth (the velum).

[Say, "Listen to /b/. Bill, ban, boy, bean. Please repeat."]

[Continue as in step 1.]

| ban | pan | dill | till | gill | kill |
|---|---|---|---|---|---|
| bill | pill | die | tie | girl | curl |
| boast | post | dean | teen | ghost | coast |

## VOCABULARY: Numbers 51-60

Teacher reviews the numbers 41-50 and introduces 51-60. Model the numbers 51-60 and have the student repeat.

Follow the procedures described in Unit B to teach saying, reading, and writing the numbers.

## ORAL EVALUATION

1. Using a calendar, review the days of the week. Student should be able to give five of these fairly quickly.

[Help your student to distinguish between Tuesday and Thursday.]

2. Review the chart words.

   Student must know all of these words to read the story in Lesson 1 of *Skill Book 1.*

[Using p. 18 of *ESOL Illustrations*, point to the pictures, asking, "What's this?"]

This is a bird.
       cup.
       dish.
       fish.
       girl.
       hand.

3. Review the subject pronouns with *have/has.*

   Student must be able to use all of the subject pronouns introduced with *have* and *has.* If he cannot, review at the beginning of your next session.

[Do the Replacement Drill in this lesson.]

I have a cup.
You have a cup.
The girl has a cup. She has a cup.
The boy has a cup. He has a cup.
The girls have cups. They have cups.
The men have cups. They have cups.

4. Review the possessive pronouns *my, your, his,* and *her.*

[Do the Substitution Drill that follows the Structure Focus: Possessive Pronouns in this lesson. If the student can respond fairly quickly, do only one or two parts of this Drill.]

5. Review the prepositional phrases with *in: in my hand, in your hand, in her hand.*

[Place a book in the student's hand, and ask, "What do you have in your hand?" Continue with other items.]

After reviewing parts 4 and 5 above, the student should know all the possessive pronouns introduced so far. If he does not, be sure to review at your next session.

# II. Reading

## CHART 1: Page 2

The illustrations below show how you should use your hands to teach each step of the chart. Note carefully the position of the hands and fingers.

If you are tutoring a student, sit next to him, and use his book. If you are teaching a group, you may need to use the large wall charts. (The first five charts and stories are available separately.)

Open your student's *Skill Book 1* to Lesson 1, page 2.

| **Do this:** | **Say this:** |
| --- | --- |
| Point to Lesson 1. | Teacher: Lesson 1. Read: *Lesson 1.* |
| | Student: Lesson 1. |
| | |
| Point to Chart 1. | Teacher: Chart 1. Read: *Chart 1.* |
| | Student: Chart 1. |
| | Teacher: Good! |

## Line 1

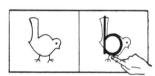

Teacher: [Point to the bird.]
What's this?
Student: It's a bird.

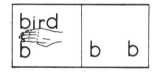

Teacher: [Trace the letter as you would write it.]
Say *bird*.
Student: Bird.

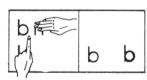

Teacher: Read *bird*.
Student: Bird.

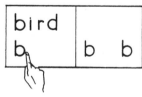

Teacher: [Cover all but the first letter of the word.]
*Bird* begins with /b/. Repeat: /b/.
[In making the sound /b/, start to say *bird* but give only the first sound. Try not to make any vowel sound.]
Student: /b/.

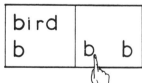

Teacher: /b/.
Student: /b/.

Teacher: /b/.
Student: /b/.

| | |
|---|---|
| bird<br>b \| b   b | Teacher: /b/.<br>Student: /b/. |
| bird<br>b \| b   b | Teacher: The sound is /b/.<br>          The name is *b*. Say *b*.<br>Student: *b*. |
| bird<br>b \| b   b | Teacher: What's the name? *b*. Say *b*.<br>Student: *b*. |
| bird<br>b \| b   b | Teacher: What's the sound? /b/. Repeat: /b/.<br>Student: /b/. |

**Line 2**

| | |
|---|---|
| [cup images] | Teacher: [Point to the cup.]<br>          What's this?<br>Student: It's a cup. |
| [cup images] | Teacher: [Trace the letter as you would write it.]<br>          Say *cup*.<br>Student: Cup. |
| cup<br>c \| c   c | Teacher: Read *cup*.<br>Student: Cup. |
| c \| c   c | Teacher: *Cup* begins with /k/. Repeat: /k/.<br>          [Say /k/ very quickly, with no vowel sound. Be sure to<br>          use the /k/ sound as in *cup,* not /s/ as in *city.*]<br>Student: /k/. |
| cup<br>c \| c   c | Teacher: /k/.<br>Student: /k/. |

```
cup
c        c    c
```

Teacher: /k/.
Student: /k/.

```
cup
c    c    c
```

Teacher: /k/.
Student: /k/.
Teacher: Good!

```
cup
c    c    c
```

Teacher:  The sound is /k/.
          The name is c. Say c.
Student: c.

```
cup
c    c    c
```

Teacher:  What's the name?
Student: c.

Teacher:  What's the sound?
Student: /k/.

**Review previous letters on chart**

```
bird
b    b    b
```

[Always review all previous sounds on the chart, going up the last column of letters.]

Teacher:  What's the sound?
Student: /b/.

```
bird
b    b    b
```

[Review all names of letters, going down the last column.]

Teacher:  What's the name?
Student: b.

```
cup
c    c    c
```

Teacher:  What's the name?
Student: c.

**Line 3**

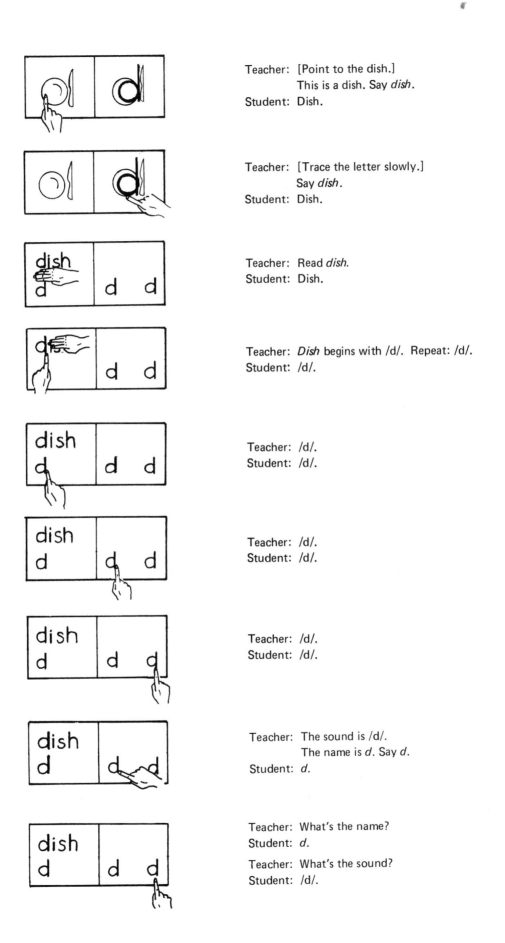

Teacher: [Point to the dish.]
         This is a dish. Say *dish*.
Student: Dish.

Teacher: [Trace the letter slowly.]
         Say *dish*.
Student: Dish.

Teacher: Read *dish*.
Student: Dish.

Teacher: *Dish* begins with /d/. Repeat: /d/.
Student: /d/.

Teacher: /d/.
Student: /d/.

Teacher: /d/.
Student: /d/.

Teacher: /d/.
Student: /d/.

Teacher: The sound is /d/.
         The name is *d*. Say *d*.
Student: *d*.

Teacher: What's the name?
Student: *d*.

Teacher: What's the sound?
Student: /d/.

**Review previous letters on chart**

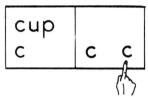

Teacher: What's the sound?
Student: /k/.

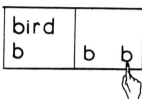

Teacher: What's the sound?
Student: /b/.

Teacher: What's the name?
Student: *b.*

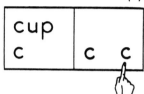

Teacher: What's the name?
Student: *c.*

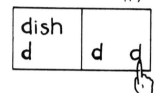

Teacher: What's the name?
Student: *d.*

**Line 4**

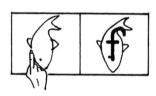

Teacher: What's this?
Student: It's a fish.

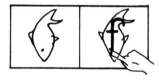

Teacher: [Trace the letter slowly.]
Say *fish.*
Student: Fish.

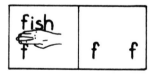

Teacher: Read *fish.*
Student: Fish.

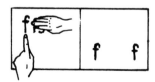

Teacher: *Fish* begins with /f/. Repeat: /f/.
Student: /f/.

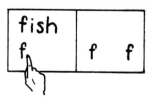

Teacher: /f/.
Student: /f/.

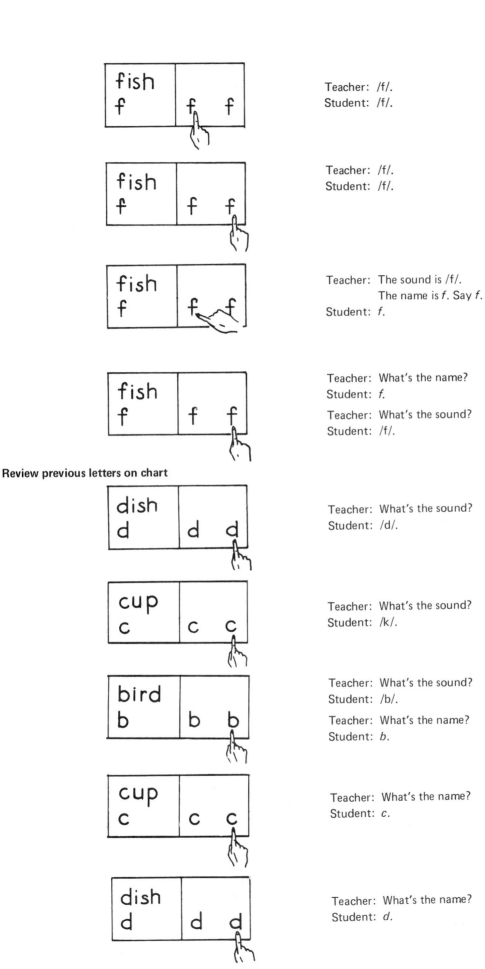

**Teacher:** /f/.
**Student:** /f/.

**Teacher:** /f/.
**Student:** /f/.

**Teacher:** The sound is /f/.
The name is *f*. Say *f*.
**Student:** *f*.

**Teacher:** What's the name?
**Student:** *f*.

**Teacher:** What's the sound?
**Student:** /f/.

**Review previous letters on chart**

**Teacher:** What's the sound?
**Student:** /d/.

**Teacher:** What's the sound?
**Student:** /k/.

**Teacher:** What's the sound?
**Student:** /b/.

**Teacher:** What's the name?
**Student:** *b*.

**Teacher:** What's the name?
**Student:** *c*.

**Teacher:** What's the name?
**Student:** *d*.

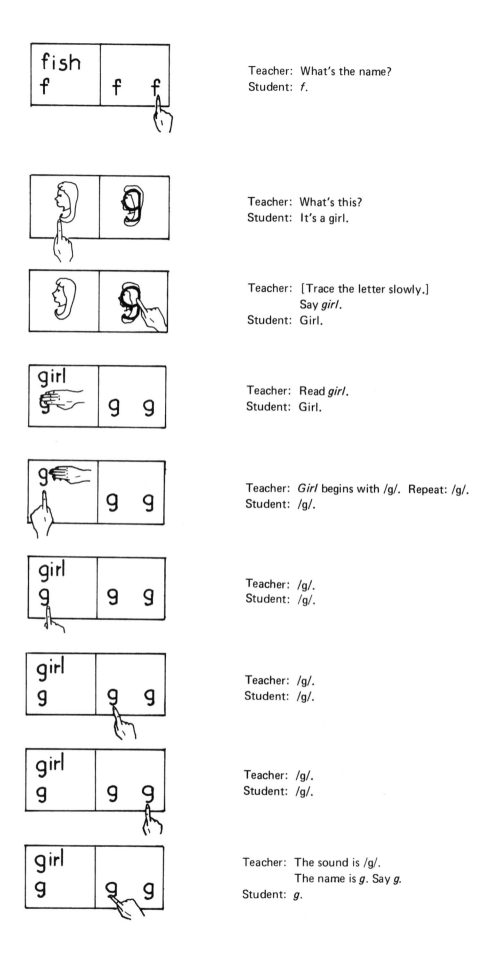

Teacher: What's the name?
Student: *f*.

**Line 5**

Teacher: What's this?
Student: It's a girl.

Teacher: [Trace the letter slowly.]
Say *girl*.
Student: Girl.

Teacher: Read *girl*.
Student: Girl.

Teacher: *Girl* begins with /g/. Repeat: /g/.
Student: /g/.

Teacher: /g/.
Student: /g/.

Teacher: /g/.
Student: /g/.

Teacher: /g/.
Student: /g/.

Teacher: The sound is /g/.
The name is *g*. Say *g*.
Student: *g*.

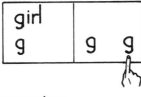

Teacher: What's the name?
Student: *g.*

Teacher: What's the sound?
Student: /g/.

**Review previous letters on chart**

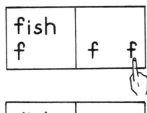

Teacher: What's the sound?
Student: /f/.

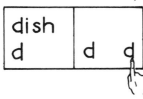

Teacher: What's the sound?
Student: /d/.

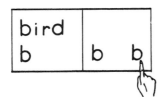

Teacher: What's the sound?
Student: /k/.

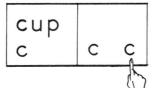

Teacher: What's the sound?
Student: /b/.

Teacher: What's the name?
Student: *b.*

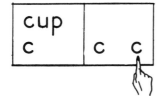

Teacher: What's the name?
Student: *c.*

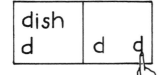

Teacher: What's the name?
Student: *d.*

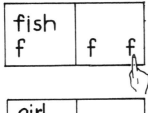

Teacher: What's the name?
Student: *f.*

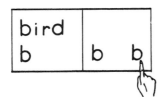

Teacher: What's the name?
Student: *g.*

**Line 6**

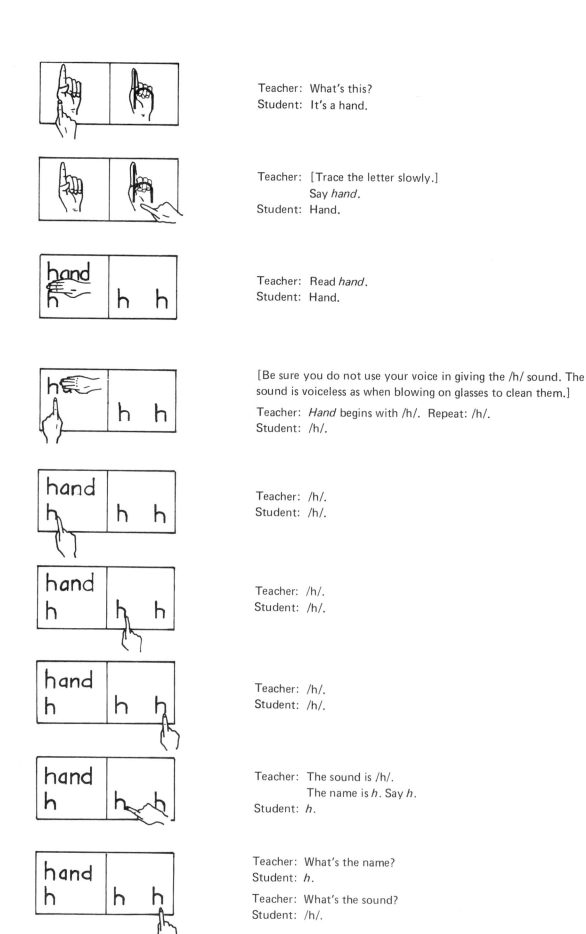

Teacher: What's this?
Student: It's a hand.

Teacher: [Trace the letter slowly.]
Say *hand*.
Student: Hand.

Teacher: Read *hand*.
Student: Hand.

[Be sure you do not use your voice in giving the /h/ sound. The sound is voiceless as when blowing on glasses to clean them.]

Teacher: *Hand* begins with /h/. Repeat: /h/.
Student: /h/.

Teacher: /h/.
Student: /h/.

Teacher: /h/.
Student: /h/.

Teacher: /h/.
Student: /h/.

Teacher: The sound is /h/.
The name is *h*. Say *h*.
Student: *h*.

Teacher: What's the name?
Student: *h*.

Teacher: What's the sound?
Student: /h/.

**Review letters on chart**

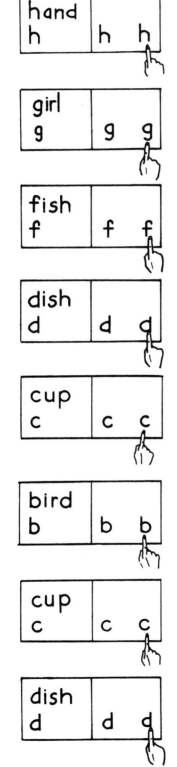

[Begin the review by teaching the concept of *letter*.]

Teacher: [Point to the last letter in each line.]
    *b* is a letter.
    *c* is a letter.
    *d* is a letter.
    *f* is a letter.
    *g* is a letter.
    *h* is a letter.

[Now review the sounds and names of all the letters, but this time, use the words *of this letter*.]

Teacher: What's the sound of this letter?
Student: /h/.

Teacher: What's the sound of this letter?
Student: /g/.

Teacher: What's the sound of this letter?
Student: /f/.

Teacher: What's the sound of this letter?
Student: /d/.

Teacher: What's the sound of this letter?
Student: /k/.

Teacher: What's the sound of this letter?
Student: /b/.

Teacher: What's the name of this letter?
Student: *b*.

Teacher: What's the name of this letter?
Student: *c*.

Teacher: What's the name of this letter?
Student: *d*.

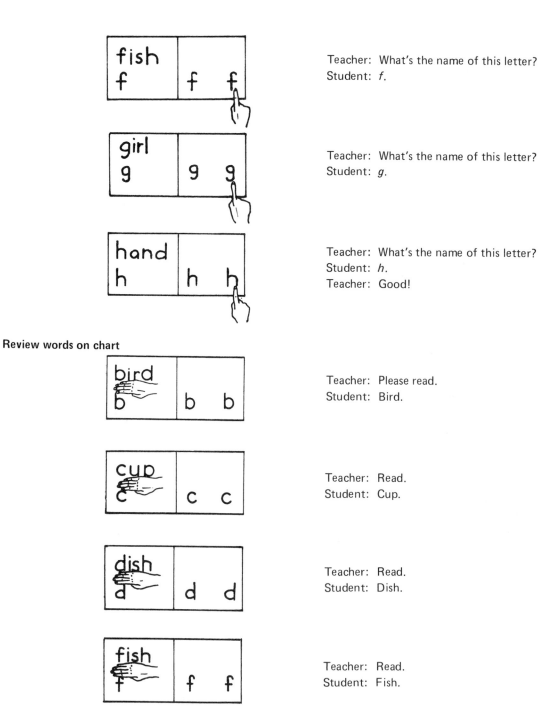

Teacher: What's the name of this letter?
Student: *f.*

Teacher: What's the name of this letter?
Student: *g.*

Teacher: What's the name of this letter?
Student: *h.*
Teacher: Good!

**Review words on chart**

Teacher: Please read.
Student: Bird.

Teacher: Read.
Student: Cup.

Teacher: Read.
Student: Dish.

Teacher: Read.
Student: Fish.

Teacher: Read.
Student: Girl.

Teacher: Read.
Student: Hand.
Teacher: Good!

Teacher: [Point to page number.] This is page 2. Read 2.
Student: 2.

## STORY: The Girl

| Do this: | Say this: |
|---|---|
| Point to the title. | Teacher: The girl. Read: *The girl*.<br>Student: The girl. |

### Paragraph 1

| | |
|---|---|
| Point to the word *bird* in chart. | Teacher: Please read.<br>Student: Bird.<br>Teacher: Good. |
| Point to the word *bird* in the first sentence. | Teacher: Read.<br>Student: Bird. |
| Run your finger under the sentence as you read it. | Teacher: This is a bird. Please read.<br>Student: This is a bird.<br>[Have your student read sentence as a whole, not word by word.] |
| Point to *cup* in the chart. | Teacher: Please read.<br>Student: Cup. |
| Point to *cup* in the second sentence. | Teacher: Read.<br>Student: Cup. |
| Run your finger under the sentence. | Teacher: Read.<br>Student: This is a cup.<br>Teacher: Good!<br>[Teach the next four sentences in exactly the same way.] |

### Paragraph 2

| | |
|---|---|
| Point to *girl* in chart. | Teacher: Please read.<br>Student: Girl. |
| Point to *girl* in first sentence. | Teacher: Read.<br>Student: Girl. |
| Point to *bird* in chart. | Teacher: Read.<br>Student: Bird. |
| Point to *bird* in first sentence. | Teacher: Read.<br>Student: Bird. |
| Run your finger under the sentence. | Teacher: The girl has a bird.<br>Please read.<br>Student: The girl has a bird. |
| Point to *cup* in chart. | Teacher: Read.<br>Student: Cup. |
| Point to *cup* in second sentence. | Teacher: Read.<br>Student: Cup. |
| Run your finger under the sentence. | Teacher: Read.<br>Student: The girl has a cup.<br><br>[Teach the next two sentences in exactly the same way.] |

## Paragraph 3

| Do this | Say this |
|---|---|
| Point to *hand* in the chart. | Teacher: Please read.<br>Student: Hand. |
| Point to *hand* in first sentence. | Teacher: Read.<br>Student: Hand. |
| Run your finger under the sentence. | Teacher: The girl has a bird in her hand.<br>Please read.<br>Student: The girl has a bird in her hand. |
| Run your finger under the second sentence. | Teacher: Read.<br>Student: The girl has a cup in her hand. |
| Run your finger under the third sentence. | Teacher: Read.<br>Student: The girl has a dish in her hand. |
| Run your finger under the last sentence. (Refer to the chart whenever the student hesitates on a key word.) | Teacher: Read.<br>Student: The girl has a fish in her hand.<br>Teacher: Good! |

## Story Words

```
this     the      in
is       has      her
a
```

Story words are new sight-reading words introduced in the story, but not in the chart. These words have been introduced orally, however. Give special attention to the story words to be sure the student can read them.

| Do this: | Say this: |
|---|---|
| Point to first sentence in paragraph 1. | Teacher: Please read.<br>Student: This is a bird. |
| Point to *this* in first sentence. | Teacher: Read.<br>Student: This. |
| Point to *this* in each of the other sentences in paragraph 1. | Teacher: Read.<br>Student: This. . .this. . .this. . .this. . .this. |
| Point to first sentence in paragraph 1 *again*. | Teacher: Please read.<br>Student: This is a bird. |
| Point to *is* in first sentence. | Teacher: Read.<br>Student: Is. |
| Point to *is* in each of the other sentences in paragraph 1. | Teacher: Read.<br>Student: Is. . .is. . .is. . .is. . . is. |

Continue in the same way for *a* (pronounced /u/) in paragraph 1. Begin by having the student read the first sentence again. Notice that you point out the story words in the same order as they appear in the sentence.

Follow the same procedure for the story words in the other two paragraphs. For each word, begin by having the student read the first sentence of the paragraph. In paragraph 2, point out only the words that are new in that paragraph: *the* (pronounced /thu/) and *has*. In paragraph 3, point out *in* and *her*.

**Review of Story**

Indicate the entire story, including the title.

Teacher: Please read.
Student: [Student reads entire story. Help him with any pronunciation difficulties.]
Teacher: Good!

Point to page number.

Teacher: This is page 3. Read *3*.
Student: 3.
Teacher: Good!

# III. Writing

## WRITING LESSON:  Page 4

Review the notes to the teacher on manuscript writing on page 24 of this manual when you make your preparations for teaching this part of the lesson.

**Do this:**

Turn in the student's book to page 4.
Point to the heading.

Turn back to Chart 1.
Point to *bird*.

Point to *b* on the chart.

Turn back to page 4, and point to the *b* in black.

Point to the dotted-line *b*.

**Say this:**

Teacher: Writing Lesson. Please read.
Student: Writing Lesson.

Teacher: Read.
Student: Bird.

Teacher: What is the sound of this letter?
Student: /b/.

Teacher: What is the name of this letter?
Student: *b*.

Teacher: What is the sound of this letter?
Student: /b/.

Teacher: What is the name of this letter?
Student: *b*.

[Trace the correct strokes on the green dot-and-arrow figure that shows how to write *b*. Trace with a pencil rather than with your finger. This will suggest the idea of writing, and the slender pencil-point will give the student a better view. Trace very lightly so that you do not actually mark on the book.]

Teacher: Write *b*.
Student: [Writes *b*.]
Teacher: Good! Again.

[Have the student write the letter several times, saying the sound each time he writes it.]

Follow the same procedure with the other letters: *h, f, d, g,* and *c.*

When you trace the green dot-and-arrow figure for *f*, which requires pencil-lifting, say "1, 2," as you trace each separate stroke.

Finally, teach the page number 4.

## HOMEWORK: Page 5

Point to the heading.

Teacher: Homework. Please read.
Student: Homework.

To explain what the student is to do, start doing a bit of page 5 as you did page 4. Then close the book and hand it to the student.

Indicate by pointing to a later time on a clock that the homework is something to be done later, not now.

Teacher: Write the homework at home.

Point to the page number.

Teacher: This is page 5. Read 5.
Student: 5.
Teacher: Good!

## READING AND WRITING EVALUATION

1. Write f, h, b, d, c, g on the board, in that order. Ask your student to say the sound for each letter. Student should be able to give all six sounds fairly quickly.

2. Write fish, dish, cup, hand, bird, girl. Ask your student to read each word. Student should be able to read all the words, although pronunciation may not be perfect.

3. Write this, the, a, her, in, is, has. Ask your student to read each word. Student should be able to read all the words, although pronunciation may not be perfect.

# Lesson 2

## OBJECTIVES

When a student completes this unit, he should be able to:

1. Say and respond to a new dialog.
2. Say the chart words, some action words, and the names of the parts of the body.
3. Use *be* + verb-*ing*.
4. Use the -*'s* possessive.
5. Use the word *and*.
6. Pronounce the sounds m/n/ng.
7. Say, read, and write the numbers 61-70.
8. Say the sound for each of these letters: *j, k, l, m, n, p*.
9. Read the following new words:
   Chart words: *jumping, kicking, leg, man, neck, pan*
   Story words: *and, man's, girl's.*
10. Read a simple story, using the new chart and story words.
11. Write the letters *j, k, l, m, n, p*.

## VISUAL AIDS

Accompanying *ESOL Illustrations for Skill Book 1*, pp. 22-24.

## REVIEW

Review any items that your student had difficulty with when doing the Oral Evaluation in Lesson 1.

# I. Conversation Skills

## DIALOG

| |
|---|
| Teacher: What are you doing? |
| Student: I'm reading a book. |
| What are you doing? |
| Teacher: I'm studying English. |

Practice the dialog, using the procedure outlined in
Unit A.

## VOCABULARY: Action Words

| | |
|---|---|
| I am walking. | I'm walking. |
| I am sitting down. | I'm sitting down. |
| I am standing up. | I'm standing up. |
| I am writing my name. | I'm writing my name. |
| I am closing my book. | I'm closing my book. |
| I am opening my book. | I'm opening my book. |

Teacher models first the full form, then the contracted form, of each pair of sentences, having the student repeat each sentence after her.

Use contractions in the Drills that follow.

[As you say the sentences, perform the action described, that is, walk, sit down, stand up, and so on.]

## DRILL: Substitution Drill with Visual Cues

Teacher performs the action, and the student says the sentences.

Be sure to perform the actions clearly.

[Open your book and say, "I'm opening my book."
Continue performing actions taught above, but have the student say the sentences.]

## DRILL: Questions and Answers (Free Reply)

Substitute the vocabulary items taught into the form of the dialog. Let the student choose his own answer.

[Say both parts of the dialog as an example.]

What are you doing?
I'm walking. What are you doing?
I'm sitting down.

## VOCABULARY: *cup, dish, pan*

| |
|---|
| The girl has a cup. |
| dish. |
| pan. |

Teacher models the sentences, having the student repeat.

(*Pan*, a chart word, is the only new vocabulary item.)

## DRILL: Substitution Drill with Visual Cues

Use the girl's possessions in the picture on p. 22 of *ESOL Illustrations.*

[Pointing to the cup, ask, "What's this?"
Let the student answer, "It's a cup." Prompt him only if necessary.]

[Repeat with *dish* and *pan*.]

## VOCABULARY: Chart Words

> The man is jumping.
> The man is kicking.

Teacher models the sentences, pointing to the pictures on p. 23 of *ESOL Illustrations*. The student repeats.

[Say, "Please repeat."]

The man is jumping.
The man is kicking.
The girl is jumping.

## DRILL: Substitution Drill with Visual Cues

Teacher points to the pictures on p. 23 of *ESOL Illustrations* to elicit the new vocabulary items.

[Ask, "What is the man doing? He's jumping. Repeat. He's jumping."]

## VOCABULARY: Parts of the Body

> This is a man.          This is his neck.
> This is his head.       This is his arm.
> This is his eye.        This is his hand.
> This is his nose.       This is his finger.
> This is his mouth.      This is his leg.
> This is his ear.        This is his foot.

Teacher models the sentences several times, using the picture on p. 24 of *ESOL Illustrations*. Have the student repeat.

Do the sentences in column 1 first, then do those in column 2.

[Point to the man and say, "This is a man. Repeat. This is a man."]

## DRILL: Substitution Drill with Visual Cues

Teacher asks questions, pointing to the various parts of the body in the picture on p. 24 of *ESOL Illustrations*.

In the answer, use the form "This is the man's leg," since it is in the Story in Lesson 2 of *Skill Book 1*.

For advanced students, you may include other parts of the body, such as *lip, wrist, ankle, knee, waist*, and so on.

| Teacher | Student |
| --- | --- |
| What's this? | |
| This is a man. | |
| | |
| What's this? | |
| This is the head. | |
| This is the man's head. | |
| | |
| Repeat. | |
| This is the man's head. | This is the man's head. |

[Continue indicating the other parts of the body, having student give the sentence.]

**STRUCTURE FOCUS: The Use of *and***

---

I have a book <u>and</u> a pen.
She has   a pen   <u>and</u> a pencil.

---

Teacher models the sentences several times, having the student repeat. Do not stress the word *and*.

[Hold up a book, saying, "I have a book. . ."
Hold up a pen also as you say, "and a pen. Repeat.
I have a book and a pen."]

[Continue the drill, holding up or indicating items.]

a pen and a pencil
a pencil and an eraser
a book and a pencil
a table and a chair
a window and a door

**DRILL: Substitution Drill with Visual Cues**

Continue the drill above, indicating combinations of items already taught. Use pictures of the items when necessary. Have the student say the sentences. Prompt him only if necessary.

a girl and a boy
a cup and a dish
a bird and a fish
a desk and a chair
a blackboard and an eraser
a clock and a window

**STRUCTURE FOCUS: *be* + verb-*ing***

---

| | |
|---|---|
| I am walking. | I'm walking. |
| You are walking. | You're walking. |
| The man is walking. | The man's walking. |
| The girl is jumping. | The girl's jumping. |

---

Teacher models first the full form, then the contracted form, of each pair of sentences, having the student repeat each sentence after her.

Perform the action yourself, or use the pictures on p. 23 of *ESOL Illustrations* when appropriate.

**Note:** This tense, made with *be* and a verb ending in *-ing*, indicates an action in progress at the moment of speaking.

[Say, "Listen to *I am, I'm.*]

Teacher: I am walking. I'm walking.

Teacher: I am walking.
Student: I am walking.

Teacher: I'm walking.
Student: I'm walking.

[Continue the same way with the other sentence pairs.]

## DRILL: Substitution Drill with Vocal Cues

Model the contracted form, and have the student use the contracted form.

| Teacher | Student |
|---|---|
| The man's walking. | The man's walking. |
| He | |
| He's walking. | He's walking. |
| She | She's walking. |
| I | |
| You | |
| The girl | |
| She | |
| The man | |
| You | |

## DRILL: Questions and Answers

Ask questions about the pictures on p. 23 of *ESOL Illustrations* and questions appropriate to what the student is doing.

| Teacher | Student |
|---|---|
| What are you doing? | I'm sitting down. |
| What is the man doing? | He's walking. |
| What is the girl doing? | She's jumping. |
| What is the man doing? | He's kicking. |
| What is the man doing? | He's jumping. |

## STRUCTURE FOCUS: Possessives with -'s

> This is the man's leg.
> This is the girl's neck.
> This is the girl's pan.
> This is the man's dish.

1. Teacher models the sentences several times, having the student repeat.

   Use the picture on p. 22 of *ESOL Illustrations*.

   Practice this pattern very well since it occurs in the Story in Lesson 2 of *Skill Book 1*.

   [Say, "Listen to /z/ in *the man's leg*."]

2. Using items that belong to the student, teacher models sentences like those suggested here. Use the student's name, and use only objects whose names have already been taught. Have the student repeat the sentences.

   [Pointing to the items, start by saying one or two sentences, such as the following.]

   This is Ann's book.
   This is Ann's pen.

   [Continue with other sentences.]

   This is Ann's paper.
   This is Ann's desk.

3. Following the procedure in step 2, the teacher uses her own first name and items that belong to her in sentences, having the student repeat.

## DRILL: Questions and Answers

Teacher asks questions with *whose* to elicit answers with the *-'s* possessive.

Ask questions about items belonging to you and questions about the picture on p. 22 of *ESOL Illustrations*.

**Class:** Elicit the names of the students in the class.

**Note:** The student need only recognize the question with *whose*; he need not produce it at this time.

[Ask, "Whose book is this?"
Point to someone else's book—not that of the student you are speaking to. Answer, "It's Bob's."]

| Teacher | Student |
|---|---|
| Whose pen    is this? | It's Bob's. |
| Whose paper is this? | |
| Whose pencil is this? | |
| Whose chair  is this? | |
| Whose pan    is this? | |
| Whose hand  is this? | |
| Whose arm    is this? | |
| Whose finger is this? | |

## PRONUNCIATION: m/n/ng

1. Teacher models pairs of words contrasting the /m/ and /n/ sounds as in *tam* and *tan*. Have the student repeat.

   Then contrast the /n/ and /ng/ as in *tang* in the same way.

   Do not explain the meaning of the words.

   **Note:** This drill contrasts the voiced nasal sounds /m/, /n/, and /ng/.

   For /m/, the lips are closed.

   For /n/, the tongue touches the tooth ridge.

   For /ng/, the tongue touches the back of the mouth (velum).

   The air stream comes through the nose for these three sounds.

2. Teacher contrasts the three sounds. Follow steps 2, 3, and 4 of the Pronunciation section in Unit D.

3. Practice the sounds by using them in phrases and sentences. Do not explain vocabulary.

[Say, "Listen to /m/ and /n/."
Prolong the two sounds as you say them.]

| | |
|---|---|
| map | nap |
| sum | sun |
| comb | cone |
| meat | neat |
| mail | nail |

[Now have the student repeat the pairs after you.]

[Say, "Listen to /n/ and /ng/."
Prolong the two sounds as you say them.]

| | |
|---|---|
| sun | sung |
| ran | rang |
| ton | tongue |
| thin | thing |
| tan | tang |

[Now have the student repeat the pairs after you.]

| | | |
|---|---|---|
| sum | sun | sung |
| tam | tan | tang |
| Tim | tin | ting |

| | |
|---|---|
| a black pan | The mail is here. |
| Tom's son | The nail is here. |
| I'm Ann. | |
| I'm Bob Samson. | The boy rang. |
| The sun's shining. | The boy ran. |

## VOCABULARY: Numbers 61-70

Teacher reviews the numbers 51-60 and introduces 61-70. Model the numbers 61-70 and have the student repeat.

Follow the procedures described in Unit B to teach saying, reading, and writing the numbers.

## ORAL EVALUATION

1. Review the contracted forms of *be* with verbs ending in *-ing* as well as the meaning of the action verbs taught.

   The student must know *jumping* and *kicking* as well as four other verbs.

[Perform the action and ask, "What am I doing?" Give the answer, "You're walking."]

[Have the student say the other sentences as you perform the action.]

| | |
|---|---|
| You're walking. | You're closing your book. |
| You're sitting down. | You're opening your book. |
| You're standing up. | You're jumping. |
| You're writing your name. | You're kicking. |

2. Review *cup, dish,* and *pan*, all of which are necessary for reading the Story in Lesson 2.

3. Review the parts of the body.

   The student must know *leg, neck,* and *hand* to read the Story in Lesson 2; he should know five other parts of the body as well.

[Use the girl's possessions in the picture on p. 22 of *ESOL Illustrations.* Ask, "What's this?"]

[Using the picture on p. 23 of *ESOL Illustrations*, see if the student can identify the parts of the body that have been taught.]

4. Review the *-'s* possessive form with the parts of the body, as: "This is the man's leg."

   The student must be able to use *the man's leg, the man's neck,* and *the man's hand* in order to read the Story in Lesson 2.

[Use the procedure in the Substitution Drill that follows Vocabulary: Parts of the Body.]

# II. Reading

Before beginning the Lesson 2 chart, check the student's Homework for Lesson 1. If the student has done his homework, praise him. If he has not, try again to get across the idea. Open his book to page 5, saying "Your homework?" with a rising intonation. If the student has not done the homework, be careful not to look disappointed. Have him do it now.

By the time the student has finished the Homework, he should be making letters that are recognizable. At this point, however, his letters need not be neat, aligned, or of uniform size.

## CHART 2: Page 6

Open your student's book to Lesson 2, page 6.

**Do this:**
Point to Lesson 2.

**Say this:**
Teacher: Lesson 2. Read: *Lesson 2.*
Student: Lesson 2.

Point to Chart 2.

Teacher: Chart 2. Read: *Chart 2.*
Student: Chart 2.
Teacher: Good!

**Line 1**
Do this:

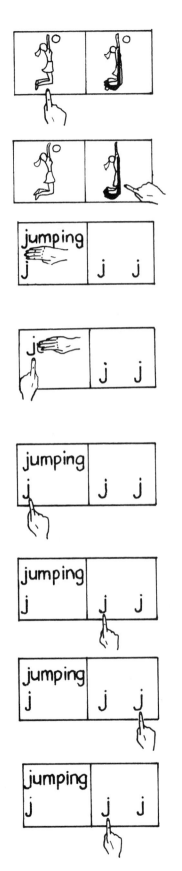

**Say this:**

Teacher: [Point to the girl jumping.]
What's the girl doing?
Student: The girl is jumping.


Teacher: [Trace the letter as you would write it.]
Say *jumping*.
Student: Jumping.


Teacher: Read *jumping*.
Student: Jumping.


Teacher: [Cover all but the first letter of the word.]
*Jumping* begins with /j/. Repeat: /j/.
[In making the sound /j/, start to say *jumping* but give only the first sound. Try not to make any vowel sound.]
Student: /j/.


Teacher: /j/.
Student: /j/.


Teacher: /j/.
Student: /j/.


Teacher: /j/.
Student: /j/.


Teacher: The sound of this letter is /j/.
The name of this letter is *j*. Say *j*.
Student: *j*.

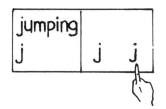

Teacher: What's the name of this letter?
Student: *j*.

Teacher: What's the sound of this letter?
Student: /j/.

Teach the rest of the chart in exactly the same way. For line-by-line instructions refer to instructions in Lesson 1 for teaching Chart 1. Be sure to review the sounds and names of the letters and the words. Be sure to have the student read the page number.

## STORY: The Girl and the Man

**Do this:**

Point to the title.

**Say this:**

Teacher: The girl and the man. Read.
Student: The girl and the man.

## Paragraph 1

Point to the word *man* in chart.

Teacher: Please read.
Student: Man.
Teacher: Good!

Point to *man* in the first sentence.

Teacher: Read.
Student: Man.

Run your finger under the sentence.

Teacher: Read.
Student: This is a man.

[Have your student read the sentence as a whole, not word by word.]

Teach the rest of paragraph 1 and paragraphs 2 and 3 in exactly the same way. Go from the key word in the chart to the key word in the sentence (from the known to the unknown).

## Paragraph 4

**Do this:**

Point to *leg* in chart.

**Say this:**

Teacher: Please read.
Student: Leg.

Point to *leg* in first sentence.

Teacher: Read.
Student: Leg.

Run your finger under the sentence.

Teacher: This is the man's leg.
Please read.
Student: This is the man's leg.

Point to *neck* in chart.

Teacher: Read.
Student: Neck.

Point to *neck* in second sentence.

Teacher: Read.
Student: Neck.

Run your finger under the sentence.

Teacher: Read.
Student: This is the man's neck.
Teacher: Good!

Teach the rest of the story in the same way. Then have your student read the complete story by himself, from title to page number at the bottom of the page. Make any corrections that are necessary.

## STORY WORDS

| **Do this:** | **Say this:** |
| --- | --- |
| Run your finger under the sentence, *This is the man's leg*. | Teacher: Please read.<br>Student: This is the man's leg.<br>Teacher: Good! |
| Point to *man's*. | Teacher: Read.<br>Student: Man's. |
| Now cover the *'s*. | Teacher: Read.<br>Student: Man.<br>Teacher: Good! |

Have your student read the rest of the *man's* on the page, as you point. Then point out *girl's* and compare it to *girl* in exactly the same way. Finally, point out *and* in the title.

## READING HINTS

Work to help your student pronounce both individual words and entire sentences correctly. As your student reads, listen to his pronunciation and correct the grossest errors (that is, words which are so distorted that they are not understandable). First correct the word itself, then say it in the sentence and have the student repeat the entire sentence. Do this three or four times at most.

Can you hear the endings of the words the student says? Dropping the ending is a common error, which will cause spelling problems later on.

# III. Writing

## CHECKUP: Page 8

| **Do this:** | **Say this:** |
| --- | --- |
| Turn to page 8 in the student's book. Point to the heading. | Teacher: Checkup. Please read.<br>Student: Checkup.<br>Teacher: Good. |
| Point to the bird. | Teacher: What's this?<br>Student: It's a bird.<br><br>Teacher: *Bird* begins with what sound? /b/. Repeat: /b/.<br>Student: /b/.<br><br>Teacher: What is the name of this letter? *b*. Say *b*.<br>Student: *b*.<br>Teacher: Good! Write *b*.<br><br>[Be sure the student uses the guidelines correctly. If he does not, simply write one *b* correctly. He will follow your example.] |

| **Do this:** | **Say this:** |
|---|---|

Point to the cup.

Teacher: What's this?
Student: It's a cup.

Teacher: *Cup* begins with what sound?
Student: /k/.

[If the student cannot give the sound, supply it for him, and ask him to repeat.]

Teacher: Good! What is the name of this letter?
Student: *c.*

[Again, if the student cannot give the answer, supply it and ask him to repeat.]
Teacher: Good! Write *c.*

Do *dish, fish, girl,* and *hand* in exactly the same way. When the student has finished writing, let him check his work against Chart 1. If he has made a mistake, have him correct it now.

Then point to the page number. "This is page 8. Read *8.*"

## LISTEN AND WRITE: Page 9

Point to the heading:

Teacher: Listen and Write. Read.
Student: Listen and Write.
Teacher: Good!

Teacher: Listen. Bird.
        *Bird* begins with what sound?
Student: /b/.

Teacher: What is the name of this letter?
Student: *b.*
Teacher: Write *b.*

[Indicate that he is to write *b* in column 1, line 1. If your student hesitates in writing the letter, refer him to the reading chart. If he makes a mistake, have him write the letter correctly in the second column.]

Proceed in the same way with these words: *fish, dish, hand, girl, cup.*

## WRITING LESSON: Page 10

| Do this: | Say this: |
|---|---|
| Point to heading. | Teacher: Writing Lesson. Read.<br>Student: Writing Lesson. |
| Turn back to Chart 2. Point to *leg*. | Teacher: Read.<br>Student: Leg. |
| Point to *l* on the chart. | Teacher: What's the sound of this letter?<br>Student: /l/.<br><br>Teacher: What's the name of this letter?<br>Student: *l*. |
| Turn back to page 10, and point to the *l* in black. | Teacher: What's the sound of this letter?<br>Student: /l/.<br><br>Teacher: What's the name of this letter?<br>Student: *l*.<br><br>[Trace the correct stroke *very* lightly over the green dot-and-arrow figure for *l*.] |
| Point to the dotted-line *l*. | Teacher: Write *l*.<br>Student: [Writes *l*.]<br>Teacher: Good! Again.<br><br>[Have the student write the letter several times, saying the sound each time he writes it.] |

Follow the same procedure with the other letters: *k, j, p, n, m*.

When you trace the green dot-and-arrow figure for *k* and *j*, which require pencil-lifting, say "1, 2," as you trace each separate stroke.

Finally, have the student read the page number: "This is page 10. Read *10*."

## HOMEWORK: Page 11

| | |
|---|---|
| Point to the heading. | Teacher: Homework. Read.<br>Student: Homework. |
| Indicate entire page 11, then entire page 10. | Teacher: Do this page [page 11] like this [page 10]. |
| Point to the page number. | Teacher: This is page 11. Read *11*.<br>Student: 11.<br>Teacher: Good. |

## READING AND WRITING EVALUATION

1. Write *m, l, p, k, n, j* on the board, in that order. Ask your student to say the sound for each letter.
   Student should be able to recall at least four sounds correctly.

2. Write *girl, girl's, man, man's,* and *pan, jumping, neck, kicking, leg.* Ask your student to read the words.
   Student should be able to read all the words correctly.

# Lesson 3

## OBJECTIVES

When a student completes this unit, he should be able to:

1. Say and respond to a new dialog.
2. Say the chart words, the names of the months of the year, and some action words.
3. Use the third person singular -s form of the verb with a singular noun, a person's name, or with *he* or *she*, as in "The man looks at the tent."
4. Use the non-*s* form of the verb with *I* and *you*, as in "I look at the book."
5. Pronounce the -s ending of the third person singular verbs.
6. Say, read, and write the numbers 71-80.
7. Say the sound for each of these letters: *r, s, t, v, w, y*.
8. Read the following new words:
   Chart words: *river, snake, tent, valley, woman, yells*
   Story words: *at, look*.
9. Read a simple story, using the new chart and story words.
10. Write the letters *r, s, t, v, w, y*.

## VISUAL AIDS

1. A current calendar, showing the names of the months.
2. Accompanying *ESOL Illustrations for Skill Book 1*, p. 25.

## REVIEW

Review any items that your student had difficulty with when doing the Oral Evaluation in Lesson 2.

# I. Conversation Skills

## DIALOG

| |
|---|
| Teacher: Are you from Puerto Rico? |
| Student: Yes, I'm from San Juan. |
| Teacher: That's a beautiful city. |
| Student: Yes, it is. |

1. Teach the dialog, using the procedure outlined in Unit A.

2. Vary the dialog by using the native country and hometown of your student.

## VOCABULARY: Months of the Year

| | |
|---|---|
| It's January. | It's July. |
| It's February. | It's August. |
| It's March. | It's September. |
| It's April. | It's October. |
| It's May. | It's November. |
| It's June. | It's December. |

Using a calendar, the teacher points to the names of the months and models the sentences, having the student repeat.

[Be sure the student imitates your pronunciation as he repeats the sentences after you. Help him with the months that are difficult for him to pronounce.]

## DRILL: Substitution Drill with Visual Cues

1. Teacher asks, "What month is this?" and student answers.

   Student need only recognize the question at this point; he need not produce it.

   [Point to various months on the calendar and ask, "What month is this?" If the student cannot answer, say: "It's January. Repeat. It's January."]

2. Drill on the actual month and day the class is being taught. For example, say, "Today is April 15th." (Say *fifteenth*, as you normally would, even though the ordinal numbers have not yet been taught.)

   [Say the date in the frame "Today is _____." Have the student repeat after you.]

## VOCABULARY: Chart Words

| |
|---|
| This is a river. |
| This is a snake. |
| This is a tent. |
| This is a valley. |

Pointing to the pictures on p. 25 of *ESOL Illustrations*, the teacher models the sentences several times, having the student repeat.

[Listen carefully to your student's pronunciation since these words may be difficult for him to pronounce.]

## DRILL: Substitution Drill with Visual Cues

Use the pictures on p. 25 of *ESOL Illustrations*.

[Point to the pictures one by one and say, "What's this? This is a river. Please repeat. This is a river."]

## VOCABULARY: Action Words

| | |
|---|---|
| I am looking at the girl. | I'm looking at the girl. |
| I am reading. | I'm reading. |
| I am speaking. | I'm speaking. |
| I am yelling. | I'm yelling. |

Performing the action described, the teacher models each pair of sentences, first the full form, then the contracted form. Have the student repeat each sentence after you.

Be sure to make a difference between "speaking" and "yelling" as you perform the actions. These words will help your student understand the Story in Lesson 3 of *Skill Book 1*.

**Note:** These sentences review the *be* + verb-*ing* pattern taught in Lesson 2.

[Before modeling the first pair of sentences, say: "Listen to *looking*." Continue the same way with other sentence pairs.]

## DRILL: Questions and Answers

Teacher asks questions which elicit statements containing the action words being taught.

Review *jumping* and *kicking* in this drill.

Have the student use contractions in his answers.

[While looking at a book, ask and answer.]

| Teacher | Student |
|---|---|
| Am I looking at the girl? | |
| No, you're looking at the book. | |
| | |
| Please repeat. | |
| No, you're looking at the book. | No, you're looking at the book. |
| | |
| [Look at the pen.] | |
| Am I looking at a cup? | No, you're looking at a pen. |
| | |
| [Look at a pencil.] | |
| Am I looking at a pen? | No, you're looking at a pencil. |
| | |
| [Look at an eraser.] | |
| Am I looking at a book? | No, you're looking at an eraser. |
| | |
| [Look at the door.] | |
| Am I looking at the window? | No, you're looking at the door. |
| | |
| [Yell as you ask.] | |
| Am I speaking? | No, you're yelling. |
| | |
| [Speak softly.] | |
| Am I yelling? | No, you're speaking. |
| | |
| [Kick a leg.] | |
| Am I jumping? | No, you're kicking. |
| | |
| [Jump.] | |
| Am I kicking? | No, you're jumping. |

## STRUCTURE FOCUS: The -s Verb Form

```
I look  at the book.
You look  at the book.
The man looks at the book.
I yell.
You yell.
The girl yells.
```

Teacher models each set of three sentences several times.

Have the student repeat each of the three sentences after you.

**Note:** The third person singular simple present tense ends in -s. This -s form of verbs is pronounced in the same way as the -s plural ending of nouns. Refer to the Note in the Pronunciation section of Unit C for a complete description.

[Say, "Listen to *look* and *looks*."
Then model the three sentences, and have student repeat.]

[Do the same with *yell* and *yells*.]

## DRILL: Substitution Drill with Vocal Cues

Teacher models cue and response, then says only the cue.

| Teacher | Student |
|---|---|
| I look at the book. | I look at the book. |
| She | |
| She looks at the book. | She looks at the book. |
| The girl | The girl looks at the book. |
| The man | |
| I | |
| Ann | |
| You | |
| He | |
| Bob | |

## PRONUNCIATION: The -s Verb Form

Teacher models the pronunciation of the -s form of verbs, having the student repeat.

**Note:** The -s form of verbs has the same three variations in pronunciation as the -s plural ending of nouns: /s/, /z/, and /uz/.

For the principles governing the use of these three sounds, look again at the Note in the Pronunciation section of Unit C.

[Say, "Listen to the /s/ in *kicks*." Prolong the /s/ sound. Have the student imitate you.]

kicks
jumps
writes
speaks
sits
walks

[Say, "Listen to the /z/ in *opens*." Prolong the /z/ sound. Have the student imitate you.]

opens
stands
yells
studies
reads

[Say, "Listen to the /uz/ in *closes*." Prolong the /uz/ sound. Have the student imitate you.]

closes
misses
uses
passes
washes

## DRILL: Transformation Drill

Teacher says the non-*s* form of the verb; the student says the -*s* form.

[Use a beckoning gesture to show when the student is to speak.]

| Teacher | | Student |
|---|---|---|
| open | He opens. | He opens. |
| yell | | He yells. |
| stand | | He stands. |
| close | | |
| miss | | |
| pass | | |
| speak | | |
| write | | |
| use | | |
| jump | | |
| sit | | |

## VOCABULARY: Numbers 71-80

Teacher reviews the numbers 61-70 and introduces 71-80. Model the numbers and have the student repeat.

Follow the procedures described in Unit B to teach saying, reading, and writing the numbers.

## ORAL EVALUATION

1. Review the months of the year.

   Student should be able to say 8 to 10 of the months.

   Student should be able to say the actual month and date *if* you are doing the Oral Evaluation on the same day he practiced this item.

   Make notes of the months the student does not know or has special difficulty pronouncing.

[Pointing to months on the calendar, ask: "What month is this?"]

2. Review the chart words.

   Student must know all these words to read the Story in Lesson 3 of *Skill Book 1.*

3. Review the action words: *jumping, kicking, looking at, reading, speaking, yelling.*

4. Review the third person singular. Be sure that your student does not omit the *-s* ending.

[Point to the pictures on p. 25 of *ESOL Illustrations.* Do not prompt your student. Give him time to answer.]

This is a river.
         snake.
         tent.
         valley.

[Do the Question and Answer Drill that follows Vocabulary: Action Words in this lesson.]

[Say, "I look at the book. The girl looks at the book."]

| Teacher | | Student |
|---|---|---|
| I read the book. | The girl | The girl reads the book. |
| I speak. | The boy | |
| I yell. | The man | |
| I jump. | The girl | |
| I kick. | She | |

# II. Reading

Before you begin the chart for Lesson 3, check student's homework for Lesson 2. If he did not do it, have him complete it now. Be sure he understands any corrections you make.

## CHART 3: Page 12

Teach the chart as you taught the previous ones. (For *yells,* say: "The man *yells.* Say *yells.*")
Remember to trace the shape of the letter with your finger as you point to the second column.
Remember to review the letters at the completion of each line: review the sounds going up the chart, the names coming down. In reviewing, always point to the last letter in each line.

Review the words and point out the page number before beginning the story. If the student does not remember a word, point to the picture in column 1. Give help only when needed.

## STORY: The Snake

Teach the story exactly as you did for Lessons 1 and 2. When your student has read the entire story, be sure he can identify the new story words by themselves: *at, look.* Point out the quotation marks. Try to get the idea across that quotation marks contain what someone says (or yells). Remember, your student's very limited vocabulary makes such explanations as "these marks mean..." and so on, meaningless. All you want to do now is to see that he notices the quotation marks.

# III. Writing

## CHECKUP: Page 14

**Do this:**

Turn in student's book to page 14. Point to the heading.

**Say this:**

Teacher: Checkup. Read.
Student: Checkup.
Teacher: Good!

Point to the girl jumping.

Teacher: What's the girl doing?
Student: The girl is jumping.
Teacher: *Jumping* begins with what sound?
Student: /j/.
Teacher: Good! What is the name of this letter?
Student: *j*.
Teacher: Good! Write *j*.

Point to the man kicking.

Teacher: What's the man doing?
Student: The man is kicking.
Teacher: *Kicking* begins with what sound?
Student: /k/.
Teacher: Good! What is the name of this letter?
Student: *k*.
Teacher: Good! Write *k*.

Point to the leg.

Teacher: What's this?
Student: It's a leg.
Teacher: Good! *Leg* begins with what sound?
Student: /l/.
Teacher: Good! What is the name of this letter?
Student: *l*.
Teacher: Good! Write *l*.

Do the rest of the page exactly as you just did with *leg*. When the student has finished writing, let him check his work against the appropriate charts. Then help him read the page number.

## LISTEN AND WRITE: Page 15

**Do this:**

Point to the heading.

**Say this:**

Teacher: Listen and Write. Read.
Student: Listen and Write.
Teacher: Good!

Teacher: Listen. Leg. *Leg* begins with what sound?
Student: /l/.
Teacher: Good! What is the name of this letter?
Student: *l*.
Teacher: Good! Write *l*.

Proceed in the same way with these words: *kick, jump, pan, neck, man.* If your student makes any mistakes, help him to write the correct answer in the second column. Then teach him the page number.

## WRITING LESSON: Page 16

From now on, you do not have to refer back to the chart unless the student cannot remember the sound or name of a letter.

| **Do this:** | **Say this:** |
|---|---|
| Point to the heading. | Teacher: Writing Lesson. Read.<br>Student: Writing Lesson. |
| Point to the *t* in black. | Teacher: What's the sound of this letter?<br>Student: /t/. |
| | Teacher: What's the name of this letter?<br>Student: *t*. |
| | [Trace the green dot-and-arrow figure for *t*. Since *t* requires pencil-lifting, say "1, 2" as you make the separate strokes.] |
| Point to the dotted-line *t*. | Teacher: Write *t*. |
| | [Have the student write the letter several times, saying the sound each time.] |

Follow the same procedure with the other letters: *r, s, v, w,* and *y*. Then teach the page number.

## HOMEWORK: Page 17

| | |
|---|---|
| Point to the heading. | Teacher: Homework. Read.<br>Student: Homework.<br>Teacher: Do this [indicate entire page] at home. |
| Point to page number. | Teacher: This is page 17. Read *17*.<br>Student: 17.<br>Teacher: Good! |

## READING AND WRITING EVALUATION

1. Write *t, r, v, s, y, w*. Ask your student to say the sound for each letter. Student should be able to give four sounds correctly without prompting.

2. Write *yells, tent, valley, river, snake*. Ask your student to read the words. Student should be able to read four of these words correctly.

3. Write *Look at, man, woman*. Ask your student to read the words. Student should be able to read all words correctly, though perhaps not quickly.

# Lesson 4

## OBJECTIVES

When a student completes this unit, he should be able to:

1. Say and respond to a new dialog.
2. Say the chart words, additional food items, some adjectives used to describe food, and the verbs *put, pick up*, and *put down*.
3. Use *give...to, get...for, thank...for* in some sentences.
4. Contrast *in* and *on* in some phrases.
5. Use *a/an* and numbers with count nouns and not with non-count nouns.
6. Use *a/an* correctly before nouns.
7. Pronounce the vowel sounds in *pan, pain, pen, pin.*
8. Say, read, and write the numbers 81-90.
9. Say the short vowel sound for each of these letters: *a, e, i, o, u.*
10. Read the following new words:
    Chart words: *apple, egg, in, olive, up*
    Story words: *an, picks, he, his, gives, to, she, puts.*
11. Read a simple story, using the new chart and story words.
12. Write the letters *a, e, i, o, u.*
13. Write the words *up, in, leg, man.*

## VISUAL AIDS

1. Accompanying *ESOL Illustrations for Skill Book 1*, pp. 26-30. To help your student recognize the food items on pp. 26-27, color them in ahead of time.

2. If you can do so, it would also be helpful to bring as many of the actual objects as possible:

| | | | | | |
|---|---|---|---|---|---|
| apple | banana | olive | carton of milk | sugar (cube) | dish |
| orange | lemon | carton of eggs | glass of water | coffee | box |

## REVIEW

Review any items that your student had difficulty with when doing the Oral Evaluation in Lesson 3.

# I. Conversation Skills

## DIALOG

> Teacher: Is the pencil on the table?
> Student: No, it isn't.
> It's in the box.

1. Teach the dialog, using the procedure outlined in Unit A.

2. Vary the dialog by substituting items already taught, e.g. "Is the pen on the desk?"

## VOCABULARY: Food Items

| Count Nouns | Non-count Nouns |
| --- | --- |
| This is an apple. | This is milk. |
| This is an orange. | This is bread. |
| This is a banana. | This is butter. |
| This is an egg. | This is sugar. |
| This is an olive. | This is coffee. |
| This is a lemon. | This is water. |

Teacher models the sentences several times, having the student repeat. Do the count nouns first, then the non-count nouns.

Be sure the student repeats *a* or *an* when he should, but do not stress the article as you say the sentences.

Be sure, too, that the student does not use *a* or *an* where he should not.

As you say the sentences, point to pictures on pp. 26-28 of *ESOL Illustrations,* or hold up items you have on hand.

[Pick up an apple or point to the picture and say, "This is an apple. Please repeat."]

[Continue with the rest of the food items listed.]

## DRILL: Substitution Drill with Visual Cues

Ask the student, "What's this?" as you indicate the various food items. Answer the question yourself two or three times as a model of what you expect.

[Pick up an apple or point to the picture and say, "What's this? This is an apple." Gesture for the student to repeat the answer.]

[Continue with the rest of the food items.]

## VOCABULARY: *eat* and *drink*

| | |
| --- | --- |
| I'm eating an apple. | I'm drinking water. |
| You're eating an orange. | You're drinking coffee. |
| He's eating an egg. | He's drinking milk. |

Teacher models the sentences several times, having the student repeat.

If you have the items with you, you can actually perform the actions of eating and drinking. If not, use the pictures at the top of p. 30 of *ESOL Illustrations.*

[Before modeling the "eating" sentences, say, "Listen to *eating.*"]

[Before modeling the "drinking" sentences, say, "Listen to *drinking.*"]

## DRILL: Substitution Drill with Vocal Cues

In this drill, student must use both the food item and the appropriate verb in the sentence. He must also use or *not* use *a/an* correctly.

| Teacher | Student |
|---|---|
| apple | |
| I'm eating an apple. | I'm eating an apple. |
| milk | |
| I'm drinking milk. | I'm drinking milk. |
| banana | I'm eating a banana. |
| egg | |
| coffee | |
| orange | |
| olive | |
| water | |
| bread | |

## VOCABULARY: Adjectives

> This is a sour   lemon.
> This is a sweet orange.
> This is a big   egg.
> This is a little   egg.
>
> This is hot coffee.
> This is cold water.

Teacher models the sentences, having the student repeat.

Use pictures on pp. 26-28 of *ESOL Illustrations* or actual items.

**One-to-one:** Have the student taste something sour, something sweet, and so on.

**Note:** Note that the adjective precedes the noun.

[Use appropriate facial expressions and hand gestures to give the meaning of the adjectives as you say the sentences.]

## DRILL: Questions and Answers

Teacher asks questions containing the adjectives and indicates the expected reply.

[Ask, "What's sweet?" and answer, "The orange is sweet." Indicate the object as you ask the question.]

| | |
|---|---|
| What's sweet? | (orange) |
| What's sour? | (lemon) |
| What's big? | (egg) |
| What's little? | (egg) |
| What's hot? | (coffee) |
| What's cold? | (water) |

**VOCABULARY:** *get...for, give...to, thank...for,* **and** *says thank you*

| Bob | gets | an apple | for | the boy. |
|-----|------|----------|-----|----------|
| Bob | gives | an apple | to | the boy. |
| The boy | says | thank you. | | |
| The boy | thanks | Bob | for | the apple. |

Teacher models the sentences several times, having the student repeat.

Use the pictures on p. 29 of *ESOL Illustrations*, following the numbered sequence.

[Pointing to picture 1, say, "The boy looks at the apples." The student need not repeat. You are just setting the scene.]

[Pointing to picture 2, say, "Listen to *gets...for*. Bob gets an apple for the boy." Have the student repeat.]

[Continue in the same way, using picture 3 for *gives...to* and using picture 4 for both *says thank you* and *thanks...for*.]

## DRILL: Questions and Answers

Model question and answer until student can answer by himself.

| Teacher | Student |
|---------|---------|
| What does Bob get for the boy? | He gets an apple for the boy. |
| What does Bob give to the boy? | He gives an apple to the boy. |
| What does the boy say? | He says thank you. |
| What does the boy thank Bob for? | He thanks Bob for the apple. |

## DRILL: Substitution Drill with Visual Cues

Use actual objects as well as pictures. The objects and their colors can be different from those suggested here so long as you use only words that have already been taught.

[Hold up a yellow pencil and say, "What does Bob get for the boy? He gets a yellow pencil for the boy. Please repeat. He gets a yellow pencil for the boy."]

[Continue holding up items or indicating pictures as you ask, "What does Bob get for the boy?"]

a blue pen
a green book
a brown eraser
a sweet orange
a little egg
a sweet apple
a sour lemon

[Repeat the same procedure with *give...to*, using the question "What does Bob give to the boy?"]

[Repeat the same procedure again with *thank...for*, using the question "What does the boy thank Bob for?"]

## VOCABULARY: *pick up / put down*

> I pick up the pencil.
> I put down the pencil.

1. Teacher models sentences with *pick up*, having the student repeat.

   Say the *verb* as you are carrying out the action.

   Vary the sentences by picking up items already taught, e.g. book, pen, apple.

   [Pick up the pencil as you say the verb.]

   | Teacher | Student |
   |---|---|
   | I pick up the pencil. | |
   | You pick up the pencil. | |
   | Repeat. | |
   | You pick up the pencil. | You pick up the pencil. |

   [Continue with other items.]

2. Teacher gives commands, using "Pick up the _____."

   Student carries out the action.

   [Say to the student, "Please pick up the pencil." If he does not, show him what to do, then repeat the command. Continue with other items on hand.]

3. Teacher models sentences with *put down*, having the student repeat.

   [Put down the pencil as you say the verb.]

   | Teacher | Student |
   |---|---|
   | I put down the pencil. | |
   | You put down the pencil. | |
   | Repeat. | |
   | You put down the pencil. | You put down the pencil. |

4. Teacher gives commands, using "Put down the _____."

   Student carries out the action.

   [Put the pencil in the student's hand and say, "Please put down the pencil." Continue with other items on hand.]

## STRUCTURE FOCUS: Count and Non-count Nouns

> | Count Nouns | Non-count Nouns |
> |---|---|
> | This is a   pen. | This is paper. |
> | This is a   book. | This is bread. |
> | This is an apple. | This is sugar. |
> | This is an egg. | This is milk. |

Teacher models the sentences several times, having the student repeat. Do the count nouns first, then the non-count nouns.

[As you say the sentence "This is a pen," do *not* emphasize the *a*.]

**Note:** Nouns in English can be divided into those which are countable (*pen, book, girl, boy*) and those which are non-countable (*paper, coffee, butter*).

With count nouns, we use *a/an*, numbers (*two apples*), and usually an *-s* plural.
With non-count nouns, we do not use *a/an* or numbers, nor do we commonly use an *-s* plural (e.g. *milk*).

As you teach count and non-count nouns, you can review many of the nouns already taught. Most of them are count nouns with *-s* plurals (*girl, eraser*). A few are count nouns with irregular plurals (*man, woman, child, housewife*). *Paper* is a non-count noun when used in sentences such as "I need paper to write on."

The use of modifiers (*some, any, many, much*) with count and non-count nouns will be introduced later.

## DRILL: Substitution Drill with Vocal Cues

Teacher gives the model sentence and the cues.

| Teacher | Student |
|---|---|
| This is a book. | This is a book. |
| | |
| clock | This is a clock. |
| bread | This is bread. |
| dish | |
| blackboard | |
| milk | |
| sugar | |
| lemon | |
| paper | |
| butter | |
| pencil | |

## DRILL: Transformation Drill

1. Before beginning the drill, teacher models the plural of the count nouns several times.

[Say the sentences several times, first giving the count nouns and their plural forms, then the non-count nouns. Indicate by shaking your head that the non-count nouns have no plural.]

**Teacher**

This is a book.
These are books.

This is a pen.
These are pens.

This is water.
[Shake your head.]
This is water.

This is bread.
[Shake your head.]
This is bread.

2. Now teacher begins the transformation drill.

[Use hand gestures to indicate when the student is to speak. Shake your head if student tries to use a non-count noun in the plural.]

| Teacher | Student |
|---|---|
| This is a pen. | These are pens. |
| This is bread. | This is bread. |
| This is milk. | |
| This is a pencil. | |
| This is a banana. | |
| This is sugar. | |
| This is coffee. | |
| This is a table. | |
| This is water. | |
| This is a lemon. | |
| This is an orange. | |
| This is bread. | |

## STRUCTURE FOCUS: Contrasting *in/on*

> I put the apple <u>in</u> the dish.
> I put the apple <u>on</u> the table.

Teacher models the sentences several times, having the student repeat.

Use the pictures at the bottom of p. 30 in *ESOL Illustrations* as needed.

If the object is available, put the apple in the dish as you say the word *in*. Put the apple on the table as you say *on*.

[Putting an apple in the dish, say:
"I put the apple in the dish."]

[Putting the apple on the table, say:
"I put the apple on the table."]

[Continue with other items already taught, as:
"I put the orange in the dish."
"I put the orange on the table."]

## DRILL: Substitution Drill with Visual Cues

Teacher performs the action; student makes the sentences.

[Following the procedure above, put a pencil *in* a book and say:
"I put the pencil in the book."]

[Now put the pencil *on* the book and say:
"I put the pencil on the book."]

pen                    I put the pen in the book.
                       I put the pen on the book.

pencil
eraser
paper

## PRONUNCIATION: Contrasting *a/an*

> I have a pen.        I have an egg.
>        a pencil.             an apple.
>        a book.              an olive.
>        a table.             an orange.
>        a hand.              an arm.
>        a nose.              an eye.

Teacher models the sentences, being sure not to stress the article. Have the student repeat.

Do the sentences with *a* first, then those with *an*.

**Note:** Use *a* before words beginning with consonant sounds. Use *an* before words beginning with vowel sounds.

It is the beginning *sound*, not the spelling that is important. For example, compare *an hour* with *a house,* *an uncle* with *a unit.*

[Say, "Listen to *a*," before you model the sentences with *a*. Be sure to give *a* the normal pronunciation /uh/, not the long /ā/ sound.]

[Say, "Listen to *an*," before you model the sentences with *an*.]

## DRILL: Substitution Drill with Vocal Cues

Teacher gives as cues the singular nouns without *a* or *an*. Student puts the word in a sentence, adding *a* or *an* as appropriate.

| Teacher | Student |
| --- | --- |
| I have a pen. | I have a pen. |
| pencil | I have a pencil. |
| egg | I have an egg. |
| book | |
| olive | |
| arm | |
| neck | |
| nose | |
| eye | |
| apple | |
| hand | |

## DRILL: Expansion Drill

Teacher models the adjective, then the key sentence, then the expanded sentence with the adjective.

Continue this way until the student can make the expanded sentence easily by himself.

**Note:** Notice that sometimes adding the adjective requires changing *a* to *an*, for example:

black   This is *an* olive.
          This is *a*   black olive.

Listen carefully to your student's responses to see that he makes such changes in a natural, unstressed manner.

| Teacher | Student |
| --- | --- |
| sour | |
| This is a lemon. | |
| This is a sour lemon. | This is a sour lemon. |
| sweet | |
| This is an apple. | This is a sweet apple. |
| black | |
| This is an olive. | This is a black olive. |
| little | |
| This is an egg. | This is a little egg. |
| yellow | |
| This is a banana. | This is a yellow banana. |
| big | |
| This is a book. | This is a big book. |
| brown | |
| This is an egg. | This is a brown egg. |
| green | |
| This is an olive. | This is a green olive. |
| big | |
| This is a desk. | This is a big desk. |
| blue | |
| This is a pen. | This is a blue pen. |
| white | |
| This is a cup. | This is a white cup. |
| little | |
| This is an eraser. | This is a little eraser. |
| black | |
| This is a pan. | This is a black pan. |

## PRONUNCIATION: a/ā/e/i

See the Pronunciation section in Unit D for the steps to follow in teaching the vowel sounds. The sounds /a/ and /e/ as in *pan* and *pen* were taught in Unit D.

1. Review the vowel sounds /a/ and /e/ as in *pan* and *pen*.

2. Contrast /ā/ with /e/ (*pain* with *pen*).

3. Contrast /e/ with /i/ (*pen* with *pin*).

4. Contrast /ā/ with /a/ (*pain* with *pan*).

5. Review the four sounds in sentences.

**Minimal pairs**

| | |
|---|---|
| pan | pen |
| bad | bed |
| mat | met |
| batter | better |
| sand | send |

| | |
|---|---|
| pain | pen |
| gate | get |
| taste | test |
| sail | sell |
| main | men |

| | |
|---|---|
| pen | pin |
| head | hid |
| check | chick |
| left | lift |
| better | bitter |

| | |
|---|---|
| pain | pan |
| hate | hat |
| plane | plan |
| snake | snack |

**Sentences**

Is the pan black?
This bag is better.
Where's the pen?
Where's the pan?

Where's Ed's pen?
Where's the pain?
Where's the pen?

This is a check.
This is a chick.
Is this a pen?
Is this a pin?

Is Dan's hat black?
Is this a snake?
Is this a snack?

Where's the pain?
Where's the pin?
Where's the pen?
Where's the pan?

## VOCABULARY: Numbers 81-90

Teacher reviews the numbers 71-80 and introduces 81-90. Model the numbers and have the student repeat.

Follow the procedures described in Unit B to teach saying, reading, and writing the numbers.

## ORAL EVALUATION

1. Review the vocabulary on food items, and count and non-count nouns.

   Student should be able to identify nine of the food items fairly quickly.

   He should be able to use *a/an* correctly with most count nouns and to omit *a/an* with non-count nouns.

   Make notes of the nouns the student has difficulty with.

   [Do the Substitution Drill that follows Structure Focus: Count and Non-count Nouns, *except* give visual cues. Point to the appropriate pictures in *ESOL Illustrations.*]

2. Review *eat* and *drink*.

   Student should be able to use the appropriate verb with the various food items, for the most part.

   [Do the Substitution Drill that follows Vocabulary: *eat* and *drink*.]

3. Review the adjectives *sweet, sour, big, little, hot,* and *cold*.

   Student should be able to place the adjective correctly in the sentence word order.

   [Do the Expansion Drill on adding adjectives to sentences in this lesson.]

4. Review verbs.

   a. Review *get...for, give...to,* and *thank...for.*

   [Use the Substitution Drill that follows Vocabulary: *get...for,* etc.]

   b. Review *pick up* and *put down.*

   Student must know all these verbs.

   [Place in front of the student a book, a pen, a pencil, and an eraser.]

   [Pick up the book, saying: "I pick up the book."
   Put down the book, saying: "I put down the book."]

   [Ask the student to perform these actions:

   Please pick up the pen.
       Pick up the pencil.
       Put down the pen.

   Please pick up the book.
       Put down the pencil.

   Please pick up the eraser.
       Put down the book.
       Put down the eraser.]

# II. Reading

Before you begin the chart for Lesson 4, check student's homework for Lesson 3. If he did not do it, have him complete it now. Be sure he understands any corrections you make.

## CHART 4: Page 18

Teach the chart as you taught the previous ones. (For *in*, say: "She's putting it *in*. Say *in*."
For *up*, say: "His arms are *up*. Say *up*.")

Some vowel sounds in English may sound similar to speakers of other languages. Be sure to make as much distinction between the sounds as possible. The sound /a/ is as in *apple*. The sound /e/ is as in *hen*. The sound /o/ is as in *pot*. Be sure your student drops his lower jaw and opens his mouth wide for this sound.

After you have finished the chart, teach the words *vowel* and *vowels*. (You will need to be able to use the word *vowel* when you do the writing sections of the next lesson, Lesson 5.)

| **Do this:** | **Say this:** |
|---|---|
| Point to *a* on the chart. | Teacher: *A* is a vowel. [Repeat several times.] |
| Point to *e* on the chart. | Teacher: *E* is a vowel. [Repeat several times.] |
| | [Continue the same way with the rest of the vowels on the chart.] |
| Finally, indicate all five vowels by running your finger down the letters at the far right of the chart. | Teacher: These are vowels. [Repeat about five times.] |

Since you are teaching the word *vowel* and *vowels* for the student's recognition only, the student need not repeat these sentences after you.

### STORY: The Apple, the Egg, and the Olive

Review the chart words one more time before you begin the story. Teach the story exactly as you did in the previous lessons. Be sure the student can read these new story words by themselves: *an, picks up, he, his, gives, to, she, puts.*

# III. Writing

### CHECKUP: Page 20

Follow the same procedure for this section as you did in the previous lesson. Refer the student to the reading charts if he does not remember how to write a letter.

### LISTEN AND WRITE: Page 21

Follow the same procedure as in the previous lesson. Your student will write the letter for the beginning sound of each word. Have him write in the first column. If he misses a letter, have him write it correctly in the second column.

**Do this:**

Dictate these words: *snake, river, valley, woman, tent, yells.*

**Say this:**

Teacher: Listen. Snake. *Snake* begins with what sound?
Student: /s/.
Teacher: What is the name of this letter?
Student: *s.*
Teacher: Write *s.* [Point to line 1, column 1.]

## WRITING LESSON: Page 22

Teach your student to write the vowels exactly as you taught the previous writing lessons. Teach the writing of the words like this:

| Do this: | Say this: |
|---|---|
| Point to *up.* | Teacher: Read.<br>Student: Up |
| Point to the *u.* | Teacher: Good! *Up* begins with what sound?<br>Student: /u/.<br>Teacher: Good! What's the name of this letter?<br>Student: *u.* |
| Point to the *p.* | Teacher: What's the sound of this letter?<br>Student: /p/.<br>Teacher: What's the name of this letter?<br>Student: *p.*<br>Teacher: Good! Write *up.* |

Teach the student to write *in, leg,* and *man* in exactly the same way.

Remember always to have the student read everything on the page, including headings and page numbers.

## HOMEWORK: Page 23

| Do this: | Say this: |
|---|---|
| Point to the heading. | Teacher: Please read.<br>Student: Homework. |
| Point to the letters, one at a time. | Teacher: What's the name of this letter?<br>Student: *a.*<br>Teacher: What's the name of this letter?<br>Student: *e.* |
| Point to the words, one at a time. | Teacher: Read.<br>Student: Up.<br>Teacher: Read.<br>Student: In. |
| Point to the page number. | Teacher: This is page 23. Read *23.*<br>Student: 23.<br>Teacher: Good! Do this page at home. |

## READING AND WRITING EVALUATION

1. For each of the five vowels on the chart—*a, e, i, o, u*—say the key word and the sound. Ask the student to name the letter and write it.

   Student should be able to name and write at least three letters correctly.

2. Write the following words, one group at a time. Ask the student to read the words.

   | a | picks | to |
   |---|---|---|
   | an | apple | his |
   | and | puts | in |
   | hand | gives | up |
   | | olive | |
   | | egg | |

Student should be able to read correctly all the words in each group, although pronunciation may not be perfect.

# Lesson 5

## OBJECTIVES

When a student completes this unit, he should be able to:

1. Say and respond to a new dialog.
2. Say the chart words and names for money (coins and *a dollar*).
3. Read some prices of $1.00 and less.
4. Use the verbs *buy...for,* and *sell...for.*
5. Use the object form of the singular personal pronouns: *me, you, him, her, it.*
6. Use the object form of the plural personal pronouns: *us, you, them.*
7. Ask some typical questions and give answers in a shopping situation.
8. Pronounce the sounds /sh/, /ch/, and /j/.
9. Say, read, and write the numbers 91-100.
10. Say the sound of each of these letters or letter combinations (digraphs): *x, z, qu, sh, ch,* and *th* as in *thanks.*
11. Read the following new words:
    Chart words: *box, zipper, quarter, shop, children, thank*
    Story words: *get, sells, for, him, they.*
12. Read a simple story, using the new chart and story words.
13. Write *x, z, qu, sh, ch, th.*
14. Write the following words from dictation: *in, man, up, cup.*

## VISUAL AIDS

1. Have on hand: a dollar bill, a half dollar, a quarter, a dime, a nickel, and a penny.
2. Accompanying *ESOL Illustrations for Skill Book 1,* pp. 31-32.

## REVIEW

Review any items that your student had difficulty with when doing the Oral Evaluation in Lesson 4.

# I. Conversation Skills

## DIALOG

| |
|---|
| Teacher:  Are you ready to order? |
| Student:  Yes. I'd like a cup of black coffee. |
| Teacher:  Anything else? |
| Student:  No, thank you. |
| Teacher:  That's thirty cents. |

Teach the dialog, using the procedure outlined in Unit A.

## VOCABULARY: Money

```
This is a dollar.
This is a half dollar.
This is a quarter.
This is a dime.
This is a nickel.
This is a penny.

This is money.
```

Teacher models the sentences several times, having the student repeat.

Put the coins and a dollar bill on the table.

[Hold up a dollar bill, saying: "This is a dollar." Gesture for the student to repeat after you.]

[Continue with the rest of the items.]

[End by indicating all the money on the table and saying, "This is money."]

## DRILL: Substitution Drill with Visual Cues

1. Teacher asks questions which elicit the names of the money units being taught.

[Holding up a dollar, ask: "What's this?" If the student cannot answer, prompt him.]

[Continue with *quarter, nickel, penny, dime, half dollar.*]

[Indicating all the money, ask: "What's this?"]

2. Teacher models the values of the coins in numbers and cents.

   Do not use the dollar bill in this drill.

[Hold up a penny.]

Teacher: Please repeat.
　　　　　This is a penny. This is one cent.
Student: This is a penny. This is one cent.

[Continue with the other coins.]

3. Teacher writes the numbers and symbols for the money units taught. Write on the blackboard or on paper.

   **Note:** The cent sign (¢) and the dollar sign ($) are introduced at this time.

[As you write $1.00, say: "This is a dollar. Please repeat. This is a dollar."]

[As you write 50¢, say: "Please repeat. This is a half dollar. This is fifty cents."]

[Continue with 25¢, 10¢, 5¢, 1¢.]

## DRILL: Transformation Drill

In this drill, the student changes the name of the coin to its equivalent in numbers and cents, as *half dollar* to *fifty cents.*

Teacher places all the coins on the table. The dollar bill is not used in this drill.

[As you pick up a quarter, say: "Pick up a quarter."]

[As you replace the money, say: "I put down twenty-five cents."]

[Indicate that the student is to follow your directions. Say, "Pick up a dime," and see that he performs the action.]

[Next say, "Repeat. I put down ten cents." See that the student performs the action of replacing the money as he repeats.]

[Continue with the other coins. If the student hesitates over the number, prompt him.]

| Teacher | Student |
|---|---|
| Pick up a penny. | I put down one cent. |
| Pick up a dime. | I put down ten cents. |
| Pick up a nickel. | I put down five cents. |
| Pick up a quarter. | I put down twenty-five cents. |
| Pick up a half dollar. | I put down fifty cents. |
| [If this drill goes easily, add these.] | |
| Pick up two nickels. | I put down ten cents. |
| Pick up two dimes. | I put down twenty cents. |

## VOCABULARY: Some Chart Words

```
This is a box.
This is a zipper.
This is a shop.

These are children.
```

Using pictures on p. 31 of *ESOL Illustrations*, teacher models the sentences several times, having the student repeat.

**Note:** *Quarter, thank,* and *children,* which are on Chart 5, have already been taught. *Children* is included here for review.

[Point to the box, saying: "This is a box." Gesture to the student to repeat after you. Continue with the other items.]

## DRILL: Substitution Drill with Visual Cues

Teacher points to pictures on p. 31 of *ESOL Illustrations*, eliciting the chart words taught.

[Pointing to the box, ask: "What's this?" Prompt the student if he cannot answer.]

## VOCABULARY: *sell...for, buy...for*

```
The man sells the box for a quarter.
The girl buys the box for a quarter.
```

Using the pictures on p. 32 of *ESOL Illustrations*, teacher models the sentences several times, having the student repeat.

[Using the top picture, say:
"The man sells the box for a quarter."
Point to the man, the box, and the 25¢ sign as you say *man, box,* and *quarter* in the sentence.]

[Using the bottom picture, say:
"The girl buys the box for a quarter."
Point to the girl, the box she has, and the quarter as you say *girl, box,* and *quarter* in the sentence.]

## DRILL: Questions and Answers

1. Teacher asks questions; student answers with the sentences given in the box.

2. Teacher varies the drill by substituting items already taught for *the box*, e.g. "The man sells the pen for a quarter."

   **Note:** This sentence frame will be drilled again later in this lesson.

Teacher: What does the man do?
Student: The man sells the box for a quarter.

Teacher: What does the girl do?
Student: The girl buys the box for a quarter.

[Hold up the item you want the student to substitute in his answer. Model the answers as necessary.]

## STRUCTURE FOCUS: Singular Object Pronouns

|  |  |
|---|---|
|  | Bob looks at me. |
|  | Bob looks at you. |
| Bob looks at the man. | Bob looks at him. |
| Bob looks at the girl. | Bob looks at her. |
| Bob looks at the box. | Bob looks at it. |

1. Teacher models the sentences with *me* and *you* several times, using gestures. Have the student repeat.

[Say, "Listen to me." Gesturing to yourself, say: "Bob looks at me." Have the student repeat.]

[Do *you* the same way, except gesture to your student.]

2. Teacher models the rest of the sentences in pairs—noun and pronoun. Have the student repeat the sentence with the object pronoun.

| Teacher | Student |
|---|---|
| Listen to *him*. | |
| Bob looks at the man. | |
| Bob looks at him. | |
| Repeat. | |
| Bob looks at him. | Bob looks at him. |

[Do *girl—her* and *box—it* the same way.]

## DRILL: Replacement Drill

Teacher models a sentence with an object noun. Student replaces it with the correct object pronoun.

| Teacher | Student |
|---|---|
| I have the book. | I have it. |
| I have the pen. | |
| I look at the girl. | |
| I look at the pencil. | |
| I look at the man. | |
| | |
| The man sells the pen. | |
| The man sells the fish. | |
| The girl has the cup. | |
| The man kicks the box. | |
| The man looks at the boy. | |

# STRUCTURE FOCUS: Plural Object Pronouns

| | |
|---|---|
| Bob looks at Ann and you. | Bob looks at you. |
| Bob looks at Ann and me. | Bob looks at us. |
| Bob looks at the children. | Bob looks at them. |
| Bob looks at the boxes. | Bob looks at them. |

Teacher models the sentences in pairs several times. Have the student repeat the sentence with the plural object pronoun.

**One-to-one:** To teach *you* plural, introduce your student to an imaginary "Ann" sitting next to him. Gesture to the space next to him and say, "This is Ann. Ann is a student."

As you say, "Bob looks at Ann and you," gesture to "Ann," then to your student.

Gesture to both your student and imaginary "Ann" as you say, "Bob looks at you."

**Class:** You may omit the sentence with *Ann and you*. Gesture to the whole class as you say, "Bob looks at you."

[Say, "Listen to *you*."]

| Teacher | Student |
|---|---|
| Bob looks at Ann and you. | |
| Bob looks at you. | |
| Repeat. | |
| Bob looks at you. | Bob looks at you. |

[Continue the same way with the other sentence pairs.]

# DRILL: Replacement Drill

Teacher models a sentence. Student replaces the object in the sentence with a plural object pronoun.

| Teacher | Student |
|---|---|
| I look at the children. | I look at them. |
| He looks at Ann and me. | He looks at us. |
| She looks at the boxes. | She looks at them. |
| Ann looks at the girl and me. | Ann looks at us. |
| Ann looks at Bob and you. | Ann looks at you. |
| Ann has the nickels. | Ann has them. |
| Bob has the books. | Bob has them. |

## DRILL: Questions and Answers

1. Teacher models the first two questions and answers
   several times, having the student repeat the answers.

   Then simply ask the question. The student is to use
   an object pronoun in a long answer.

   **Note:** At this point, the student is not asked to
   make the question. Notice, however, that the
   student has had practice in responding to this
   question pattern in Lesson 3.

| Teacher | Student |
|---|---|
| Is the man looking at the girl? | Yes, he's looking at her. |
| Is the man looking at the book? | Yes, he's looking at it. |
| Is the man looking at Ann? | Yes, he's looking at her. |
| Is the man looking at Bob? | Yes, he's looking at him. |
| Is the man kicking the chair? | Yes, he's kicking it. |
| Is the man kicking the box? | Yes, he's kicking it. |
| Is the man looking at the chair? | Yes, he's looking at it. |
| Is the man looking at the teacher? | Yes, he's looking at her. |
| Is the girl looking at the man? | Yes, she's looking at him. |
| Is the man looking at the children? | Yes, he's looking at them. |
| Is the man looking at the pens? | Yes, he's looking at them. |
| Is the man looking at the students? | Yes, he's looking at them. |

2. Teacher models first two questions and answers,
   having student repeat the answers.

   Then simply ask the question.

   **Note:** This drill gives the student practice in making
   the switch from *you* in the question to *me* in the
   answer, and vice versa. This switch is often difficult.

| Teacher | Student |
|---|---|
| Is the man looking at you? | Yes, he's looking at me. |
| Is the man looking at me? | Yes, he's looking at you. |
| Is the teacher looking at you? | Yes, she's looking at me. |
| Is the teacher looking at me? | Yes, she's looking at you. |
| Is the student looking at you? | Yes, he's looking at me. |
| Is the student looking at me? | Yes, he's looking at you. |

| | Teacher | Student |
|---|---|---|
| 3. Teacher models first two questions and answers, having student repeat the answers.<br><br>Then simply ask the question.<br><br>**Note:** This drill gives the student practice in using *us* and *you* plural appropriately in answers to questions. | Is the man looking at Ann and me? | Yes, he's looking at you. |
| | Is the man looking at you and me? | Yes, he's looking at us. |
| | Is the waiter looking at Bob and me? | Yes, he's looking at you. |
| | Is the waiter looking at you and me? | Yes, he's looking at us. |
| | Is the waitress looking at you and me? | Yes, she's looking at us. |
| | Is the waitress looking at Bob and me? | Yes, she's looking at you. |

## GENERAL REVIEW

**Note:**

This review will teach the student the sentence structures needed to buy things as well as reviewing items previously taught.

Try to have on hand as many of the following items as possible:

| book | pen | clock | cup | apple | banana | milk | egg | box |
|---|---|---|---|---|---|---|---|---|
| eraser | pencil | pan | dish | orange | coffee | sugar | bread | zipper |

Set up an imaginary shop in the classroom. Make price tags or signs for each item. Use amounts already taught: 1¢, 5¢, 10¢, 25¢, 50¢, and $1.00. Set up the items on the "counter" (your desk or table). As clerk, the teacher should stand behind the counter.

**Procedure**

1. Introduce the shop to the student, and review the names of its "merchandise."

   [Indicating the counter and the items on it, say: "This is a shop." Have the student repeat.]

   [Indicate the items in the shop one by one, saying, for example: "This is a pen. This is a cup." Have the student repeat.]

2. Practice *sell...for,* and *buy...for*. To practice the third person singular *-s,* use the name Ann or Bob or your student's name.

   Teacher models both the first sentence and the student response several times, having the student repeat the response. Then continue with only the teacher's role.

   As you say the price of each item, indicate its price tag or sign.

   Change places with your student halfway through the drill so he can practice *sell* as well as *buy*.

| Teacher | Student |
|---|---|
| I sell the book for a quarter. | Ann buys the book for a quarter. |
| I sell the cup for a dime. | Ann buys the cup for a dime. |
| I sell the banana for a nickel. | |
| I sell the bread for a half dollar. | |
| I sell the sugar for a dollar. | |
| I sell the pencil for a nickel. | |
| I sell the clock for a dollar. | |

3. Practice changing names of coins to their equivalents in numbers and cents.

   Model the first sentence and response as in step 2.

| Teacher | Student |
|---|---|
| I sell the book for a quarter. | I buy the book for twenty-five cents. |
| I sell the cup for a dime. | I buy the cup for ten cents. |
| [Continue as in step 2.] | |

4. Model both the question and the answer until the student understands the drill.

| Teacher | Student |
|---|---|
| How much is the pencil? | |
| The pencil is a nickel. | |
| Please repeat. | |
| The pencil is a nickel. | The pencil is a nickel. |
| | |
| How much is the pen? | The pen is a quarter. |
| How much is the book? | |
| How much is the apple? | |
| | |
| [Continue with all the items in the shop.] | |

**Note:**

For additional practice for more advanced students or for review on another day, use a newspaper supermarket ad or a catalog to practice prices. Ask, "How much is this?" In this drill, of course, you will have many different prices to practice.

## PRONUNCIATION: ch/j/sh

**Note:**

The /ch/ and /sh/ sounds are unvoiced.
The /sh/ sound is made with the teeth close together and the tongue close to the tooth ridge.
The /ch/ sound is made like /sh/, but the tongue touches the tooth ridge.
The /j/ sound is a voiced sound. In making this sound, the tongue touches the tooth ridge.

**Procedure:**

See the Pronunciation section in Unit D for the steps to follow.

1. Contrast /ch/ with /j/ (cheap with jeep).

**Minimal pairs**

| | | **Sentences** |
|---|---|---|
| cheap | jeep | The jar is chilled. |
| chill | Jill | Jill is jumping. |
| etch | edge | The chap is leaving. |
| char | jar | Jane is leaving. |
| chip | gyp | Jane's chin is cut. |
| chain | Jane | Jill goes to church. |

2. Contrast /ch/ with /sh/ (cheap with sheep).

| | | |
|---|---|---|
| share | chair | These shoes are cheap. |
| sheep | cheap | It's chilly. |
| shoe | chew | I'm not sure. |
| shop | chop | Let's wash the dog. |
| washing | watching | Let's watch the dog. |
| wish | witch | Sue's not sure. |
| | | She sells shells. |

## VOCABULARY: Numbers 91-100

Teacher reviews the numbers 81-90 and introduces 91-100. Model the numbers and have the student repeat. For 100, say "one hundred."

Follow the procedures described in Unit B to teach saying, reading, and writing the numbers.

## ORAL EVALUATION

1. Review the names for money and reading prices.

[Write 25¢ on the board.
Say: "This is twenty-five cents. This is a quarter."]

[Write 10¢. Have the student give you two responses.
Continue with 50¢, 5¢, 1¢.]

[For $1.00, only one response is required: "This is a dollar."]

2. Review the chart words.

Student must know all these words to read the Story in Lesson 5.

[Using p. 31 of *ESOL Illustrations,* point to pictures and ask, "What's this?" or "What are these?"]

This is a   box.
         zipper.
         shop.
These are children.

3. Review *sell...for, buy...for.*

Do the Question and Answer Drill that follows Vocabulary: *sell...for, buy...for.*]

[If the student has difficulty, do steps 2 and 3 of the General Review.]

4. Review the object pronouns.

It is important for the student to know all the object pronouns. If he cannot do the drill easily and quickly, review it at the beginning of your next session.

[Do steps 1-3 of the Question and Answer Drill that follows Structure Focus: Plural Object Pronouns.]

# II. Reading

Before you begin the chart for this lesson, check student's homework for the previous lesson. If he did not do it, have him complete it now.

## CHART 5:  Page 24

The first three lines of the chart are taught in the same general way as previous charts. Don't forget to trace the letters as they are written in column 2. The last three lines introduce the consonant diagraphs *sh, ch,* and *th.* (A consonant digraph is a combination of two consonants that produce a single sound.)

**Do this:**

**Line 1**

Point to the box.

Trace the letter *x* on the box.

Point to the word *box.*

Cover all but the last letter of the word *box.*

**Say this:**

Teacher:  What's this?
Student:  It's a box.

Teacher:  Say *box.*
Student:  Box.

Teacher:  Read *box.*
Student:  Box.

Teacher:  *Box* ends with /ks/. Repeat: /ks/.
Student:  /ks/.
Teacher:  [Continue as you have with previous charts.]

| **Do this:** | **Say this:** |

## Line 2

| Point to the zipper. | Teacher: What's this?<br>Student: It's a zipper. |

| Trace the letter *z*. | Teacher: Say *zipper*.<br>Student: Zipper. |

| Point to the word *zipper*. | Teacher: Read *zipper*.<br>Student: Zipper. |

| Cover all but the first letter of the word *zipper*. | Teacher: *Zipper* begins with /z/. Repeat: /z/.<br>Student: /z/.<br>Teacher: [Continue as you have with previous charts.] |

## Line 3

| Point to the quarter. | Teacher: What's this?<br>Student: It's a quarter. |

| Trace the letter *q*. | Teacher: Say *quarter*.<br>Student: Quarter. |

| Point to the word *quarter*. | Teacher: Read *quarter*.<br>Student: Quarter. |

| Cover all but the first two letters of the word *quarter*. | Teacher: *Quarter* begins with /kw/. Repeat: /kw/.<br>Student: /kw/. |

| Point to *qu* under *quarter*. | Teacher: /kw/.<br>Student: /kw/. |

| Point to next *qu*. | Teacher: /kw/.<br>Student: /kw/.<br>Teacher: Good! The sound is /kw/.<br>The names of the letters are *q u*.<br>What are the names of the letters?<br>Student: *q u*.<br>Teacher: What's the sound?<br>Student: /kw/.<br>Teacher: Good! |

## Line 4

| Point to the shop. | Teacher: This is a shop. Say *shop*.<br>Student: Shop. |

| Point to the word *shop*. | Teacher: Read *shop*.<br>Student: Shop. |

| Cover all but the first two letters of the word *shop*. | Teacher: *Shop* begins with /sh/. Repeat: /sh/.<br>Student: /sh/. |

| | |
|---|---|
| Point to next *sh*. | Teacher: /sh/.<br>Student: /sh/. |
| Point to next *sh*. | Teacher: /sh/.<br>Student: /sh/. |
| Point to last *sh*. | Teacher: /sh/.<br>Student: /sh/. |
| Point to last *sh*. | Teacher: The sound is /sh/.<br>The names of the letters are *s h*.<br>What are the names of the letters?<br>Student: *s h*.<br>Teacher: Good! What's the sound?<br>Student: /sh/. |

Do lines 5 and 6 as you did line 4. (For *children*, say: "These are children. Say *children*." For *thank*, say: "He says thank you. Say *thank*.") If the student has difficulty distinguishing /sh/ and /ch/, make a note to review step 2 in the Pronunciation section of this lesson. Finally, review sounds, names of letters, and words as in the previous charts. Be sure to teach the page number.

## STORY: The Shop

Teach the story exactly as you have in previous lessons, going from the key word in the chart to the story, and so on.

Be sure the student can read these new words by themselves: *get, sells, for, him, they*. Be sure your student reads *sells*, not *sell*.

# III. Writing

## CHECKUP: Page 26

Before you begin this section, review the word *vowel* and the sounds of the five short vowels. Turn back to the chart on page 18.

**Do this:**

Point to *a*.

**Say this:**

Teacher: *A* is a vowel.
What is the sound of this vowel? /a/. Repeat.
Student: /a/.
Teacher: [Continue with the other four vowels.]

Now turn back to the Checkup on page 26.

**Do this:**

Point to *f_sh*.

**Say this:**

Teacher: This word is *fish*.
Please write the vowel.
Student: [Writes *i*.]
Teacher: Good!

Do the entire page in the same way. When the student has filled in the blanks, make any corrections necessary, referring him to the proper reading charts. Then have him read all the words on the page.

Remember to have the student read the heading and page number on every page.

## LISTEN AND WRITE: Page 27

As in previous lessons, the student is to write just the beginning sound of the words you dictate. The words are: *apple, egg, in, olive.*

On the longer guidelines, the student is to write these entire words: *up, cup.*

## WRITING LESSON: Page 28

Teach this as you did in previous lessons.

## HOMEWORK: Page 29

Ask your student to read the words in class and to write them at home.

## READING AND WRITING EVALUATION

1. Write *qu, th, x, sh, z, ch.* Ask your student to say the sound for each letter or combination of letters. Student should be able to give the correct sound for at least three.

2. Write the following words, one group at a time. Ask the student to read the words.

   | | |
   |---|---|
   | sells | children |
   | shop | quarter |
   | box | him |
   | thank | zipper |
   | for | get |

   Student should be able to read correctly four words in each group.

3. Ask your student to write these words: *in, man, up, cup.*
   Student should be able to write at least three correctly.

4. Dictate the numbers 1-25 for your student to write. Then ask him to read the numbers he has written. Student should be able to write and to read nearly all the numbers correctly.

# Lesson 6

## OBJECTIVES

When a student completes this unit, he should be able to:

1. Say and respond to a new dialog.
2. Say the chart words and names for some family relationships.
3. Make questions with *do/does* and the verb *have*; give short affirmative and negative answers.
4. Pronounce the sounds /d/, /t/, voiced /th/ as in *this*, and unvoiced /th/ as in *thank*.
5. Say the name and sound for each of these capital letters: *A, B, C, D, E, F.*
6. Recognize that names of persons begin with capital letters.
7. Read the following new words:
   Chart words: *Ann, Bob, Cal, Dan, Ed, Fran*
   Story words: *boy, says, you.*
8. Read a simple story, using the new chart and story words.
9. Distinguish aurally between the beginning sounds d/t, b/d, b/p, p/f, k/g and identify each sound with its symbol (letter).
10. Read the *-s* ending on some nouns and verbs.
11. Write the capital letters *A, B, C, D, E, F.*
12. Write the names *Ann, Bob, Cal, Dan, Ed, Fran.*
13. Write all the small letters previously taught.
14. Read some simple skill book instructions.

## VISUAL AIDS

1. Accompanying *ESOL Illustrations for Skill Book 1*, p. 33.
2. Snapshots of teacher's family to illustrate family relationships.

## REVIEW

Review any items that your student had difficulty with when doing the Oral Evaluation in Lesson 5.

# I. Conversation Skills

## DIALOG

| |
|---|
| Teacher: Do you have any children? |
| Student: Yes, I do. |
| I have a boy and a girl. |
| Teacher: How old are they? |
| Student: The boy is ten and the girl is thirteen. |

1. Teach the dialog, using the procedure outlined in Unit A.

2. Vary the dialog by having the student answer according to his own family situation.

## VOCABULARY: Family Relationships

| Male | Female |
|------|--------|
| I have a husband. | I have a wife. |
| I have a son. | I have a daughter. |
| I have a father. | I have a mother. |
| I have a brother. | I have a sister. |
| I have a family. | I have a family. |

Using p. 33 of *ESOL Illustrations*, teach the above family relationships. Model the sentences, having the student repeat.

[Indicating the pictures, say the sentences and have the student repeat. Finally, indicating everyone pictured, say: "I have a family."]

## DRILL: Questions and Answers

1. Teacher asks the student questions which can be answered according to student's own personal situation.

   For practice, require a long answer, as "Yes, I have a husband," instead of "Yes, I do."

   For a female student:

   | Teacher | Student |
   |---------|---------|
   | Are you a wife? | Yes, I'm a wife. |
   | Are you a mother? | No, I'm not a mother. |
   | Are you a sister? | |
   | Are you a daughter? | |

   For a male student:

   | Teacher | Student |
   |---------|---------|
   | Are you a husband? | Yes, I'm a husband. |
   | Are you a father? | |
   | Are you a brother? | |
   | Are you a sister? | |

2. Vary the drill by asking the student questions with *Do you. . .?*

   **Teacher**

   Do you have children?
   Do you have a daughter?
      a son?
      a brother?
      a sister?

3. **One-to-one:** The teacher may show pictures of her family, using the sentence patterns "This is my son. His name is _____."

   Ask the student to show pictures of his family. Be sure he uses the pattern "This is my wife," and so on. Let him identify each person in the pictures. Then ask, "What is your wife's name?" and so on.

   If the student does not have any family snapshots with him, he will probably bring them to the next session. Do this practice again at that time.

## VOCABULARY: *give. . .to*

```
I give   the pencil  to you.
Ann gives the pen     to Bob.
She gives the paper   to Dan.
```

Illustrate the use of *give. . .to* by performing the action very carefully as you model the sentences. Have the student repeat.

[Say: "Listen to *give. . .to*."
Say: "I give the pencil to you," as you actually give it to the student.]

## DRILL: Substitution Drill with Visual Cues

Teacher models the first and second expected replies, then just hands the student the items and has him say the answer.

[Hand the student a pen, saying: "What do I give to you? You give the pen to me." Have the student repeat only the answer.]

[Continue, using a book, an eraser, a pencil.]

## VOCABULARY: Names

```
Ann   is a woman's name.
Fran

Bob   is a man's name.
Cal
Dan
Ed
```

Teacher models the sentences several times, having the student repeat.

## DRILL: Substitution Drill with Vocal Cues

Teacher gives the name, and student uses it in a sentence. Model the first sentence.

| Teacher | Student |
|---|---|
| Ann | |
| Ann is a woman's name. | Ann is a woman's name. |
| Bob | |
| Dan | |
| Fran | |
| Ed | |
| Cal | |
| Ann | |

## STRUCTURE FOCUS: Questions with *do* + *have*

```
     You have a book.
Do you have a book?
     We have a pen.
Do we have a pen?
     They have a son.
Do they have a son?
```

Teacher models the statements and the questions several times, having the student repeat both.

[Say, "Listen to *do*."]

**Note:** Use *do* plus *have* to make questions with *I, you, we,* and *they.* The pattern with *do* (and *does*) is another of the basic question patterns in English. We use a rising intonation pattern with this type of question. See Unit E, Structure Focus: Questions with *is.*

Lr

## DRILL: Transformation Drill

Teacher gives a statement and indicates through examples that the student is to transform (change) the statement into a question.

[Say, "Listen," then model the statement and the question. Indicate by using a Beckoning gesture that you want the student to repeat the question. Prompt him if he needs help.]

| Teacher | Student |
|---|---|
| You have a book. | |
| Do you have a book? | Do you have a book? |
| We have a pen. | |
| Do we have a pen? | Do we have a pen? |
| They have a son. | |
| You have a brother. | |
| You have books. | |
| They have children. | |
| We have a family. | |

## STRUCTURE FOCUS: Questions with *does + have*

The teacher has  a book.
Does the  teacher have a book?

The man  has  a brother.
Does the  man  have a brother?

Teacher models the statements and the questions several times, having the student repeat both.

**Note:** Use *does* to make questions with the third person singular (*he, she, it*). We use a rising intonation pattern with this type of question.

## DRILL: Transformation Drill

Teacher gives a statement and indicates through examples that the student is to transform the statement into a question.

[Say, "Listen," then indicate with a Beckoning gesture that you expect the student to repeat the question. Prompt him if he needs help.]

| Teacher | Student |
|---|---|
| The teacher has a book. | |
| Does the teacher have a book? | Does the teacher have a book? |
| The child has an apple. | Does the child have an apple? |
| The woman has a son. | |
| The man has a brother. | |
| She has a sister. | |
| He has a brother. | |
| They have two sons. | Do they have two sons? |
| You have three children. | |
| Ann has two daughters. | |
| Bob has two children. | |
| We have two sons. | |
| Ann has a family. | |

**STRUCTURE FOCUS:** Short Answers with *do/don't, does/doesn't*

| | | |
|---|---|---|
| <u>Do</u> | you have a book? | Yes, I <u>do.</u> |
| <u>Do</u> | you have a snake? | No, I <u>don't.</u> |
| <u>Does</u> | the teacher have a pen? | Yes, she <u>does.</u> |
| <u>Does</u> | the teacher have a fish? | No, she <u>doesn't.</u> |

Teacher models the questions with the affirmative and negative short answers several times. Have the student repeat the answers after you.

**Note:** *Do* and *does* are used to form questions and to make short affirmative and negative answers. Do not use the full forms, *do not* and *does not*, since native speakers almost always use the contracted forms, *don't* and *doesn't*.

Use a falling intonation pattern in these short answers.

[Say, "Listen to *do* and *don't*." As you say the answers, nod your head for the affirmative answers; shake it for the negative.]

## DRILL: Short Answers with *do* (Free Reply)

Teacher asks the student questions which will elicit affirmative and negative answers. Use only items already taught.

| Teacher | Student |
|---|---|
| Do you have a brother? | (Yes, I do.) |
| Do you have a sister? | (No, I don't.) |
| a son? | |
| a daughter? | |
| a family? | |

## DRILL: Short Answers with *does*

Teacher places items (e.g. pen, book, eraser) on her desk or table, then asks questions which will elicit affirmative and negative answers.

| Teacher | Student |
|---|---|
| Does the teacher have a pen? | Yes, she does. |
| Does the teacher have an egg? | No, she doesn't. |
| a cup? | |
| a book? | |
| an olive? | |
| a pencil? | |
| an apple? | |
| a banana? | |
| an eraser? | |

## STRUCTURE FOCUS: Review *is/are*

Review Unit E, Structure Focus: Affirmative Short Answers and Structure Focus: Negative Short Answers for answers with *be*.

When your student can do this review material with ease, proceed with the following drill.

## DRILL: Short Answers (Free Reply)

Teacher asks the questions and answers a few of them until student knows what to do.

If the student seems unsure of how to answer some of the questions, indicate by nodding or shaking your head how he might answer.

| Teacher | Student |
| --- | --- |
| Are you Spanish? | (Yes, I am.) *or* (No, I'm not.) |
| Are you Chinese? | (No, I'm not.) |
| Do you have a brother? | (Yes, I do.) |
| Does the teacher have a pen? | |
| Are you a waiter? | |
| Do you have a son? | |
| Is the teacher German? | |
| Does the teacher have a daughter? | |
| Are you a student? | |
| Do I have a pen? | |
| Is this a pencil? | |
| Does the teacher have a clock? | |
| Does the teacher have a family? | |

## DRILL: Reply and Rejoinder

Teacher asks questions which will elicit a negative short answer from the student. Then have him give the correct information.

[Ask the question, "Are you Spanish?"
As you answer, shake your head, saying: "No, I'm not. I'm German." Indicate by using a Beckoning gesture that you want the answer, not the question.]

| Teacher | Student |
| --- | --- |
| Are you Chinese? | No, I'm not. I'm Spanish. |
| Are you German? | No, I'm not. I'm Polish. |
| Are you Polish? | |
| Are you American? | |
| Are you Spanish? | |
| Are you Korean? | |
| Are you American? | |

## PRONUNCIATION: /d/, /t/, and /th/ (voiced and unvoiced)

See Unit D, Pronunciation, for the steps to follow in teaching the /d/ and /t/ sounds and the voiced and unvoiced /th/ sounds (as in *thy* and *thigh*).

**Note:** The /d/ sound is voiced, and the /t/ sound is unvoiced. Both are made with the tip of the tongue touching the tooth ridge, not the teeth.

The /th/ has two sounds: /th/ as in *this* and *thy* is a voiced sound; /th/ as in *thing* and *thigh* is an unvoiced sound. Both are made with the tip of the tongue between the teeth. Watch your student's mouth to see that his tongue actually protrudes.

| /t/ | /d/ | Sentences: |
| --- | --- | --- |
| tore | door | Today is Tuesday. |
| trip | drip | It's ten to two. |
| at | ad | Type a letter. |
| seat | seed | Dan is daring. |
| tab | dab | Where's Ed? |

| /t/ | /th/ (unvoiced) | Sentences: |
| --- | --- | --- |
| tank | thank | Thank you, Tom. |
| tick | thick | I taught the lesson. |
| taught | thought | We thought he was right. |
| oats | oaths | It's thick. |

| /d/ | /th/ (voiced) | Sentences: |
|-----|-----|-----|
| dare | their | What day is this? |
| day | they | Today is Thursday. |
| doze | those | Thank you, Ted. |
| sued | soothe | I didn't do it. |

| /th/ (voiced) | /th/ (unvoiced) | Sentences: |
|-----|-----|-----|
| thy | thigh | Either you do it or not. |
| either | ether | The baby's teething. |
| teethe | teeth | They gave him ether. |

## ORAL EVALUATION

1. Review vocabulary on family relationships.

   Student should be able to name six of these fairly quickly. If not, review them at the next session.

   [Using p. 33 of *ESOL Illustrations* and pointing to the various pictures, ask, "What do you have?"]

2. Review *give. . .to*.

   [Do the Question and Answer Drill that follows the Structure Focus: *give. . .to* in this lesson.]

3. Review questions with *do/does* plus *have*.

   If the student cannot form questions with *do/does* plus *have* fairly quickly, be sure to write this in your notebook. If necessary, practice this question pattern at next session since this is a *very important* basic pattern.

   [Do the Transformation Drill that follows the Structure Focus: Questions with *does + have* in this lesson.]

4. Review short answers with *do/does*.

   Student must be able to answer questions with *do/does* fairly quickly. If he cannot, review at the next session.

   [Do the Drill on Short Answers that follows the Structure Focus: Review *is/are* in this lesson.]

# II. Reading

Always check the student's homework from the previous lesson before beginning a new chart.

## CHART 6: Page 30

The charts for Lessons 6-9 are taught in the same way, so learn the following procedure well.

**Do this:**

Point to headings.

**Say this:**

Teacher: Lesson 6. Read.
Student: Lesson 6.

Teacher: Chart 6. Read.
Student: Chart 6.

### Line 1

Point to *a* on the chart.

Teacher: What's the name of this letter?
Student: *a*.

Teacher: Good! What's the sound of this letter?
Student: /a/.

| **Do this:** | **Say this:** |
|---|---|
| Point to *A* on the chart. | Teacher: The name of this letter is *capital A*. What's the name of this letter? |
| | Student: *Capital A*. |
| | Teacher: Good! The sound of this letter is /a/. [Be sure to pronounce /a/ as in *apple*.] Repeat: /a/. |
| | Student: /a/. |
| | Teacher: What's the name of this letter? |
| | Student: *Capital A*. |
| | Teacher: What's the sound of this letter? |
| | Student: /a/. |
| Point to *A* in *Ann*. | Teacher: What's the sound? |
| | Student: /a/. |
| Point to *nn* in *Ann*. | Teacher: What's the sound? |
| | Student: /n/. |
| Point to the letters in *Ann* again, more quickly. | Teacher: Again. |
| | Student: /a/. . ./n/. |
| | Teacher: Good! Ann. |
| Point to last *Ann* on chart. | Teacher: Read. |
| | Student: Ann. |
| | Teacher: Good! *Ann* is a woman's name. |

## Line 2

| | |
|---|---|
| Point to *b* on chart. | Teacher: What's the name of this letter? |
| | Student: *b*. |
| | Teacher: Good! What's the sound of this letter? |
| | Student: /b/. |
| Point to *B* on the chart. | Teacher: The name of this letter is *capital B*. What's the name of this letter? |
| | Student: *Capital B*. |
| | Teacher: Good! What's the sound of this letter? |
| | Student: /b/. |
| | Teacher: What's the name of this letter? |
| | Student: *Capital B*. |
| Point to *B* in *Bob*. | Teacher: What's the sound? |
| | Student: /b/. |
| Point to *o* in *Bob*. | Teacher: What's the sound? |
| | Student: /o/. |
| Point to *b* in *Bob*. | Teacher: What's the sound? |
| | Student: /b/. |
| Point to the letters in *Bob* again, more quickly. | Teacher: Good! Again. What's the sound? |
| | Student: /b/. . ./o/. . ./b/. |
| | Teacher: Good! Bob. |
| Point to last *Bob* on chart. | Teacher: Read. |
| | Student: Bob. |
| | Teacher: Good! *Bob* is a man's name. |

Do the rest of the page in exactly the same way. From now on, the student will be sounding out most words. Let him figure them out as much as he is able, but be sure to correct pronunciation. Since English first names are not familiar to most students, be sure to tell whether each name is a man's or a woman's name.

## STORY: Thank You

From now on, teach the story in this way:

1. Help the student read any new story words (new words that appear in the story but not in the chart). If these words consist only of consonant and vowel sounds he has learned, have him sound out the words.

   In Lesson 6, the new story words are *boy, says, you.*

2. Ask the student to read the first paragraph silently. (You can convey the idea of *silently* by putting a finger over your lips.)

3. Ask questions to check the student's comprehension of the paragraph. Be sure to use only question forms he has already learned to respond to in the Conversation Skills sections. Allow him to give short answers when appropriate.

4. Ask the student to read the first paragraph aloud. If he cannot read it fairly smoothly or if he makes gross pronunciation errors, you read it and have him imitate you, one line at a time. Then have the student read the paragraph aloud again.

5. Do the rest of the story as you did the first paragraph, one paragraph at a time.

6. Read the story to your student, sentence by sentence. Speak at a normal rate and with natural intonation. Slowing down would cause unnatural stress on some words. Have the student repeat each sentence after you. Have him say it, not read it. Have him say each sentence several times, until he is imitating your intonation as well as pronunciation.

7. Now have the student read the entire story—including the title—aloud. When he has finished, teach the page number.

Sample comprehension questions you may use for the Lesson 6 story are given below.

| Paragraph 1 | Teacher | Student |
|---|---|---|
| | Is Ann a woman? | Yes, she is. |
| | Is Dan a boy? | Yes, he is. |
| | Is Fran a girl? | Yes, she is. |
| Paragraph 2 | What does Ann give to Bob? | She gives a bird to Bob. (A bird.) |
| | What does Ann give to Cal? | She gives a cup to Cal. (A cup.) |
| | What does Ann give to Ed? | She gives an egg to Ed. (An egg.) |

[Point to each person in the illustration and ask, "What's his (her) name?"
The student should be able to identify the adult woman as Ann and should be able to tell which child is which from the object each one is holding.]

| Paragraph 3 | What does Bob thank Ann for? | He thanks Ann for the bird. |
|---|---|---|
| | What does Dan thank Ann for? | He thanks Ann for the dish. |
| | What does Fran thank Ann for? | She thanks Ann for the fish. |
| Paragraph 4 | What does Fran give to Ann? | She gives an apple to Ann. |
| | Does Ann say thank you? | Yes, she does. |

## SKILLS PRACTICE: Beginning Sounds d/t, b/d, b/p, p/f, k/g

**Note:**

From now on, each lesson in *Skill Book 1* will contain a Skills Practice in the Reading section. Many exercises in the Skills Practice will require the student to discriminate between two similar sounds (/b/ and /p/, for example). The student will be asked to identify each sound when he hears it and to associate the sound with the letter that represents it.

Although a few of the words in these exercises are words that the student has learned to read, many are words he does not know at all. *Do not explain the meaning of any words.* The meaning is not important to the purpose of the exercise, and trying to explain would take too much time.

In order to focus the student's attention on sound recognition in these exercises, do not let him look at what you are reading. Do not write anything for him, either, except what you are specifically told to write.

In this Skills Practice, you will write several pairs of letters for the student. You should have several small sheets of paper with you so you can write each pair on a separate sheet. The student should see only the pair of letters you are working with at the momemt.

This first Skills Practice shows exactly what you are to do and what you are to say to your student. Similar exercises in later lessons will follow the same pattern.

### 1. Beginning sounds d/t

**Step 1:** **Write the letters.** Write the letters *d* and *t* on a piece of paper and place it in front of your student. Write the letters fairly large and spaced well apart.

For a class, write the letters very large and spaced very far apart on the blackboard.

**Step 2:** **Chart words.** First, demonstrate thoroughly to the student the pattern this exercise will follow and the way he will be expected to respond.

Begin with the chart words the student already knows.

| **Do this:** | **Say this:** |
|---|---|
| | Listen: dish, dish. |
| | What sound does it begin with? |
| | dish, dish. |
| Pointing to *d*, give the sound /d/ yourself. | /d/. |
| Continuing pointing to the *d* as you ask and answer this question. | What is the name of this letter? |
| | *d*. |
| | Listen: tent, tent. |
| | What sound does it begin with? |
| | tent, tent. |
| Point to the *t*. | /t/. |
| Continue pointing to the *t*. | What is the name of this letter? |
| | *t*. |

**Now, repeat step 2,** this time allowing the student to answer. Be sure that he points to the correct letter as he gives the sound and name.

**Step 3:** **Example pair 1.** Now, demonstrate with a minimal pair. (A minimal pair consists of two words that sound exactly alike except for the two sounds you are contrasting, for example *Dan* and *tan.*)

| **Do this:** | **Say this:** |
|---|---|
| | Listen: Dan, Dan.<br>What sound does it begin with?<br>Dan, Dan. |
| Point to the *d*. | /d/. |
| Continue pointing to the *d*. | What is the name of this letter?<br>*d*. |
| | Listen: tan, tan.<br>What sound does it begin with?<br>tan, tan. |
| Point to the *t*. | /t/. |
| Continue pointing to the *t*. | What is the name of this letter?<br>*t*. |

**Step 4:** **Example pair 2.** Demonstrate with a second minimal pair. This time, beckon for the student to answer. Be sure that he points to the correct letter, as well as giving the sound.
Supply the answers if the student cannot.

**Say this:**

Listen: tent, tent.
What sound does it begin with?
tent, tent.

[Student should give the sound *and* point to the letter.]

What is the name of this letter?

Listen: dent, dent.
What sound does it begin with?
dent, dent.

[Student should give the sound *and* point to the letter.]

What is the name of this letter?

**Step 5:** **Minimal pairs.** Continue this process with the rest of the minimal pairs listed below. Vary the order in which you give the words in the pair; sometimes, give the *d* word first, sometimes, the *t* word.

| /d/ | /t/ | /d/ | /t/ |
|---|---|---|---|
| dab | tab | dime | time |
| dank | tank | din | tin |
| dell | tell | dip | tip |
| den | ten | door | tore |
| Dick | tick | duck | tuck |
| die | tie | do | to |

If the student cannot answer, or if he makes a mistake, repeat the word, give the sound, and point to the letter.

If the student can identify quickly and correctly the beginning sounds of all the words in the first column of minimal pairs, you do not need to do the second column.

Do the following exercises on beginning consonant sounds exactly as you did the first one.

## 2. Beginning sounds b/d

Write letters: *b* and *d*

Chart words: dish/bird

Example pair 1: Dan/ban

Example pair 2: big/dig

Minimal pairs:

| /b/ | /d/ | /b/ | /d/ |
|------|------|------|------|
| bug | dug | beer | deer |
| bad | dad | bike | dike |
| bay | day | bill | dill |
| bell | dell | bore | door |
| boo | do | bunk | dunk |
| buck | duck | bust | dust |
| bump | dump | buy | die |

## 3. Beginning sounds b/p

Write letters: *b* and *p*

Chart words: pan/bird

Example pair 1: pan/ban

Example pair 2: big/pig

Minimal pairs:

| /b/ | /p/ | /b/ | /p/ |
|------|------|------|------|
| Ben | pen | ban | pan |
| bet | pet | bad | pad |
| buy | pie | back | pack |
| bat | pat | bath | path |
| big | pig | beg | peg |

## 4. Beginning sounds p/f

Write letters: *p* and *f*

Chart words: pan/fish

Example pair 1: pan/fan

Example pair 2: four/pour

Minimal pairs:

| /p/ | /f/ | /p/ | /f/ |
|------|------|------|------|
| pat | fat | pun | fun |
| pad | fad | past | fast |
| pan | fan | pill | fill |
| pig | fig | pop | fop |
| pin | fin | pull | full |
| pit | fit | pour | four |

## 5. Beginning sounds k/g

**Note:** In this exercise, all the words that begin with the /k/ sound are spelled with a beginning letter *c*.

Write letters: *c* and *g*

Chart words: cup/girl

Example pair 1: Cal/gal

Example pair 2: girl/curl

Minimal pairs:

| /k/ | /g/ | /k/ | /g/ |
|------|------|------|------|
| cap | gap | come | gum |
| cot | got | came | game |
| cold | gold | cave | gave |
| curl | girl | coat | goat |
| cash | gash | cuff | guff |

# III. Writing

## CHECKUP: Page 32

| Do this: | Say this: |
|---|---|
| Point to heading. | Teacher: Checkup. Please read. |
| | Student: Checkup. |
| Point to first picture. | Teacher: What's this? |
| | Student: It's a box. |
| Point to blank. | Teacher: Please write the letter. |

Follow the same procedure with the rest of the page. When the student has finished writing, check his work, then have him read every word on the page. Then teach him the page number ("This is page 32. Read *32.*").

## REVIEW: Page 33

| | |
|---|---|
| Point to heading. | Teacher: Review. Please read. |
| | Student: Review. |
| Point to first letter, *b*. | Teacher: What's the name of this letter? |
| | Student: *b*. |
| | Teacher: What's the sound of this letter? |
| | Student: /b/. |
| | Teacher: Good! Please write *b*. |

Ask the same questions for every letter on the page. Be sure the student writes the letters correctly. Then teach the page number.

## WRITING LESSON: Page 34

| | |
|---|---|
| Point to heading. | Teacher: Writing Lesson. Please read. |
| | Student: Writing Lesson. |
| Point to *A*. | Teacher: What's the name of this letter? |
| | Student: *Capital A.* |
| | Teacher: What's the sound of this letter? |
| | Student: /a/. |
| Trace the green dot-and-arrow figure for *A*. | Teacher: Write *capital A* like this: 1, 2, 3. |
| | Student: [Writes *A*.] |
| | Teacher: Good! Again. |

Do the same with the rest of the capital letters. When the student writes the words at the bottom of the page, be sure he makes the capital letters correctly.

## HOMEWORK: Page 35

The homework assignment is self-explanatory. If the assignment seems too simple for your student, you may choose to give him some new vocabulary words to study at home in addition. Choose the words for their immediate usefulness to your student. Do not give him more than three to five additional words.

## READING AND WRITING EVALUATION

1. Dictate these letters for your student to write: *a, A, D, c, E, F, b.*
   Student should be able to write all these letters correctly.

2. Write *bird, girl, river, valley, zipper, egg, woman, leg.* Ask your student to read each word.
   Student should be able to read all the words, although his pronunciation may not be perfect.

3. Ask your student to write:  *Ann, Bob, Cal, Dan, Ed, Fran.*
   Student should be able to write at least three correctly, using a capital letter at the beginning.

4. Write *Lesson, Chart, Checkup, Review, Writing Lesson, Listen and Write, Homework.*
   Ask your student to read each item.

   Student should be able to read at least five correctly.

# Lesson 7

## OBJECTIVES

When a student completes this unit, he should be able to:

1. Say and respond to a new dialog.
2. Say new vocabulary, including the chart words, words for recreation, and expressions with *go*.
3. Make questions with *be* + verb-*ing* and make short affirmative and negative answers.
4. Pronounce the vowel sounds in *leave* and *live*.
5. Say the name and sound for each of these capital letters: *G, H, I, J, K, L*.
6. Read the following new words:
   Chart words: *Glenn, Hill, Indian, Jill, Kim, Liz*
   Story words: *lives, are, looking, girls, fishing.*
7. Read a simple story, using the new chart and story words.
8. Distinguish aurally between the beginning sounds s/z, s/sh, sh/ch, j/ch and identify each sound with its symbol (letter).
9. Write the capital letters *G, H, I, J, K, L.*
10. Write the names *Glenn, Hill, Indian, Jill, Kim, Liz.*

## VISUAL AIDS

Accompanying *ESOL Illustrations for Skill Book 1,* pp. 34-37.

## REVIEW

Review any items that your student had difficulty with when doing the Oral Evaluation in Lesson 6.

# I. Conversation Skills

## DIALOG

| | |
|---|---|
| Teacher: | Are you going home after class? |
| Student: | No, I'm not. |
| | I'm going swimming. |
| Teacher: | Where are you going swimming? |
| Student: | I'm going swimming in the river. |

Teach the dialog, using the procedure outlined in
Unit A.

## VOCABULARY:
### Chart and
### Story Words

| | | |
|---|---|---|
| This is Glenn Hill. | He | lives in Indian Valley. |
| This is Liz Hill. | She | lives in Indian Valley. |
| This is Kim Hill. | She | lives in Indian Valley. |
| This is Jill Hill. | She | lives in Indian Valley. |
| This is Ed Hill. | He | lives in Indian Valley. |
| These are the Hills. | They | live  in Indian Valley. |
| | I | live  in _____. |

Using p. 34 of *ESOL Illustrations*, teacher models each
pair of sentences several times, having the student
repeat each sentence. With the last sentence, use the
name of the community where the student lives.

## DRILL: Substitution Drill with Vocal Cues

Teacher models the cue and response, then says only the cue. The student uses *live* or *lives* correctly in the sentence with the cue word. Use the name of the student's community throughout this drill.

| Teacher | Student |
|---|---|
| I | |
| I live in _____. | I live in _____. |
| She | |
| We | |
| He | |
| You | |
| Ann | |
| They | |
| I | |
| Bob | |

## VOCABULARY: Review Family Relationships

Glenn Hill is the father.
Liz Hill is the mother.
Glenn and Liz are husband and wife.

Glenn and Liz have one son.
The son is Ed.

Glenn and Liz have two daughters.
The daughters are Kim and Jill.

Kim and Jill are sisters.
Ed is Kim and Jill's brother.

This is the Hill family.

Teacher models the sentences several times, having the student repeat. Use p. 34 of *ESOL Illustrations*.

## DRILL: Questions and Answers

Use p. 34 of *ESOL Illustrations*.

[Point to Glenn Hill in picture. Say: "Whose father is this? This is Kim's father. Repeat. This is Kim's father."]

| Teacher | Student |
|---|---|
| Whose mother is this? | This is Kim's mother. |
| Whose wife is this? | This is Glenn's wife. |

[Continue with the rest of the items.]

## VOCABULARY: Recreation

| Glenn and Liz Hill | are | fishing in the river. |
|---|---|---|
| Ed | is | swimming in the river. |
| Kim | is | jumping rope. |
| Jill | is | playing ball. |

Teacher models the sentences several times, having the student repeat. Use p. 34 of *ESOL Illustrations*.

## DRILL: Questions and Answers

Use p. 34 of *ESOL Illustrations.*

[Pointing to Glenn Hill, say: "What is Glenn doing?
He's fishing in the river. Please repeat.
He's fishing in the river."]

| Teacher | Student |
|---|---|
| What is Jill doing? | She's playing ball. |
| What is Kim doing? | |
| What is Ed doing? | |
| What is Glenn doing? | |
| What is Liz doing? | |

## VOCABULARY: Expressions with *go*

The woman is going home.
She is going downtown.

She is going to work.
She is going to class.
The man is going to church.
He is going to bed.

Using pp. 35-37 of *ESOL Illustrations*, teacher models the sentences several times, having student repeat.

**Note:** Notice that *going home* and *going downtown* do not use *to*, but *going to class* and the other expressions do.

[Pointing to picture, say: "The woman is going home. Please repeat. The woman is going home."]

[Continue with remaining items.]

## DRILL: Questions and Answers

Use pp. 35-37 of *ESOL Illustrations.*

[Point to appropriate picture as you ask each question.]

| Teacher | Student |
|---|---|
| Where is the woman going? | She is going home. |
| Where is the man going? | He is going to church. |

[Continue with other items.]

## STRUCTURE FOCUS: Review Statements with *be* + verb-*ing*

Statements with *be* + verb-*ing* were introduced in Lesson 2.

Before you teach the question pattern, review the statement pattern. Turn back to Lesson 2 and review the Structure Focus: *be* + verb-*ing* and the Drills that follow it.

**STRUCTURE FOCUS:** Questions with *is* + verb-*ing*

| | | |
|---|---|---|
| The woman | is | going home. |
| Is the woman | | going home? |
| The man | is | going to church. |
| Is the man | | going to church? |

Teacher models the statements and the questions, having the student repeat both.

[Say, "Listen to *is*."]

**Note:** To make questions in this pattern, the word order changes. "The woman is going home" becomes "Is the woman going home?" We use a rising intonation pattern with this type of question.

**DRILL:** Transformation Drill

Teacher gives a statement and indicates through examples that the student is to transform (change) the statement into a question.

**Teacher**

The woman is going home.
She is going downtown.
The man is going to church.
He is going to bed.
Jill is jumping.
Kim is picking up the cup.
Liz is walking.
The teacher is opening her book.
She is closing her book.
Kim is looking at her mother.
Jill is reading a book.
She is eating an apple.
He is drinking water.

**Student**

Is the woman going home?

**STRUCTURE FOCUS:** Questions with *am/are* + verb-*ing*

| | |
|---|---|
| I am | going home. |
| Am I | going home? |
| You are | going to class. |
| Are you | going to class? |
| We are | going to church. |
| Are we | going to church? |
| They are | going to bed. |
| Are they | going to bed? |

Teacher models the statements and questions, having the student repeat both.

Use a rising intonation pattern for the questions.

The vocabulary has already been introduced, but you may refer to pp. 35-37 of *ESOL Illustrations* if necessary.

[Before modeling the statement and question with *am*, say: "Listen to *am*."]

[Say: "Listen to *are*," before modeling the other statements and questions.]

## DRILL: Transformation Drill

Teacher gives a statement, which the student transforms into a question.

| Teacher | Student |
|---|---|
| I am going home. | Am I going home? |
| You are going to class. | Are you going to class? |
| We are going to church. | |
| We are looking at the book. | |
| They are going downtown. | |
| We are looking at the blackboard. | |
| They are yelling. | |
| I am sitting down. | |
| You are picking up the pencil. | |
| They are thanking the teacher. | |
| You are going to work. | |

## REVIEW DRILL: Transformation Drill

This drill tests the student's ability to make questions with *is, are,* and *am*.

| Teacher | Student |
|---|---|
| The man is selling the blue book. | Is the man selling the blue book? |
| The women are buying sweet oranges. | Are the women buying sweet oranges? |
| Bob is picking up the sour lemon. | |
| The girl is looking at the big eggs. | |
| The men are buying the black pans. | |
| The woman is selling white bread. | |
| She is picking up the green apple. | |
| Jill is eating a sweet orange. | |
| The girls are drinking cold water. | |
| You are buying brown eggs. | |
| I am going home. | |
| You are going downtown. | |
| Ann is going to work. | |
| We are going to class. | |
| They are going to church. | |
| The child is going to bed. | |

**STRUCTURE FOCUS:** Short Answers with *he/she/we/they* and *be*

> Is Ann going home?
> Yes, she is.
>
> Are Jill and Glenn going fishing?
> Yes, they are.
>
> Is Bob going to church?
> Yes, he is.
>
> Are you and I going downtown?
> No, we aren't.

Teacher models the questions and short answers several times, having the student repeat both.

[Say, "Listen to *Yes* and *No*."]

Use a rising intonation in the questions and a falling intonation (final) in the answers.

**Note:** When a name is used in the question, a subject pronoun is used as a substitute in the answer.
"Is *Glenn* fishing? Yes, *he* is."

## DRILL: Questions and Answers

Use pictures on pp. 35-37 of *ESOL Illustrations* as visual cues.

| Teacher | Student |
|---|---|
| Is the woman going home? | Yes, she is. |
| Is the woman going to church? | No, she isn't. |
| Is Ann going home? | |
| Are Glenn and Jill going fishing? | |
| Is Kim going to church? | |
| Are you and I going downtown? | |
| Are you and Kim going to church? | |
| Is the man going to bed? | |

**STRUCTURE FOCUS:** Short Answers with *I/you* and *be*

> Am I sitting down?
> Yes, you are.
>
> Am I standing?
> No, you aren't.
>
> Are you sitting down?
> Yes, I am.
>
> Are you standing?
> No, I'm not.

Teacher models the questions and answers several times, having the student repeat both.

Use gestures to indicate the pronouns since the change from *Am I* to *You are* and from *Are you* to *I am* is difficult for many students.

[Say, "Listen to *I* and *you*."
Use gestures to indicate yourself and say "Am I reading?"
Shake your head, shift your body and say, "No, you aren't."]

| Teacher | Student |
|---|---|
| Am I sitting? | Yes, you are. |
| Am I writing? | No, you aren't. |
| Am I looking at you? | |
| Am I yelling? | |
| Am I drinking water? | |
| Am I picking up the book? | |
| Are you sitting? | Yes, I am. |
| Are you jumping? | No, I'm not. |
| Are you looking at me? | |
| Are you going downtown? | |
| Are you going home? | |
| Are you eating an apple? | |

## REVIEW DRILL: Short Answers with *be* (Free Reply)

The drill tests the student's ability to answer a variety of questions beginning with *am, is,* and *are.* Repeat it again or make other questions (using only vocabulary already introduced) if your student cannot answer these questions.

| Teacher | Student |
|---|---|
| Are you reading? | (No, I'm not.) |
| Am I sitting down? | (Yes, you are.) |
| Is Glenn fishing in the river? | |
| Is Kim jumping rope? | |
| Is Liz swimming in the river? | |
| Are Kim and Jill playing ball? | |
| Are you and I going downtown? | |
| Is the man going to church? | |
| Are the man and the woman going to class? | |
| Are you and I going home? | |
| Am I eating a banana? | |

## PRONUNCIATION: /ē/ and /i/ as in *leave* and *live*

See the Pronunciation section in Unit D for the procedure to follow in teaching the vowel sounds /ē/ as in *leave* and /i/ as in *live.*

The student might need extra practice in hearing the difference between the two sounds.

**Note:** These two vowel sounds present a problem for students of a variety of backgrounds since /ē/ and /i/ rarely both occur in other languages. Generally, students are apt to have more trouble with /i/ than with /ē/. Notice that the lips are more tense and spread when making /ē/ than /i/, where the lips are in a more relaxed position.

| /ē/ | /i/ |
|---|---|
| leave | live |
| ease | is |
| peak | pick |
| heel | hill |
| steal | still |
| he's | his |

**Sentences**

This is a heel.
This is a hill.

Is he leaving?
Is he living?

Is Liz Kim's mother?
Kim and Jill are sisters.
Kim lives in Indian Valley.
He's still sleepy.

This is a sheep.
This is a ship.

## ORAL EVALUATION

1. Review the chart words. All of these are necessary for reading the story.

2. Review vocabulary on recreation (*fishing, swimming, jumping rope,* and *playing ball*). These will be practiced again later.

3. Review expressions with *go*. Student should be able to name four of these, using *to* correctly.

4. Review formation of questions with *be* + verb-*ing*.

5. Review short answers with *be*.

Student must be able to do items 4 and 5 above fairly well. If not, review at the next session.

[Do the Question and Answer Drill following Vocabulary: Family Relationships.]

[Do the Question and Answer Drill that follows Vocabulary: Recreation. Use p. 34 of *ESOL Illustrations*.]

[Do the Question and Answer Drill that follows Vocabulary: Expressions with *go*.]

[Do the Review Drill: Transformation Drill.]

[Do the Review Drill: Short Answers with *be*.]

# II. Reading

Check the student's homework from Lesson 6. Make any corrections needed and explain them.

## CHART 7: Page 36

**Do this:**
Point to headings.

**Say this:**
Teacher: Please read.
Student: Lesson 7, Chart 7.

## Line 1

Point to *g* on the chart.

Teacher: What's the name of this letter?
Student: *g*.

Teacher: Good! What's the sound of this letter?
Student: /g/.

Point to *G* on the chart.

Teacher: The name of this letter is *capital G*. What's the name of this letter?
Student: *Capital G*.

Teacher: Good! The sound of this letter is /g/. Repeat: /g/.
Student: /g/.

Teacher: What's the name of this letter?
Student: *Capital G*.

Teacher: What's the sound of this letter?
Student: /g/.

Point to *G* in *Glenn*.

Teacher: What's the sound?
Student: /g/.

Point to *l* in *Glenn*.

Teacher: What's the sound?
Student: /l/.

Point to *e* in *Glenn*.

Teacher: What's the sound?
Student: /e/.

Point to *nn* in *Glenn*.

Teacher: What's the sound?
Student: /n/.

| Point to letters in *Glenn* again, more quickly. | Teacher: Again. |
| | Student: /g/.../l/.../e/.../n/. |
| | Teacher: Good! Glenn. |
| | |
| Point to last *Glenn* on chart. | Teacher: Please read. |
| | Student: Glenn. |
| | Teacher: Good! Glenn is a man's name. |

## Line 2

Point to *h* on the chart.

Teacher: What's the name of this letter?
Student: *h.*

Teacher: Good! What's the sound of this letter?
Student: /h/.

Point to *H* on the chart.

Teacher: The name of this letter is *capital H.*
What's the name of this letter?
Student: *Capital H.*

Teacher: Good! The sound of this letter is /h/. Repeat: /h/.
Student: /h/.

Teacher: What's the name of this letter?
Student: *Capital H.*

Teacher: What's the sound of this letter?
Student: /h/.

Point to *H* in *Hill.*

Teacher: What's the sound?
Student: /h/.

Point to *i* in *Hill.*

Teacher: What's the sound?
Student: /i/.

Point to *ll* in *Hill.*

Teacher: What's the sound?
Student: /l/.

Point to letters in *Hill* again, more quickly.

Teacher: Again.
Student: /h/.../i/.../l/.
Teacher: Good! Hill.

Point to last *Hill* on chart.

Teacher: Please read.
Student: Hill.
Teacher: Good! Hill is Glenn's family name.

## Lines 3-6

Do the rest of the chart the same way.

## STORY: Indian Valley

To teach the story, follow steps 1-7 in the Story section of Lesson 6. The new story words are: *lives, are, looking, girls, fishing*. Use the questions below to check comprehension.

| | Teacher | Student |
|---|---|---|
| **Paragraph 1** | [Point to the man in the picture.] | |
| | Is this man Glenn Hill? | Yes, he is. |
| | [Indicate entire area in picture.] | |
| | Is this Indian Valley? | Yes, it is. |
| **Paragraph 2** | Do Glenn and Liz live in Indian Valley? | Yes, they do. |
| | Does Jill live in Indian Valley? | Yes, she does. |
| | Does Kim live in Indian Valley? | Yes, she does. |
| **Paragraph 3** | Where are Glenn and Liz? | They're at the river. |
| | Are Jill and Kim at the river? | Yes, they are. |
| **Paragraph 4** | What is Jill doing? | She's jumping. |
| | What is Kim doing? | She's kicking. |
| | Are Glenn and Liz looking at the girls? | Yes, they are. |
| **Paragraph 5** | What are Glenn and Liz doing? | They're fishing. |

Finally, have the student point to each person in the picture.

## SKILLS PRACTICE: Beginning Sounds s/z, s/sh, sh/ch, j/ch

Do these exercises exactly as you did the ones in Lesson 6. The pattern for what you are to say is given below.

```
Listen:  snake    ,  snake    .
         What sound does it begin with?
          snake   ,  snake    .
          /s/ .                              [Point to letter.]
         What is the name of this letter?    [Continue pointing to letter.]
           s .
```

**Note:**  For the sounds /sh/ and /ch/, the last question should be: "What are the names of the letters?"

## 1. Beginning sounds s/z

| | | Minimal pairs: | /s/ | /z/ |
|---|---|---|---|---|
| Write letters: | s and z | | sue | zoo |
| Chart words: | snake/zipper | | sap | zap |
| Example pair 1: | sing/zing | | seal | zeal |
| Example pair 2: | zip/sip | | sink | zinc |
| | | | see | Z |
| | | | sing | zing |
| | | | sip | zip |

## 2. Beginning sounds s/sh

| | | Minimal pairs: | /s/ | /sh/ |
|---|---|---|---|---|
| Write letters: | s and sh | | see | she |
| Chart words: | snake/shop | | sip | ship |
| Example pair 1: | sell/shell | | sack | shack |
| Example pair 2: | shop/sop | | sag | shag |
| | | | said | shed |
| | | | sin | shin |
| | | | sock | shock |
| | | | suck | shuck |
| | | | sell | shell |

## 3. Beginning sounds sh/ch

| | | Minimal pairs: | /sh/ | /ch/ |
|---|---|---|---|---|
| Write letters: | sh and ch | | sheep | cheap |
| Chart words: | shop/children | | sheet | cheat |
| Example pair 1: | shop/chop | | sheer | cheer |
| Example pair 2: | chair/share | | sherry | cherry |
| | | | shoe | chew |
| | | | shill | chill |
| | | | shin | chin |
| | | | ship | chip |
| | | | shock | chock |
| | | | shore | chore |
| | | | shuck | chuck |

## 4. Beginning sounds j/ch

| | | Minimal pairs: | /j/ | /ch/ |
|---|---|---|---|---|
| Write letters: | j and ch | | jet | Chet |
| Chart words: | jumping/children | | jug | chug |
| Example pair 1: | jump/chump | | junk | chunk |
| Example pair 2: | chill/Jill | | jump | chump |
| | | | Jane | chain |
| | | | jar | char |
| | | | jeep | cheap |
| | | | jeer | cheer |
| | | | Jerry | cherry |
| | | | jest | chest |
| | | | joke | choke |
| | | | Joyce | choice |

## SKILLS PRACTICE: Adding -s

Write these pairs of words on the board or on a sheet of paper. Then have the student read each pair (without and with the -s). Be sure the student is pronouncing *all* the endings.

| girl | girls | | thank | thanks |
|------|-------|---|-------|--------|
| egg  | eggs  | | get   | gets   |
| cup  | cups  | | sell  | sells  |
| pan  | pans  | | yell  | yells  |
|      |       | | look  | looks  |
|      |       | | kick  | kicks  |

# III. Writing

## CHECKUP: Page 38

Dictate the following sentences, and have the student fill in the missing names in the blanks. He may look back to Chart 6 for help in spelling the names. When he has completed the sentences, ask him to read them aloud.

Ann has an apple.      Fran has a fish.      Dan has a dish.
Bob has a bird.        Cal has a cup.        Ed has an egg.

Do the letters at the bottom of the page like this:

| **Do this:** | **Say this:** |
|---|---|
| Point to *a*. | Teacher: What's the name of this letter?<br>Student: *a*. |
| | Teacher: What's the sound of this letter?<br>Student: /a/. |
| | Teacher: Good! Write *capital A*.<br>Student: [Writes *A*.] |
| Point to the *A* student wrote. | Teacher: What's the sound of this letter?<br>Student: /a/. |

Do the rest of the letters the same way. Then teach the page number.

## LISTEN AND WRITE: Page 39

| **Do this:** | **Say this:** |
|---|---|
| | Teacher: Listen. Bob.<br>*Bob* begins with what sound?<br>Student: /b/. |
| | Teacher: What's the name of the letter?<br>Student: *Capital B*. |
| Point to the first space in column 1. | Teacher: Good! Write *capital B*.<br>Student: [Writes *B*.] |

Have the student write the letters in column 1. If he makes a mistake, help him look back to Chart 6 on page 30 to see how the letter should be written. Then have him write it again in column 2.

Do the rest of the page the same way. The words are: *Ann, Cal, Dan, Fran, Ed.*

## WRITING LESSON: Page 40

Don't forget to teach the heading and the page number. On this page, the student simply copies the letters and words. When he has finished, review the names and sounds of the letters and ask him to read the words.

## HOMEWORK: Page 41

The student is to write the capital letter beside the corresponding small letter. In the sentences, he fills in the missing letter. When you check the homework at your next session, be sure he has filled in capital letters.

## READING AND WRITING EVALUATION

1. Dictate these letters for your student to write:
   *i, l, G, I, g, L, k, H, J, h, j, K.*

   Student should be able to write at least 10 out of 12 correctly.

2. Ask your student to write these names:
   *Glenn, Indian, Hill, Kim, Jill, Liz.*

   Student should be able to write four correctly.

# Lesson 8

## OBJECTIVES

When a student completes this unit, he should be able to:

1. Say and respond to a new dialog.
2. Say the chart words and the names of some animals (pets).
3. Use *this/that, these/those*.
4. Use *do/does* in negative statements.
5. Use *be* in negative statements.
6. Pronounce the sounds /l/ and /r/ in initial and medial positions.
7. Say the name and sound for each of these capital letters: *M, N, O, P, Q, R.*
8. Read the following new words:
   Chart words: *Mr., Mrs., Ned, Oliver, Pam, Queen, Robert.*
   Story words: *Oliver's, pup, runs, pets, pup's.*
9. Read a simple story, using the new chart and story words.
10. Distinguish aurally between the beginning sounds m/n, l/r, r/w, v/w, f/v and identify each sound with its symbol (letter).
11. Read nouns ending in -'s in some phrases.
12. Write the capital letters *M, N, O, P, Q, R.*

## VISUAL AIDS

Accompanying *ESOL Illustrations for Skill Book 1*, pp. 38-40.

## REVIEW

Review any items that your student had difficulty with when doing the Oral Evaluation in Lesson 7.

# I. Conversation Skills

## DIALOG

| |
|---|
| Teacher: Do you have a pet? |
| Student: Yes, I do. |
|            I have a cat and a dog. |
| Teacher: Do they fight? |
| Student: No, they don't. |
|            They eat and sleep together. |

Teacher models the dialog, using the procedure outlined in Unit A.

Vary the dialog by making it appropriate for your student's situation, e.g. "I have two cats."

## VOCABULARY: Chart Words

> This is Mr. Oliver.
> This is Mrs. Oliver.
>
> This is Ned Oliver.
> This is Pam Oliver.
> This is Robert Oliver.
>
> This is Queen.
> Queen is Mr. Oliver's pup.

Using p. 38 of *ESOL Illustrations*, teacher models the sentences, having the student repeat.

## VOCABULARY: Animals (Pets)

> This is a pup.
> This is a dog.
>
> This is a kitten.
> This is a cat.
>
> This is a fish.
> This is a bird.
> This is a snake.

Using p. 39 of *ESOL Illustrations*, teacher models the sentences several times, having the student repeat.

*Fish, bird,* and *snake* have been introduced before.

## DRILL: Substitution Drill with Visual Cues

Use pictures on p. 39 of *ESOL Illustrations* as visual cues.

[Pointing to the pup, say: "What's this? This is a pup. Repeat. This is a pup."]

[Continue with the rest of the items.]

## VOCABULARY: Action Words

> The pup <u>runs</u> to Mr. Oliver.
> Mr. Oliver <u>pets</u> the pup.
> He <u>picks up</u> the pup.
> He <u>puts</u> the pup in a box.

Using the picture sequence on p. 40 of *ESOL Illustrations*, teacher models the sentences several times, having the student repeat.

## DRILL: Questions and Answers

Use p. 40 of *ESOL Illustrations.*

[Pointing to the appropriate picture, say:
"What does the pup do? He runs to Mr. Oliver. Repeat.
He runs to Mr. Oliver."]

[Continue with the remaining items.]

## STRUCTURE FOCUS: *this/that*

| | |
|---|---|
| This is a pen. | That is a pen. |
| This is a pencil. | That is a pencil. |
| This is a book. | That is a book. |

Teacher models each pair of sentences, having the student repeat.

Place a pen, pencil, and book near you and a pen, pencil, and book at some distance from you.

**Note:** *This* is used to indicate an object near the speaker; *that*, an object not so near. *This* and *that* are used with singular count and non-count nouns. *This* was introduced in Unit A; *that* is a new item.

[Say: "Listen to *this* and *that*." As you say "This is a pen," indicate the pen near you.
As you say "That is a pen," indicate the pen away from you.]

[Continue with the rest of the items.]

## DRILL: Substitution Drill with Visual Cues

1. Sitting beside the student, place a pen, pencil, book, and an eraser near you and the student.

   As a further drill, open to a page of the *ESOL Illustrations* already presented that you think your student needs to review (e.g. names of family, relationships, food, money). Place the book close to both of you.

[Indicating the pen, say: "What's this? This is a pen. Repeat. This is a pen."]

[Continue with the rest of the items.]

2. Now place the pen, pencil, and other items at a distance from both you and your student.

[Indicating the pen away from you, say:
"What's that? That's a pen. Repeat. That's a pen."]

[Continue with the rest of the items.]

## STRUCTURE FOCUS: *these/those*

| | |
|---|---|
| These are pens. | Those are pens. |
| These are pencils. | Those are pencils. |
| These are books. | Those are books. |

Teacher models each pair of sentences, having the student repeat.

Place pens, pencils, books near you and pens, pencils, books at some distance from you.

**Note:** *These* is used to indicate objects near the speaker; *those*, to indicate objects not so near. *These* and *those* are used with plural count nouns. *These* was introduced in Unit C. *Those* is a new item.

[Say, "Listen to *these* and *those*." As you say "These are pens," indicate the pens near you.
As you say "Those are pens," indicate the pens at a distance.]

## DRILL: Substitution Drill with Visual Cues

Follow the Drill given for *this* and *that*, making it plural.

## STRUCTURE FOCUS: Negative Statements with *be* + verb-*ing*

|  |  |
|---|---|
| I'm not | sitting. |
| You aren't | walking. |
| She isn't | standing. |
| We aren't | jumping. |
| They aren't | kicking. |

Teacher models the sentences several times, having the student repeat.

Shake your head as you say the negative contraction.

[Before modeling the first sentence, say: "Listen to *I'm not*."]

[Say: "Listen to *aren't*" or "Listen to *isn't*" before modeling the other sentences.]

## DRILL: Transformation Drill

Teacher makes an affirmative statement; student transforms it into a negative statement.

[Say: "The girl is yelling."
Shake your head and say: "The girl isn't yelling. Repeat. The girl isn't yelling."]

| Teacher | Student |
|---|---|
| I'm picking up my book. | I'm not picking up my book. |
| Glenn is fishing in the river. | |
| You are reading a book. | |
| They are going home. | |
| I am closing the door. | |
| Liz is going to church. | |
| Kim and Jill are going to class. | |
| Ed is playing ball. | |
| I am opening the door. | |
| He is going to bed. | |
| Ann is going downtown. | |
| Fran is drinking coffee. | |

## STRUCTURE FOCUS: Negative statements with *don't*

```
        I       live in _____ (city).
        I don't live in Indian Valley.
  You          have a dog.
  You don't have a cat.
      We       have a fish.
      We don't have a bird.
  They         live in _____ (city).
  They don't live in Indian Valley.
```

Teacher models the sentences several times, having the student repeat.

Use the name of the city or town you live in.

**Note:** Negative statements with *I, you, we, they* are made with *do not,* usually contracted to *don't.*

[Say "Listen to *don't.*"
Shake your head as you say the negative sentences.]

## DRILL: Transformation Drill

The student transforms an affirmative statement into a negative one.

| Teacher | Student |
|---|---|
| I have a dog. | I don't have a dog. |
| You have a cat. | |
| They have a kitten. | |
| We have a bird. | |
| They have a pup. | |
| I have a snake. | |
| You have a kitten. | |
| I have a fish. | |

## STRUCTURE FOCUS: Negative statements with *doesn't*

```
      He          lives in Indian Valley.
      He doesn't live in _____ (city).
     She          buys bread.
     She doesn't buy bread.
  The dog         has a pup.
      It  doesn't have a kitten.
```

Teacher models each pair of sentences several times, having the student repeat the negative sentence.

**Note:** Negative statements with verbs like *live* and *buy* in the third person singular present tense are made with *does not*, usually contracted to *doesn't* in spoken English. Students commonly make the mistake of pronouncing the *-s* verb ending where it does not occur, as *She doesn't lives here,* or *She doesn't has a dog.*

(An asterisk before a phrase or sentence means that this form is unacceptable to native speakers of English.)

[Say, "Listen to *doesn't.*"]

## DRILL: Transformation Drill

The student transforms an affirmative statement into a negative one.

| Teacher | Student |
|---|---|
| He lives in Indian Valley. | He doesn't live in Indian Valley. |
| She goes to class. | |
| The girl opens the book. | |
| The boy has a dog. | |
| She opens the door. | |
| Mr. Oliver has a cat. | |
| It opens. | |
| The man goes to church. | |
| The woman eats olives. | |

## DRILL: Reply and Rejoinder

Teacher asks questions which elicit negative answers. The student then adds the appropriate affirmative information.

If the student cannot supply the information, prompt him by suggesting an answer. Do this only until he catches on to the drill. For practice, accept only full answers, not short answers such as "No, I'm not."

[Ask, "Are you standing?" Shake your head, saying: "No, I'm not standing. I'm sitting. Please repeat. No, I'm not standing. I'm sitting."]

1. The first drill is with *be*.

| Teacher | Student |
|---|---|
| Are you walking? | No, I'm not walking. I'm sitting. |
| Are they looking at the blackboard? | |
| Are you going home? | |
| Is Kim going to bed? | |
| Are they going downtown? | |
| Is Jill swimming in the river? | |

2. This drill is with *do/does*.

| Teacher | Student |
|---|---|
| Do you have a cat? | No, I don't have a cat. I have a dog. |
| Do you live in Indian Valley? | |
| Do you have a kitten? | |
| Do you have a pup? | |
| Does Jill live in _____ (city)? | |
| Do you have an eraser? | |
| Does Liz play ball? | |

3. This drill is with *be/do/does*.

| Teacher | Student |
|---|---|
| Is Glenn jumping? | No, he's not jumping. He's fishing. |
| Do you live in Indian Valley? | |
| Are you swimming in the river? | |
| Are they going to class? | |
| Do you have a cat? | |
| Does the man go to class? | |
| Is the man going to bed? | |
| Is Kim jumping rope? | |
| Does Glenn live in _____ (city)? | |

## PRONUNCIATION: /l/ and /r/

See Unit D, Pronunciation, for the procedure to follow in teaching the /l/ and /r/ sounds.

**Note:** Both /l/ and /r/ are voiced sounds. When making the /l/ sound, the tip of the tongue touches the tooth ridge. When making the /r/ sound, the tip of the tongue curves upward and toward the back of the mouth and the lips are somewhat rounded.

| /l/ | /r/ | Sentences |
|---|---|---|
| lace | race | Lots of luck. |
| lake | rake | I'll see you later. |
| lead | read | Lil's gone. |
| lip | rip | Jill's wrong. |
| load | road | The berries are blue. |
| collect | correct | I'll collect them. |
| belly | berry | I'll correct them. |
| filing | firing | It's long. |
| elect | erect | It's wrong. |
| jelly | Jerry | |

## ORAL EVALUATION

1. Review the chart words (names) necessary for the reading.

   [Using p. 38 of *ESOL Illustrations*, say the names, having the student repeat after you.]

2. Review names for pets. Since some of these are review items, student should be able to name all of them.

   [Using p. 39 of *ESOL Illustrations*, ask, "What's this?"]

3. Review action words necessary for the reading.

   [Using p. 40 of *ESOL Illustrations*, ask questions, such as, "What does the pup do?"]

4. Review *this/that, these/those*. The student should be able to make a difference between the singular and plural forms. If he cannot answer fairly quickly, review at your next session.

   [Do Substitution Drills following Structure Focus: *this/that* and *these/those*.]

5. Review negative statements with *be/do/does*. This is an important basic pattern. Review it at the next session if your student cannot make negative statements fairly quickly.

   [Do the Reply and Rejoinder Drill in this lesson as a review of this pattern.]

# II. Reading

Before you begin the chart, check and correct your student's homework from Lesson 7. If he has not finished it, ask him to finish now.

## CHART 8: Page 42

**Do this:**

Point to headings.

**Say this:**

Teacher: Please read.
Student: Lesson 8, Chart 8.

## Line 1

Point to *m* on the chart.

Teacher: What's the name of this letter?
Student: *m*.

Teacher: Good! What's the sound of this letter?
Student: /m/.

| | |
|---|---|
| Point to *M* on the chart. | Teacher: The name of this letter is *capital M.* <br> What's the name of this letter? <br> Student: *Capital M.* <br><br> Teacher: Good! The sound of this letter is /m/. Repeat: /m/. <br> Student: /m/. <br><br> Teacher: What's the name of this letter? <br> Student: *Capital M.* <br><br> Teacher: What's the sound of this letter? <br> Student: /m/. |
| Point to first *Mr.* | Teacher: This is *Mr.* Please read *Mr.* <br> Student: *Mr.* |
| Point to first *Mrs.* | Teacher: This is *Mrs.* Please read *Mrs.* <br> Student: *Mrs.* |
| Point to last *Mr.* | Teacher: Please read. <br> Student: *Mr.* |
| Point to last *Mrs.* | Teacher: Please read. <br> Student: *Mrs.* |
| Point to first *Mr.* again. | Teacher: Mr. Hill is a man. Please repeat. <br> Student: Mr. Hill is a man. |
| Point to first *Mrs.* again. | Teacher: Mrs. Hill is a woman. Please repeat. <br> Student: Mrs. Hill is a woman. |
| Point to last *Mr.* | Teacher: Mr. Hill is the husband. Please repeat. <br> Student: Mr. Hill is the husband. |
| Point to last *Mrs.* | Teacher: Mrs. Hill is the wife. Please repeat. <br> Student: Mrs. Hill is the wife. |

## Line 2

| | |
|---|---|
| Point to *n* on the chart. | Teacher: What's the name of this letter? <br> Student: *n.* <br><br> Teacher: Good! What's the sound of this letter? <br> Student: /n/. |
| Point to *N* on the chart. | Teacher: The name of this letter is *capital N.* <br> What's the name of this letter? <br> Student: *Capital N.* <br><br> Teacher: Good! The sound of this letter is /n/. <br> Repeat: /n/. <br> Student: /n/. <br><br> Teacher: What's the name of this letter? <br> Student: *Capital N.* <br><br> Teacher: What's the sound of this letter? <br> Student: /n/. |
| Point to *N* in *Ned.* | Teacher: What's the sound? <br> Student: /n/. |

| | |
|---|---|
| Point to *e* in *Ned*. | Teacher: What's the sound?<br>Student: /e/. |
| Point to *d* in *Ned*. | Teacher: What's the sound?<br>Student: /d/. |
| Point to the letters in *Ned* again, more quickly. | Teacher: Again.<br>Student: /n/. . ./e/. . ./d/.<br>Teacher: Good! Ned. |
| Point to last *Ned*. | Teacher: Please read.<br>Student: Ned.<br>Teacher: Good! Ned is a man's name. |

Teach the remaining lines of the chart in a similar way.

Teach *Oliver* as a sight word, i.e., tell the student the word, as you did for *Mr.* At the end of the line, say: "Ned Oliver. Oliver is Ned's family name. Ned Oliver."

Have the student sound out *Pam*, as he did *Ned*. At the end of the line, say: "Pam is a woman's name."

Write a *u* after the *q* and *Q* in the student's book just before you ask "What's the sound?" for each. Teach *Queen* as a sight word. At the end of the line, point to the pup in the picture and say: "Queen is the pup's name."

Teach *Robert* as a sight word. At the end of the line, say: "Robert is a man's name."

## STORY: Mr. Oliver's Pup

To teach the story, follow steps 1-7 in the Story section of Lesson 6. The new story words are: *Oliver's, pup, runs, pets, pup's.* Use the questions below to check comprehension.

| | Teacher | Student |
|---|---|---|
| **Paragraph 1** | [Point to the man in the picture.]<br>Is this man Mr. Oliver? | Yes, he is. |
| | [Point to the woman.]<br>Is this woman Mrs. Oliver? | Yes, she is. |
| | [Point to all three children.]<br>Are they Ned and Pam and Robert? | Yes, they are. |
| | [Point to the pup.]<br>Is this Queen? | Yes, it is. |
| | Whose pup is Queen? | Mr. Oliver's. |
| **Paragraph 2** | Does the pup run to Mr. Oliver?<br>Does the pup run to Mrs. Oliver?<br>Does the pup run to Pam? | Yes, it does.<br>Yes, it does.<br>Yes, it does. |
| **Paragraph 3** | Does Mrs. Oliver pet the pup?<br>Does Ned pet the pup's neck?<br>Does Robert pet the pup's leg? | Yes, she does.<br>Yes, he does.<br>Yes, he does. |
| **Paragraph 4** | Does Mr. Oliver pick up Queen?<br>Where does he put the pup? | Yes, he does.<br>In a box. |
| **Paragraph 5** | Does the pup have a dish?<br>Does Pam put the dish on the table? | Yes, it does.<br>No, she doesn't.<br>(She puts it in the box.) |

**Note:** Do not change the form of these questions. They are designed so that their answers follow patterns of usage that the student has already learned.

The student has not yet learned to use *it* to refer to a person, as in: "Is this Mr. Oliver? Yes, it is."

Nor has the student learned to use *he* or *she* to refer to a pet animal, as we often do, especially when the pet's name indicates its sex.

Do *not* confuse the student with these exceptions to the patterns he has learned.


## SKILLS PRACTICE: Beginning Sounds m/n, l/r, r/w, v/w, f/v

Do these exercises exactly as you did those in Lesson 6. The pattern for what you are to say is given below.

| | |
|---|---|
| Listen: ___man___ , ___man___ . | |
| What sound does it begin with? | |
| ___man___ , ___man___ . | |
| / m /. | [Point to letter.] |
| What is the name of this letter? | [Continue pointing to letter.] |
| ___m___ . | |

If the student can identify quickly and correctly the beginning sounds of all the words in the first column of minimal pairs, you do not need to do the second column.


## 1. Beginning sounds m/n

| | | | | | | |
|---|---|---|---|---|---|---|
| Write letters: | *m* and *n* | Minimal pairs: | /m/ | /n/ | /m/ | /n/ |
| Chart words: | man/neck | | map | nap | Mel | Nell |
| | | | man | Nan | mod | nod |
| Example pair 1: | man/Nan | | meat | neat | mull | null |
| Example pair 2: | nine/mine | | mail | nail | mutt | nut |
| | | | met | net | mere | near |
| | | | meal | Neil | moat | note |
| | | | moon | noon | more | nor |


## 2. Beginning sounds l/r

| | | | | | | |
|---|---|---|---|---|---|---|
| Write letters: | *l* and *r* | Minimal pairs: | /l/ | /r/ | /l/ | /r/ |
| Chart words: | leg/river | | lip | rip | lag | rag |
| | | | lamp | ramp | lash | rash |
| Example pair 1: | look/rook | | lock | rock | link | rink |
| Example pair 2: | red/led | | lot | rot | lung | rung |
| | | | late | rate | lush | rush |
| | | | lug | rug | lust | rust |
| | | | lap | rap | lack | rack |

## 3. Beginning sounds r/w

Write letters:    *r* and *w*

Chart words:    river/woman

Example pair 1:    red/wed

Example pair 2:    wing/ring

Minimal pairs:

| /r/ | /w/ | /r/ | /w/ |
|-----|-----|-----|-----|
| reek | week | rate | wait |
| rent | went | rag | wag |
| reel | we'll | rink | wink |
| rest | west | rage | wage |
| rake | wake | rise | wise |
| ring | wing | rave | wave |

## 4. Beginning sounds v/w

Write letters:    *v* and *w*

Chart words:    valley/woman

Example pair 1:    vet/wet

Example pair 2:    wine/vine

Minimal pairs:

| /v/ | /w/ | /v/ | /w/ |
|-----|-----|-----|-----|
| vent | went | vile | wile |
| vest | west | vend | wend |
| V | we | veil | wail |
| veer | we're | vain | wane |
| vet | wet | Vicks | wicks |
| vine | wine | verse | worse |
| vary | wary | | |

## 5. Beginning sounds f/v

Write letters:    *f* and *v*

Chart words:    fish/valley

Example pair 1:    fat/vat

Example pair 2:    Van/fan

Minimal pairs:

| /f/ | /v/ | /f/ | /v/ |
|-----|-----|-----|-----|
| fine | vine | fend | vend |
| fast | vast | fear | veer |
| feel | veal | file | vile |
| few | view | fuse | views |
| fail | veil | final | vinyl |
| ferry | very | fan | Van |
| fat | vat | | |

## SKILLS PRACTICE: Adding -'s

Write the following phrases on the board or on a sheet of paper. Then have the student read all the phrases.

| | | |
|---|---|---|
| the man's hand | the girl's tent | the pup's neck |
| the pup's dish | the woman's cup | Mr. Oliver's pup |

# III. Writing

## CHECKUP: Page 44

Have your student fill in the missing letter or word. This exercise is based on the story in Lesson 7. If the student does not remember the names, let him look up the answers. When he has completed the sentences, ask him to read them aloud.

Do the letters at the bottom of the page like this:

| **Do this:** | **Say this:** |
|---|---|
| Point to *g*. | Teacher: What's the name of this letter?<br>Student: *g*. |
| | Teacher: What's the sound of this letter?<br>Student: /g/. |
| | Teacher: Good! Write *capital G*.<br>Student: [Writes *G*.] |
| Point to *G* student wrote. | Teacher: What's the sound of this letter?<br>Student: /g/. |

Do the rest of the letters the same way. Then teach the page number.

## LISTEN AND WRITE: Page 45

Ask your student to write the capital letter that these names begin with:

| Bob | Dan | Fran | Hill | Kim | Ann |
|---|---|---|---|---|---|
| Cal | Ed | Glenn | Jill | Liz | Indian |

## WRITING LESSON: Page 46

The student simply copies the letters and words. Help him with anything that troubles him. Then review the sounds and names of the letters, and ask him to read the words. Don't forget to teach the page number.

## HOMEWORK: Page 47

The student is to write the capital letters beside the corresponding small letters and then to fill in the missing letters in the sentences.

## READING AND WRITING EVALUATION

1. Write these words and ask student to read them: *pup, pets, runs, pup's.*
   Student should be able to read all four correctly.

2. Write *Mr. Oliver, Mrs. Oliver.* Ask your student to read both names.
   Student should be able to read both correctly.

3. Ask your student to write these letters: *O, M, Q, N, R, P.*
   Student should be able to write all six correctly.

# Lesson 9

## OBJECTIVES

When a student completes this unit, he should be able to:

1. Say and respond to a new dialog.
2. Say new vocabulary, including the chart words and some time expressions with daily activities.
3. Use *in, on,* and *at* with some time and place expressions.
4. Make questions with *where* and *when.*
5. Pronounce the sounds /y/, /j/ in words like *yell, jell,* and the /h/ in *hill* contrasted with its absence in *ill.*
6. Say the name and sound for each of these capital letters: *S, T, U, V, W, Y.*
7. Read the following new words:
   Chart words: *Sam, Ted, Uncle, Van, Will, York*
   Story words: *on, street, pet, going, boys, birds, pups, jumps.*
8. Read a simple story, using the new chart and story words.
9. Distinguish aurally between the beginning sounds unvoiced th/t, th/f, th/s; voiced th/d, th/v, th/z; and identify each sound with its symbol.
10. Write the capital letters *S, T, U, V, W, Y.*

## VISUAL AIDS

1. A cardboard or toy clock with movable hands.
2. Accompanying *ESOL Illustrations for Skill Book 1,* p. 41.

## REVIEW

Review any items that your student had difficulty with when doing the Oral Evaluation in Lesson 8.

# I. Conversation Skills

## DIALOG

Teacher: What are you studying?
Student: I'm studying English.

Teacher: Do you study every day?
Student: Yes, I do.

Teacher: Where do you study?
Student: I study at home.

Teach the dialog, using the procedure outlined in
Unit A.

## VOCABULARY: Chart Words

```
This is Sam.
This is Van.
This is Will.
This is Uncle Ted.
The boys are visiting Uncle Ted.
```

Using p. 41 of *ESOL Illustrations*, teacher models the sentences several times, having student repeat.

[Indicate the pictures as you model the sentences.]

## DRILL: Substitution Drill with Visual Cues

Use pictures on p. 41 of *ESOL Illustrations* as visual cues.

[Pointing to picture, say: "Who is this? This is Sam. Repeat. This is Sam."]

[Continue with remaining pictures.]

## VOCABULARY: *pet shop* and Review of Animals

```
Uncle Ted has a pet shop.
Uncle Ted sells dogs at the pet shop.
                  cats
                  birds
```

Teacher models the sentences several times, having the student repeat.

Use p. 41 of *ESOL Illustrations* to show the meaning of *pet shop*.

## DRILL: Substitution Drill with Visual Cues

Use the pictures of animals on p. 39 of *ESOL Illustrations*. Do not say the cues unless necessary.

| Teacher | Student |
|---|---|
| Uncle Ted sells dogs at the pet shop. | Uncle Ted sells dogs at the pet shop. |
| cats | Uncle Ted sells cats at the pet shop. |
| birds | |
| snakes | |
| pups | |
| fish | |
| kittens | |

## VOCABULARY: Telling Time (On the Hour)

| It's | one | o'clock. |
|------|--------|----------|
| It's | two | o'clock. |
| It's | three | o'clock. |
| It's | four | o'clock. |
| It's | five | o'clock. |
| It's | six | o'clock. |
| It's | seven | o'clock. |
| It's | eight | o'clock. |
| It's | nine | o'clock. |
| It's | ten | o'clock. |
| It's | eleven | o'clock. |
| It's | twelve | o'clock. |

Teacher models the sentences several times, having the student repeat.

Draw a clock face on the blackboard or use a cardboard clock. Change the hands of the clock to indicate the various times as you model the sentences. Be sure to put the hands only on the exact hours.

[Indicate a clock face at one o'clock. Say: "What time is it? It's one o'clock. Repeat. It's one o'clock."]

[Continue with the rest of the items.]

## DRILL: Substitution Drill with Visual Cues

Practice telling time, indicating the various times above on a clock face as visual cues.

**Teacher**
[Point to clock.]
What time is it?

**Student**

It's three o'clock.

## VOCABULARY: Time Expressions with Daily Activities

| I get up | in the morning. | |
|-------------------|------|----------------|
| I get dressed | in the morning. | |
| I have breakfast | in the morning. | |
| I go to work | in the morning. | |
| I have lunch | at | noon. |
| I go shopping | in the afternoon. | |
| I have dinner | at | six o'clock. |
| I go to class | at | night. |
| I go to bed | at | night. |

Using pp. 42-45 of *ESOL Illustrations*, teacher models the sentences several times, having the student repeat.

The new vocabulary is *have breakfast/lunch/dinner* and the time expressions. The illustrations include clocks showing appropriate times for the time expressions. If your student still has difficulty understanding the time expressions, indicate the time on a cardboard clock.

[Divide the practice into four parts. Begin by saying, "Listen to *in the morning*," then modeling the sentences containing that time expression.]

[Continue with "Listen to *at noon*."]

[Go on to "Listen to *in the afternoon*."]

[Conclude with "Listen to *at night*," before the last two sentences. You do not need to say anything before modeling the sentence with *at six o'clock*.]

## DRILL: Questions and Answers

Use pp. 42-45 of *ESOL Illustrations* if your student
needs help.

| Teacher | Student |
|---|---|
| When do you get up? | I get up in the morning. |
| When do you get dressed? | |
| When do you have breakfast? | |
| When do you go to work? | |
| When do you have lunch? | |
| When do you go shopping? | |
| When do you have dinner? | |
| When do you go to class? | |
| When do you go to bed? | |

## VOCABULARY: Place Expressions with *in* and *on*

| | | | |
|---|---|---|---|
| Glenn Hill | lives | in | Indian Valley. |
| He | lives | on | Grant Street. |
| My mother | lives | in | Boston. |
| She | lives | on | Beacon Street. |
| I | live | in | _____ (city). |
| I | live | on | _____ (street). |

Teacher models the sentences several times, having the
student repeat.

[Say, "Listen to *in* and *on*."]

**Note:** Use *in* with names of countries, towns, and
cities. Use *on* with street names (no number).

For practice, use the names of cities and streets in
your area. Be sure the student practices with his own
city and street name.

## DRILL: Questions and Answers (Free Reply)

Teacher asks questions with *where* which elicit answers
using *in* and *on*.

[Say: "Where does Glenn Hill live? He lives in Indian Valley.
Repeat. He lives in Indian Valley."]

| Teacher | Student |
|---|---|
| Where does your mother live? | She lives in Boston. |
| What street does she live on? | She lives on Beacon Street. |
| Where do you live? | |
| What street do you live on? | |
| Where does Glenn Hill live? | |
| What street does he live on? | |

## DRILL: Questions and Answers

Review names of countries and nationalities by asking questions with *where* which require an answer using *in*.

[Say: "He's American.
Where does he live? He lives in the United States.
Repeat. He lives in the United States."]

| Teacher | Student |
|---|---|
| He's Italian. | |
| Where does he live? | He lives in Italy. |
| He's Spanish. | |
| Where does he live? | |
| He's Chinese. | |
| Where does he live? | |
| He's Polish. | |
| Where does he live? | |
| He's German. | |
| Where does he live? | |
| He's American. | |
| Where does he live? | |

## VOCABULARY: Place Expressions with *at*

| | | |
|---|---|---|
| He | is | at home. |
| She | is | at work. |
| They | are | at church. |
| Mr. Hill | is | at the river. |
| Sam and Will | are | at the pet shop. |

Teacher models the sentences several times, having the student repeat.

[Say: "Listen to *at*."]

**Note:** Do not confuse the student by trying to teach items not in this pattern, as: *downtown, in bed,* and *in class.*

## DRILL: Multiple-Slot Substitution Drill

Teacher says either the subject or the place as the vocal cue for the student to substitute in the sentence.

**Note:** This is a new kind of substitution drill. The student is asked to substitute items in different parts (slots) of the sentence.

If the student has difficulty, give both the cue and the sentence, having him repeat the sentence. Then do the drill again, giving only the cues.

| Teacher | Student |
|---|---|
| Ann is at home. | Ann is at home. |
| church | Ann is at church. |
| Sam | Sam is at church. |
| They | They are at church. |
| river | They are at the river. |
| Mr. Hill | Mr. Hill is at the river. |
| pet shop | Mr. Hill is at the pet shop. |
| work | Mr. Hill is at work. |
| home | Mr. Hill is at home. |
| Mr. and Mrs. Hill | Mr. and Mrs. Hill are at home. |
| church | Mr. and Mrs. Hill are at church. |

## STRUCTURE FOCUS:  Review Yes/No Questions

| | | | |
|---|---|---|---|
| Is Sam | | at the pet shop? | Yes, he is. |
| Are you | | going downtown? | No, I'm not. |
| Does Uncle Ted | live | on York Street? | Yes, he does. |
| Do they | | study in the morning? | Yes, they do. |

Review the Yes/No question pattern introduced in Units E and F and in Lessons 6 and 7. Repeat and practice only as many of the exercises as your student needs.


## STRUCTURE FOCUS:  Information Questions with *where* and *when*

| | | |
|---|---|---|
| Where is Sam? | | At the pet shop. |
| Where does Glenn Hill live? | | In Indian Valley. |
| When do you have lunch? | | At noon. |
| When do they have breakfast? | In the morning. |

Teacher models the questions and short answers several times, having the student repeat both.

Use *ESOL Illustrations*, pp. 41, 34, 43, and 44 if your student needs help in understanding the meaning of the questions and answers.

**Note:** Questions with *where* and *when* (also *what, why, whose,* and *who*) are called information questions.

In information questions, it is very important that your student use the question word order, as in "Is Sam at the pet shop?" and "Do you study at night?"

Questions beginning with *where* elicit an answer about a place; with *when*, about time; with *why*, about a reason; and with *who*, about a person. (*Who* is more common in conversational English than the formal *whom*.)

Information questions beginning with *where, when, what,* and so on, use a falling intonation pattern (final) similar to that used for statements.

[Say: "Listen to *where*" before modeling the questions with *where*.]

[Say: "Listen to *when*" before modeling the questions with *when*.]

## DRILL:  Transformation Drill

The student transforms each statement into a question beginning with *where*.

[Say: "Listen. Sam is at the pet shop. Where is Sam? Repeat. Where is Sam?"]

| Teacher | Student |
|---|---|
| Uncle Ted is at the pet shop. | Where is Uncle Ted? |
| Ann is at home. | |
| Mr. Hill is at the river. | |
| The pencil is in the book. | |
| Uncle Ted lives on York Street. | |
| Glenn is at work. | |
| My mother and father live in Germany. | |
| Glenn lives on York Street. | |
| The pet shop is on Main Street. | |
| Kim puts the snake in the box. | |
| The pen is on the table. | |

## DRILL:  Transformation Drill

Student transforms the statement into a question beginning with *when*.

[Say: "Listen. Bob gets up in the morning. When does Bob get up? Repeat. When does Bob get up?"]

| Teacher | Student |
|---|---|
| The children have lunch at noon. | When do the children have lunch? |
| Glenn goes to work at seven o'clock. | When does Glenn go to work? |
| The girls play ball in the morning. | |
| The teacher opens the door at eight o'clock. | |
| I read in the morning. | |
| Jill goes shopping in the afternoon. | |
| The boys run in the afternoon. | |
| They go to class at night. | |

## DRILL:  Short Answers (Free Reply)

Teacher asks questions with *where* and *when* which elicit short answers beginning with *in, on,* or *at*.

[Say, "Listen. When does the teacher open the door? In the morning. Repeat. In the morning."]

| Teacher | Student |
|---|---|
| Where is Sam? | (At the pet shop.) |
| When do the children have lunch? | (At noon.) |
| Where do you live? | |
| When do the girls play ball? | |
| When do you study? | |
| Where is the pet shop? | |
| When does the teacher open the door? | |

When do the boys have dinner?
Where is the pencil?
Where does your sister live?
When do you get up?
Where do your mother
and father live?

## PRONUNCIATION: /y/ and /j/

1. See Unit D, Pronunciation, for the steps to follow in teaching the /y/ and /j/ sounds.

2. Teach the /h/ sound before vowels as contrasted with the lack of /h/ before vowels.

   **Note:** Some of your students may have difficulty pronouncing /h/ before vowels. Practice the minimal pairs given in this section for these students. For those who have no difficulty, do the drill very quickly.

| /y/ | /j/ | Sentences |
|---|---|---|
| yolk | joke | It's a yellow dress. |
| Yale | jail | He drives a jeep. |
| yam | jam | The yolk is yellow. |
| yell | jell | He yelled at Jenny. |
| yet | jet | He went to Yale. |
| | | He went to jail. |

| /—/ | /h/ | Sentences |
|---|---|---|
| ill | hill | Henry's hungry. |
| eel | heel | He's angry. |
| air | hair | He's at home. |
| at | hat | He's ill. |
| is | his | |

## ORAL EVALUATION

1. Review chart words necessary for reading the story.

   [Using p. 41 of *ESOL Illustrations*, ask: "Who's this?"]

2. Review telling time on the hour.

   Student should be able to say all of the times, since the numbers have been taught and practiced before.

   [Use cardboard clock to drill telling time (on the hour only).]

3. Review time expressions: *in the morning, at noon, in the afternoon,* and *at night.*

   Student should be able to use all of these expressions.

   [Using pp. 42-45 of *ESOL Illustrations*, do the Drill that follows Vocabulary: Time Expression with Daily Activities.]

4. Review place expressions with *in* and *on.*

   [Do the two Drills on Questions and Answers the follow Vocabulary: Place Expressions with *in* and *on.*]

5. Review place expressions with *at.*

   If the student has difficulty with time and place expressions with *in, on,* and *at,* review at the next session.

   [Do the Multiple-Slot Substitution Drill.]

6. Review formation of questions with *where* and *when.*

   [Do the Transformation Drills that follow Structure Focus: Information Questions with *where* and *when.*]

7. Review short answers to questions with *where* and *when.*

   If the student cannot make these questions and answer them fairly quickly, be sure to review both at the next session.

   [Do the Short Answers (Free Reply) Drill.]

# II. Reading

Before you begin the chart, check and correct the student's homework from Lesson 8.

## CHART 9:  Page 48

Do this chart as you did those in Lessons 6 and 7.

When your student sounds out *Uncle*, remember that the final *e* is silent. Do not point to it. You may even want to draw a line through it to help your student remember that it is silent.

## STORY:  At the Pet Shop

To teach the story, follow steps 1-7 in the Story section of Lesson 6. The new story words are:
*on, street, pet, going, boys, birds, pups, jumps*. Use the questions below to check comprehension.

| | Teacher | Student |
|---|---|---|
| **Paragraph 1** | [Run your finger along the street in the picture.] | |
| | What street is this? | (It's) York Street. |
| | [Point to the man in front of the shop.] Is this man Uncle Ted? | Yes, he is. |
| | [Point to the three boys.] Are they Sam and Van and Will? | Yes, they are. |
| **Paragraph 2** | Where does Uncle Ted live? | (He lives) on York Street. |
| | [Point to the pet shop in the picture.] Whose pet shop is this? | (It's) Uncle Ted's. |
| | Where are the boys going? | They're going to the pet shop. |
| **Paragraph 3** | Are the boys at the pet shop? | Yes, they are. |
| | What are the boys looking at? | They're looking at the birds, and the pups, and the fish. |
| **Paragraph 4** | What does Will pick up? | He picks up a box. |
| | What is in the box? | A snake (is in the box). |
| | Does Van pick up the snake? | No, he doesn't. |
| | What does Van do? | He jumps and runs. |
| **Paragraph 5** | Is the snake a pet? | Yes, it is. |

## SKILLS PRACTICE: Beginning Sounds—Unvoiced th/t, th/f, th/s and Voiced th/d, th/v, th/z

Do these exercises exactly as you did those in Lesson 6. The pattern for what you are to say is given below.

Listen: _tent_ , _tent_ .

What sound does it begin with?

_tent_ , _tent_ .

/ t /.  [Point to letter.]

What is the name of this letter?  [Continue pointing to letter.]

_t_ .

**Note:** For the sounds unvoiced /th/ and voiced /th/, the last question should be: "What are the names of the letters?"

## 1. Unvoiced th/t

| Write letters: | th and t | Minimal pairs: | /th/ | /t/ |
|---|---|---|---|---|
| Chart words: | thank/tent | | thing | ting |
| | | | thick | tick |
| Example pair 1: | thank/tank | | thorn | torn |
| Example pair 2: | tin/thin | | theme | team |
| | | | thought | taught |
| | | | thug | tug |
| | | | three | tree |
| | | | threw | true |

## 2. Unvoiced th/f

| Write letters: | th and f | Minimal pairs: | /th/ | /f/ |
|---|---|---|---|---|
| Chart words: | thank/fish | | thin | fin |
| | | | think | fink |
| Example pair 1: | three/free | | thirst | first |
| Example pair 2: | Fred/thread | | thought | fought |
| | | | thresh | fresh |
| | | | threat | fret |
| | | | thrill | frill |
| | | | three | free |
| | | | thread | Fred |

## 3. Unvoiced th/s

| | | | Minimal pairs: | /th/ | /s/ |
|---|---|---|---|---|---|
| Write letters: | th and s | | | thaw | saw |
| Chart words: | thank/snake | | | theme | seem |
| Example pair 1: | thank/sank | | | thick | sick |
| Example pair 2: | sing/thing | | | thigh | sigh |
| | | | | thin | sin |
| | | | | think | sink |
| | | | | thought | sought |
| | | | | thuds | suds |
| | | | | thumb | sum |
| | | | | thump | sump |
| | | | | thank | sank |
| | | | | thing | sing |

## 4. Voiced th/d

| | | | Minimal pairs: | /th/ | /d/ |
|---|---|---|---|---|---|
| Write letters: | th and d | | | their | dare |
| Chart words: | this/dish | | | then | den |
| Example pair 1: | they/day | | | those | doze |
| Example pair 2: | Dan/than | | | though | dough |
| | | | | thy | die |
| | | | | thence | dense |
| | | | | they | day |
| | | | | than | Dan |

**Note:** *This* is not really a chart word, but the student has had ample practice with it.

## 5. Voiced th/v

| | | | Minimal pairs: | /th/ | /v/ |
|---|---|---|---|---|---|
| Write letters: | th and v | | | they'll | veil |
| Chart words: | this/valley | | | thy | vie |
| Example pair 1: | that/vat | | | thine | vine |
| Example pair 2: | Van/than | | | thou | vow |
| | | | | thee | V |
| | | | | than | Van |
| | | | | that | vat |

## 6. Voiced th/z

| | | | More words: | /th/ | /z/ |
|---|---|---|---|---|---|
| Write letters: | th and z | | | they | zeal |
| Chart words: | this/zipper | | | them | zebra |
| Example pair 1: | then/Zen | | | their | zero |
| Example pair 2: | Z/thee | | | than | zest |
| | | | | that | zinc |
| | | | | this | zip |
| | | | | those | zone |
| | | | | then | zoo |
| | | | | these | zoom |

**Note:** These two sounds have almost no minimal pairs in which the /z/ sound has a regular z spelling. Use the words given here in the same way you have been using minimal pairs.

## SKILLS PRACTICE: Adding -s

Write the following words on the board and have the student read each pair (without and with the -s).

| leg | legs | | pick | picks |
|-----|------|--|------|-------|
| wing | wings | | jump | jumps |
| | | | run | runs |
| | | | look | looks |

# III. Writing

## CHECKUP: Page 50

As before, the student is to fill in the missing word or letter and then to write the capital letters beside the corresponding small letters.

## LISTEN AND WRITE: Page 51

Ask your student to write the capital letter that these names begin with:

| Pam | Robert | Mr. | Liz | Jill | Hill |
|-----|--------|-----|-----|------|------|
| Ned | Oliver | Queen | Kim | Glenn | Indian |

Check carefully what he has written.

## WRITING LESSON: Page 52

Do this page exactly as you did the one in Lesson 8.

## HOMEWORK: Page 53

Ask your student to write the capital letters at home.

Feel free to give him some other homework, too, particularly a review of something he has been having trouble with or some new words he needs in his job.

## READING AND WRITING EVALUATION

1. Ask your student to write: *V, Y, S, U, T, W.* Then ask him to say the names and sounds.

   Student should be able to write all the letters, to give all their names, and to give at least four sounds correctly.

2. Write these words and ask your student to read them:

   | a | am | in | to | up | is |
   |---|----|----|----|----|-----|
   | an | at | on | are | and | this |

   Student should be able to read at least nine out of 12 correctly.

3. Write these words and ask your student to read them:

   | jumps | pet | going |
   |-------|--------|---------|
   | jumping | street | looking |

   Student should be able to read four correctly.

# Lesson 10

## OBJECTIVES

When a student completes this unit, he should be able to:

1. Say and respond to a new dialog.
2. Use new vocabulary about recreation.
3. Use the indirect object with *to*.
4. Use *some/any* with count and non-count nouns.
5. Make questions with *who, what,* and *whose.*
6. Use the possessive pronouns *my, your, his, her, its, our, their.*
7. Pronounce the vowel sounds in *Luke, look, luck.*
8. Say the name and sound of each of these capital letters: *X, Z.*
9. Say the names of all the small letters and capital letters (review).
10. Read all the chart words taught thus far.
11. Read a simple story, using familiar words and the following new story words: *gets, Hills.*
12. Distinguish aurally between ending sounds -p/t, -b/p, -d/t, -b/d and identify each sound with its symbol.
13. Write the capital letters *X* and *Z* as well as all the other capital letters and all the small letters.
14. Say the letters of the alphabet in order.

## VISUAL AIDS

Accompanying *ESOL Illustrations for Skill Book 1*, pp. 46-47.

## REVIEW

Review any items that your student had difficulty with when doing the Oral Evaluation in Lesson 9.

# I. Conversation Skills

## DIALOG

> Teacher: Jill, I need some dimes for a telephone call.
> Do you have any?
> Student: No, I don't. But I have some nickels.
> Teacher: Good, thank you.

Teach the dialog, using the procedure outlined in Unit A.

## VOCABULARY: Recreation

|  |  |  |
|---|---|---|
| Mr. Hill | is | fishing in the river. |
| Glenn | is | sailing. |
| Jill | is | swimming. |
| Glenn and Liz | are | camping. |
| Sam | is | hunting. |
| Will | is | hiking. |

Teacher models the sentences several times, having the student repeat. Use pp. 46-47 of *ESOL Illustrations.*

[Indicate the pictures as you model the sentences.]

## DRILL: Questions and Answers

Indicating the pictures, ask questions.

[Say: "Listen. What is Mr. Hill doing?
He's fishing in the river. Repeat. He's fishing in the river."]

| Teacher | Student |
|---|---|
| What is Glenn doing? | He's sailing. |
| What is Jill doing? | |
| What are Glenn and Liz doing? | |
| What is Sam doing? | |
| What is Will doing? | |
| What is Mr. Hill doing? | |

## STRUCTURE FOCUS: Indirect Object with *to*

| | | | |
|---|---|---|---|
| The woman | is giving | the book | to the boy. |
| The man | is selling | the book | to the girl. |
| The teacher | is reading | the book | to the student. |
| The girl | is speaking | English | to the boy. |
| The teacher | is teaching | English | to the student. |
| She | is showing | the books | to the students. |
| She | is repeating | the numbers | to the students. |

Teacher models the sentences, having the student repeat. As you model the sentence with *showing* (a new vocabulary item), illustrate by performing the action.

**Note:** Verbs like *give, sell,* and *read* can take two objects: a direct object and an indirect object (with *to*). Notice that the indirect object in the sentences being taught comes after the direct object. Word order is extremely important in English. Although you do not have to use the terminology given here with your student, it is important that he use the correct word order in English.

[Before modeling the first sentence, say: "Listen to *to the boy*."]

[Continue to call attention to the indirect object in the same way before modeling each of the remaining sentences.]

| Subject | Verb | Direct Object | Indirect Object |
|---|---|---|---|
| The woman | is giving | the book | to the boy. |
| The man | is selling | the book | to the girl. |
| The teacher | is reading | the book | to the student. |

You may print the above examples on the blackboard (without the headings). Say the sentences, having your student repeat them after you.

## DRILL: Expansion Drill

Teacher says the indirect object and the sentence. Student expands the sentence by adding the indirect object.

[Say: "Listen to *to the boy*." Pause.
"The woman's giving the book.
The woman's giving the book to the boy. Please repeat.
The woman's giving the book to the boy."]

| Teacher | Student |
|---|---|
| to the girl<br>The man's selling the book. | The man's selling the book to the girl. |
| to the boy<br>The man's selling a pen. | The man's selling a pen to the boy. |
| to the woman<br>The boy's giving the cup. | |
| to Glenn<br>Jill's giving the fish. | |
| to him<br>Kim's speaking English. | |
| to her<br>He's passing the butter. | |
| to them<br>He's repeating the numbers. | |
| to Will<br>Uncle Ted's giving the snake. | |
| to the waiter<br>The girl's giving fifty cents. | |
| to the boys and girls<br>The teacher's showing the book. | |
| to them<br>The teacher's reading the book. | |

## STRUCTURE FOCUS: *some/any*

|  | some | | any | |
|---|---|---|---|---|
| **Count Nouns:** | Mary has | some nickels. | Mary doesn't have | any nickels. |
| | Jill has | some dimes. | Jill doesn't have | any dimes. |
| | I have | some apples. | I don't have | any apples. |
| **Non-Count Nouns:** | Mary has | some milk . | Mary doesn't have | any milk . |
| | Jill has | some bread . | Jill doesn't have | any bread . |
| | I have | some water . | I don't have | any water . |

Teacher models the sentences several times, having the student repeat. Do not stress the words *some* and *any* as you say the sentences.

**Note:** *Some* means an indefinite number or quantity. It is used in *affirmative* sentences with plural count nouns and non-count nouns. *Any* is used in *negative* sentences with plural count nouns and non-count nouns.

[Say: "Listen to *some* and *any*.
Mary has some nickels. Mary doesn't have any nickels."
Continue in this order.]

## DRILL: Transformation Drill

1. Student transforms affirmative sentences with *some* to negative sentences with *any*.

[Say: "Listen. Mary has some nickels. Mary doesn't have any nickels. Repeat. Mary doesn't have any nickels."]

| Teacher | Student |
|---------|---------|
| I have some books. | I don't have any books. |
| Mary has some boxes. | |
| I have some cups. | |
| You have some pens. | |
| I have some bread. | |
| Mary has some sugar. | |
| They have some coffee. | |
| We have some paper. | |

2. Student transforms negative sentences with *any* to affirmative sentences with *some*.

[Say: "Listen. The nurse doesn't have any books. The nurse has some books. Repeat. The nurse has some books."]

| Teacher | Student |
|---------|---------|
| The waitress doesn't have any oranges. | The waitress has some oranges. |
| The man doesn't have any boxes. | |
| The housewife doesn't have any cups. | |
| The waiter doesn't have any coffee. | |
| The child doesn't have any water. | |
| The student doesn't have any books. | |
| The girl doesn't have any apples. | |

## STRUCTURE FOCUS: Information Questions with *who* and *what*

| | |
|---|---|
| Who is the woman giving the book to? | To the boy. |
| What does Jill have? | A pan. |

Teacher models the questions and short answers several times, having student repeat both.

**Note:** Questions with *who* elicit an answer about a person; *what,* about a thing; and *whose* (next section), about a possessive. *Who, what,* and *whose* are followed by question word order. These questions use a falling intonation pattern similar to that used in statements.

*Who* is the interrogative used as both subject and object in informal speech. *Whom* is the object form used in formal speech and in writing.

[Before modeling the question with *who,* say: "Listen to *who*."]

[Before modeling the question with *what,* say: "Listen to *what*."]

## DRILL: Transformation Drill

1. The student transforms statements into questions with *who*.

[Say: "Listen. Will is giving the fish to Jill. Who is Will giving the fish to? Repeat. Who is Will giving the fish to?"],

| Teacher | Student |
|---|---|
| Kim is speaking English to the girl. | Who is Kim speaking English to? |
| He is showing the books to the teacher. | |
| The teacher is reading the book to the student. | |
| Jill sells the book to the student. | |
| The girl gives the book to the teacher. | |

2. The student transforms statements into questions with *what*.

[Say: "Listen. Jill has a pan. What does Jill have? Repeat. What does Jill have?"]

| Teacher | Student |
|---|---|
| Mr. Hill gets a fish. | What does Mr. Hill get? |
| Mary has some dimes. | |
| Mr. Oliver has a pup. | |
| Mr. Hill's looking at the river. | |
| Jill's eating a banana. | |
| Kim's drinking milk. | |

## STRUCTURE FOCUS: *What does_____mean?*

| | |
|---|---|
| What does <u>dime</u> mean? | It means ten cents. |
| What does <u>nickel</u> mean? | It means five cents. |

Teacher models the question and its answer, having the student repeat both. This is to help the student understand the meaning of this question, which is an extremely useful one for him.

[Say: "Listen to *What does <u>dime</u> mean?*"]

## DRILL: Substitution Drill with Vocal Cues

Teacher gives a noun as a vocal cue. Student uses it in a question, using the frame "What does _____ mean?"

| Teacher | Student |
|---|---|
| nickel | |
| What does *nickel* mean? | What does *nickel* mean? |
| dime | |
| quarter | |
| half dollar | |
| penny | |
| family | |
| money | |

## STRUCTURE FOCUS: Possessive Pronouns

| | | | |
|---|---|---|---|
| I | have | my | book. |
| You | have | your | book. |
| He | has | his | book. |
| She | has | her | book. |
| The dog | has | its | ball. |
| We | have | our | books. |
| You | have | your | books. |
| They | have | their | books. |

Teacher models the sentences several times, especially those with the new items: *its, our, your* plural, and *their*. The others—*my, your* singular, *his*, and *her*—were introduced in Lesson 1. Have the student repeat.

[Call attention to the possessive pronoun before modeling each sentence by saying: "Listen to *my*," and so on.]

[Stress that *its* correlates with *dog, our* with *we, your* with *you*, and *their* with *they*.]

## DRILL: Substitution Drill with Vocal Cues

Student substitutes subjects and possessive pronouns in the sentence.

| Teacher | Student |
|---|---|
| I have my ball. | I have my ball. |
| You | |
| You have your ball. | You have your ball. |
| He | He has his ball. |
| She | |
| The dog | |
| The cat | |
| We | |
| You | |
| They | |
| Bob | |
| The children | |
| Ann | |

## STRUCTURE FOCUS: Information Questions with *whose*

| | |
|---|---|
| Whose book does Jill have? | She has her book. |
| Whose book does Bob have? | He has his book. |
| Whose book do you have? | I have the teacher's book. |

Teacher models each question and answer several times, having the student repeat both.

[Say: "Listen to *whose.*
Whose book does Jill have? She has her book. Repeat.
Whose book does Jill have? She has her book."]

## DRILL: Transformation Drill

The student transforms statements into questions with *whose*.

[Say: "Listen. This is the teacher's book. Whose book is this? Repeat. Whose book is this?"]

| Teacher | Student |
|---|---|
| This is Jill's fish. | Whose fish is this? |
| Queen is Mr. Oliver's pup. | Whose pup is Queen? |
| This is Kim's ball. | |
| This is my book. | |
| Those are his pens. | |
| That is her desk. | |
| The teacher is picking up his book. | |
| The teacher is reading her book. | |

## DRILL: Short Answers (Free Reply)

The student gives short answers to questions with *who, what,* and *whose*.

In this drill, the student is expected to make up his own short answers. If he cannot, prompt him, but only for as long as necessary.

[Say: "Listen.
Who is the waiter selling coffee to?
The man. Repeat. The man."]

| Teacher | Student |
|---|---|
| Who is the teacher giving a book to? | (A student.) |
| What does Glenn have? | (A book.) |
| Whose pen is this? | (Jill's.) |
| What do you have? | |
| Whose book is this? | |
| Who is the girl speaking English to? | |
| Whose pencil do you have? | |
| What does the teacher have? | |
| Who is the teacher showing the book to? | |
| Whose eraser is that? | |
| What do you have in your hand? | |
| Whose book are you looking at? | |

## PRONUNCIATION: Vowel Sounds in *Luke, look, luck*

See the Pronunciation Section in Unit D for the steps to follow in teaching the sounds.

1. Teach /ū/ as in *Luke* and /uu/ as in *look*.

   **Note:** The lips are rounded and tense when making /ū/. They are rounded but not tense when making /uu/.

| /ū/ | /uu/ | Sentences |
|---|---|---|
| Luke | look | I look at the fool. |
| cooed | could | Luke could go. |
| pool | pull | The pool is full. |
| fool | full | I pulled and pulled. |
| stewed | stood | |

2. Teach /uu/ as in *look* and /u/ as in *luck*.

| /uu/ | /u/ | Sentences |
|------|-----|-----------|
| look | luck | Lots of luck. |
| put | putt | I put the book on the table. |
| could | cud | He took the buck. |
| book | buck | It's a book. |
| took | tuck | It's a buck. |

## ORAL EVALUATION

1. Review the vocabulary about recreation.

   Student should know *fishing* and three others.

   [Use pp. 46-47 of *ESOL Illustrations*.]

2. Review verbs + *to*.

   [Do the Expansion Drill following Structure Focus: Indirect Object with *to*.]

3. Review *some* and *any*.

   Student should be able to use *some* and *any* with count and non-count nouns. If he cannot answer fairly quickly, make a note to review at the next session.

   [Do the Transformation Drill following Structure Focus: *some/any*.]

4. Review the formation of questions with *who, what,* and *whose*.

   [Do the Transformation Drills that follow Structure Focus: Information Questions with *who* and *what* and Structure Focus: Information Questions with *whose*.]

5. Review short answers to questions with *who, what,* and *whose*.

   [Do the Drill with Short Answers (Free Reply).]

   If student has difficulty with items 4 and 5, it is essential to review these items at the next session. You could combine this review with a review of *where* and *when* if your student seems to find this question pattern troublesome and needs extra practice.

# II. Reading

Before you begin the chart, check and correct the student's homework from Lesson 9. If it is not completed, have your student complete it now.

## CHART 10: Page 54

| **Do this:** | **Say this:** |
| --- | --- |
| Point to headings. | Teacher: Please read. |
| | Student: Lesson 10, Chart 10. |
| Point to *a* on chart. | Teacher: What's the name of this letter? |
| | Student: *a*. |
| | Teacher: What's the sound of this letter? |
| | Student: /a/. |
| Point to *apple*. | Teacher: Please read. |
| | Student: Apple. |
| Point to *A* on chart. | Teacher: What's the name of this letter? |
| | Student: *Capital A*. |
| | Teacher: What's the sound of this letter? |
| | Student: /a/. |
| Point to *Ann*. | Teacher: Please read. |
| | Student: Ann. |
| | Teacher: Good! |

Do the rest of the page the same way. Be very particular about your student's vowel sounds and pronunciation. Can you hear his word endings?

Remember to teach the page number.

## STORY: Fishing in the River

To teach this story, follow steps 1-7 in the Story section of Lesson 6. Do not skip anything.
The new story words are: *gets, Hills*. Use the questions below to check comprehension.

| | **Teacher** | **Student** |
| --- | --- | --- |
| **Paragraph 1** | What's the boy's name? | Ed Hill. |
| | What's the girl's name? | Jill Hill. |
| **Paragraph 2** | Are the Hills at the river? | Yes, they are. |
| | What are the Hills doing? | They're looking at the fish. |
| | What are the fish doing? | The fish are jumping. |
| **Paragraph 3** | Are Mr. and Mrs. Hill fishing? | Yes, they are. |
| | Does Mr. Hill get a fish? | Yes, he does. |
| | Does Mrs. Hill get a fish? | Yes, she does. |
| **Paragraph 4** | Are Ed and Jill swimming? | No, they aren't. (They're fishing.) |
| | Do the children get any fish? | Yes, they do. |
| **Paragraph 5** | Where are the Hills? | They're at the tent. |
| | Who puts the fish in a dish? | Mr. Hill does. |
| | Who does Mr. Hill give the fish to? | The children. |

## SKILLS PRACTICE:  Ending Sounds -p/t, -b/p, -d/t, -b/d

Before you begin these exercises, refresh the student's memory of the meaning of *ends with*. To do this, review the word *box* on Chart 5, p. 24 of *Skill Book 1*.

| **Do this:** | **Say this:** |
|---|---|
| Point to the box. | What's this? [Let student answer, "It's a box."] |
| Point to the word *box*. | Read *box*. [Let student read, "Box."] |
| Cover all but the last letter of the word *box*. | *Box* ends with /ks/.<br>*Box* ends with /ks/.<br><br>Listen: box, box.<br>      What sound does it end with?<br>      What sound does it end with?<br>      box, box.<br>      /ks/. |
| Point to the *x* under the word *box*. | What is the name of this letter?<br>*x*.<br><br>[Repeat from "Listen," this time allowing the student to answer.] |

Now you are ready to begin the exercises on ending consonant sounds. Follow nearly the same steps as you followed for beginning sounds.

**Step 1: Write the letters.** Write each pair of letters on a piece of paper (on the board for a class).

**Step 2: Example pairs 1 and 2.** Use example pairs 1 and 2 for demonstration and practice. (There are no chart words for ending sounds.)

For each example pair, go through the procedure twice. The first time, give the answers yourself; the second time, allow the student to answer.

**Step 3: Minimal pairs.** Continue the procedure with the rest of the minimal pairs, allowing the student to answer.

The pattern for what you are to say is given below.

Listen:   _cup_ , _cup_ .
What sound does it end with?
_cup_ , _cup_ .
/ _p_ /.                                  [Point to letter.]
What is the name of this letter?          [Continue pointing to letter.]
_p_.

## 1. Ending sounds -p/t

| Write letters: | p and t | | Minimal pairs: | -/p/ | -/t/ |
|---|---|---|---|---|---|
| Example pair 1: | cup/cut | | | shop | shot |
| Example pair 2: | pet/pup | | | cap | cat |
| | | | | map | mat |
| | | | | rap | rat |
| | | | | sap | sat |
| | | | | hop | hot |
| | | | | pup | putt |
| | | | | pap | pat |

## 2. Ending sounds -b/p

| Write letters: | b and p | | Minimal pairs: | -/b/ | -/p/ |
|---|---|---|---|---|---|
| Example pair 1: | cup/cub | | | pub | pup |
| Example pair 2: | Bob/bop | | | cab | cap |
| | | | | gab | gap |
| | | | | lab | lap |
| | | | | nab | nap |
| | | | | tab | tap |
| | | | | rib | rip |
| | | | | cob | cop |
| | | | | lob | lop |
| | | | | mob | mop |
| | | | | sob | sop |
| | | | | sub | sup |

## 3. Ending sounds -d/t

| Write letters: | d and t | | Minimal pairs: | -/d/ | -/t/ |
|---|---|---|---|---|---|
| Example pair 1: | Ned/net | | | Fred | fret |
| Example pair 2: | pat/pad | | | and | ant |
| | | | | ride | write |
| | | | | ad | at |
| | | | | bad | bat |
| | | | | cad | cat |
| | | | | fad | fat |
| | | | | had | hat |
| | | | | sad | sat |
| | | | | bed | bet |
| | | | | led | let |
| | | | | hid | hit |
| | | | | cod | cot |
| | | | | bud | but |
| | | | | mud | mutt |
| | | | | tend | tent |

## 4. Ending sounds -b/d

| | | Minimal pairs: | -/b/ | -/d/ |
|---|---|---|---|---|
| Write letters: | *b* and *d* | | cab | cad |
| Example pair 1: | Ed/ebb | | dab | dad |
| Example pair 2: | lib/lid | | lab | lad |
| | | | web | wed |
| | | | rib | rid |
| | | | cob | cod |
| | | | cub | cud |
| | | | sob | sod |
| | | | rob | rod |
| | | | gob | God |
| | | | bib | bid |

## SKILLS PRACTICE:  Adding - *'s*

1. Write the following phrases on the board, and ask your student to read them.

| | |
|---|---|
| Jill's pan | Will's neck |
| Jill's dish | Will's box |
| Jill's fish | Will's hand |

2. Pointing to each noun, ask the student, "Whose pan is this?" and so on.
   The student may give the short answer "Jill's."

# III. Writing

## CHECKUP:  Page 56

The student is to fill in the missing word or letters, and then to write the capital letters beside the corresponding small letters. When he has finished writing, ask him to read the sentences and to say the names and sounds of the letters.

## LISTEN AND WRITE:  Page 57

Ask your student to write the capital letters that these names begin with:

| Sam | Uncle | York | Oliver | Pam | Robert |
|---|---|---|---|---|---|
| Ted | Will | Van | Ned | Queen | Mr. |

## WRITING LESSON:  Pages 58-59

Your student is to copy the capital and small letters as shown. When he has finished, have him say or read the alphabet as quickly as he can.

## HOMEWORK: Pages 60-61

The student is to write the capital letters beside the corresponding small letters and to copy the words.
Be sure your student notices that there are two pages of homework for this lesson.

## READING AND WRITING EVALUATION

1. Ask your student to write the letters $Z$ and $X$. He should be able to write both correctly.

2. Ask your student to say the alphabet. He should be able to say it with almost no mistakes.

3. Ask your student to count from 1 to 20. Then ask him to count by 10's to 100 (start him out by saying, "10, 20 . . .").

   He should be able to say the numbers with almost no mistakes, although his pronunciation may not be perfect.

# Lesson 11

## OBJECTIVES

When a student completes this unit, he should be able to:

1. Say and respond to a new dialog.
2. Tell time, using numbers like *1:15, 2:30, 3:45*.
3. Use the expressions *now* and *every* _____ in contrasting the verb tenses as in *I am walking/I walk*.
4. Say more expressions of place and time with *in, on,* and *at*.
5. Use the expression "I'd like . . . " with some additional food items.
6. Pronounce the vowel sounds in *lock* and *luck*.
7. Say and read the numerals to 100.
8. Read the following new words:
   Chart words: *Numbers*
   Story words: *live, their, telephone number, not, Ted's.*
9. Read a simple story, using the new chart and story words and numerals.
10. Distinguish aurally between ending sounds -p/f, -f/v, -m/n, -g/k and identify each sound with its symbol.
11. Choose between *-s* and *-'s* to represent word endings he hears in sentences.
12. Read and write the alphabet, in both small and capital letters.
13. Write the numerals from *0* to *20*, and *30, 40, 50*.

## VISUAL AIDS

1. A calendar of the current month showing the days of the week.
2. A cardboard or toy clock.
3. Accompanying *ESOL Illustrations for Skill Book 1*, p. 48.
4. If possible, an apple, an orange, a banana, a sandwich, a potato, a can of soup, and cheese.

## REVIEW

Review any items that your student had difficulty with when doing the Oral Evaluation in Lesson 10.

# I. Conversation Skills

## DIALOG

> Teacher: What's your name?
> Student: My name's _____ .
>
> Teacher: Where do you live?
> Student: I live at 920 Main Street.
>
> Teacher: What's your telephone number?
> Student: My telephone number is 445-1876.

Teach the dialog, using the procedure outlined in Unit A.

This dialog is similar to the one in Unit C, but the aim here is to practice *at*.

Use your student's name, street address, and telephone number.

[Remember to say the numbers the same way you did in Unit C. For the street number 920, say: "nine twenty." For the telephone number 445-1876, say: "four, four, five," pause, "one, eight, seven, six."]

## VOCABULARY: Telling Time (On the Quarter and Half Hour)

It's 1:15.
It's 1:30.
It's 1:45.

Teacher models the sentences, having the student repeat.

Use a cardboard clock to show the time. Do not use other ways of expressing these times unless your student is more advanced.

[Pointing to the clock, which reads 1:15, say: "It's one fifteen. Please repeat. It's one fifteen."]

[Continue with 2:15, 3:15, and so on.]

[Teach 1:30 and 1:45 in the same way. For these times, say: "It's one thirty," and "It's one forty-five."
Follow 1:30 with 2:30, 3:30, and so on.
Follow 1:45 with 2:45, 3:45, and so on.]

## DRILL: Substitution Drill with Visual Cues

Teacher uses times shown on the cardboard clock as visual cues.

[Set the clock at 1:15, then ask and answer: "What time is it? It's 1:15. Repeat. It's 1:15."]

[Continue asking the time without giving the answer.]

| | | |
|------|------|-------|
| 1:30 | 3:00 | 6:00 |
| 2:45 | 4:45 | 7:30 (etc.) |
| 6:15 | 5:15 | 12:00 |

## VOCABULARY: Days of the Week (Review)

Review the days of the week. Model the sentences, having the student repeat after you.

[Pointing to a calendar, say the names of the days of the week: "It's Monday. It's Tuesday," and so on. Then have the student give the names without any prompting.]

## VOCABULARY: Use of *every*

> I have lunch    <u>every</u> day.
> I go shopping   <u>every</u> Thursday.
> I go downtown <u>every</u> Saturday.
> I go to church <u>every</u> Sunday.

Teacher models the sentences several times, having the student repeat.

To illustrate the meaning of *every*, use a calendar to indicate the repetitive nature of the action.

[Say: "Listen to *every*."
Indicating the days on the calendar, say:
"I have lunch on Sunday, Monday, Tuesday, Wednesday, Thursday, Friday, and Saturday.
I have lunch every day. Please repeat.
I have lunch every day."]

[Continue with the other sentences in the box, using the calendar to show the meaning of *every Thursday*, and so on.]

## DRILL: Substitution Drill with Vocal Cues

| Teacher | Student |
|---|---|
| I go shopping<br>   every Thursday. | I go shopping<br>   every Thursday. |
| downtown | I go downtown<br>   every Thursday. |
| to church<br>to class<br>home | |

## VOCABULARY: Use of *now*

> I'm having a class <u>now.</u>
> I'm speaking English <u>now.</u>
> I'm picking up a pencil <u>now.</u>

Teacher models the sentences several times, having the student repeat.

Perform the action as you say each sentence.

If the student has difficulty understanding, give more examples, performing the action as you say, for example: "I'm walking now," "I'm writing now," "I'm looking at my book now."

[Say: "Listen to *now*."
On a clock, indicate the exact moment that you are saying the sentence, "I'm having a class now."
Then say: "Please repeat. I'm having a class now."]

[Continue with the rest of the items.]

## DRILL: Free Reply

Teacher asks questions which elicit answers about actions the student is performing at that moment.

[Say: "What are you doing now? I'm looking at you. Please repeat. I'm looking at you."]

[Prompt the student if he cannot think of an answer to your question. For example, have him open his book, pick up a pen, or close the book.]

## STRUCTURE FOCUS: Contrast of Simple Present and Present Progressive Tenses

| | | | |
|---|---|---|---|
| I have | a class | every day. | |
| I'm having | a class | now. | |
| We speak | English | every day. | |
| We're speaking | English | now. | |

Teacher models each pair of sentences several times, having the student repeat both sentences.

[Say: "Listen to *every day* and *now*."]

**Note:** The simple present tense, as in "I have a class every day," indicates habitual action. The present progressive tense, as in "I am having a class now," indicates action going on at the moment of speaking.

Illustrate this contrast for the student by saying first a sentence like "I walk every day," and then, as you perform the action, saying: "I'm walking now."

## DRILL: Multiple-Slot Substitution Drill

Teacher gives vocal cues.

| Teacher | Student |
|---|---|
| I go to class every day. | I go to class every day. |
| now | |
| I'm going to class now. | I'm going to class now. |
| shopping | I'm going shopping now. |
| downtown | I'm going downtown now. |
| to church | I'm going to church now. |
| every Sunday | I go to church every Sunday. |
| home | I go home every Sunday. |
| Bob goes fishing every June. | Bob goes fishing every June. |
| swimming | Bob goes swimming every June. |
| now | Bob is going swimming now. |
| camping | Bob is going camping now. |
| every May | Bob goes camping every May. |

## DRILL: Transformation Drill

1. The student transforms sentences from the simple present into the present progressive.

| Teacher | Student |
|---|---|
| I have breakfast every day. | I'm having breakfast now. |
| Bob speaks English every day. | |
| Ann goes downtown every Saturday. | |
| Kim jumps rope every morning. | |
| She plays ball every morning. | |

2. The student transforms sentences from the present progressive into the simple present.

| Teacher | Student |
|---|---|
| We're speaking English now. | We speak English every day. |
| They're looking at the book now. | |
| You're going swimming now. | |
| I'm going home now. | |
| She's having lunch now. | |
| We're writing now. | |
| They're speaking English now. | |

## VOCABULARY: *in, on, at* with Place Expressions

| | |
|---|---|
| I live in Syracuse. | (city) |
| I live in New York. | (state) |
| I live in the United States. | (country) |
| I live on Main Street. | (name of street) |
| I live at 920 Main Street. | (street address) |

Teacher models the sentences several times, having the student repeat.

Use the names of your city and state, and street names familiar to your student.

**Note:** Use *in* with names of cities, states, and countries. Use *on* with street names (no number); use *at* with full street addresses (names and numbers).

You may wish to review other place expressions taught in Lesson 9.

[Say: "Listen to *in, on,* and *at.*"]

## DRILL: Substitution Drill with Vocal Cues

Teacher gives place names as vocal cues.

Use names of cities and streets familiar to your student.

[Say: "Syracuse." Pause. "I live in Syracuse. Please repeat. I live in Syracuse."]

| Teacher | Student |
|---|---|
| Boston | I live in Boston. |
| Main Street | I live on Main Street. |
| the United States | |
| New York | |
| 920 Main Street | |
| Columbus Street | |
| 86 Columbus Street | |

## VOCABULARY: *in, on, at* with Time Expressions

| | | |
|---|---|---|
| I go swimming <u>in</u> July. | (month) |
| I go downtown <u>on</u> Saturday. | (day) |
| I go to work <u>at</u> eight o'clock. | (time) |
| I go home <u>at</u> 5:30. | (time) |

Teacher models the sentences several times, having the student repeat.

[Say: "Listen to *in, on,* and *at*."]

**Note:** Use *in* with years and months, *on* with days, and *at* with exact times of day.

You may wish to review other time expressions taught in Lesson 9.

## DRILL: Substitution Drill with Vocal Cues

Teacher gives times as vocal cues.

[Say: "July." Pause. "I go swimming in July. Please repeat. I go swimming in July."]

| Teacher | Student |
|---|---|
| August | I go swimming in August. |
| 1:30 | I go swimming at 1:30. |
| Saturday | |
| June | |
| 9:30 | |
| Sunday | |
| seven o'clock | |

## VOCABULARY: *would like* + Count Nouns

| | | |
|---|---|---|
| I'<u>d</u> <u>like</u> an | apple. |
| You'<u>d</u> <u>like</u> an | orange. |
| He'<u>d</u> <u>like</u> an | egg. |
| She'<u>d</u> <u>like</u> a | banana. |
| We'<u>d</u> <u>like</u> a | potato. |
| They'<u>d</u> <u>like</u> a | sandwich. |

Teacher models the sentences several times, having the student repeat.

[Say: "Listen to *I'd like*. I'd like an apple. Please repeat. I'd like an apple."]

Use the actual objects, or use the pictures on p. 26 and the top of p. 48 in *ESOL Illustrations*.

[Continue with the rest of the items.]

Use the contracted form of *would like* as you model the sentences. Be sure the student pronounces the /d/ sound in *I'd* and the other contractions.

**Note:** *Potato* and *sandwich* are new vocabulary items. *I'd like* (*I would like*) was first introduced in the Dialog in Lesson 5.

## DRILL: Substitution Drill with Visual Cues

Indicate actual objects, or point to pictures on p. 26 and top of p. 48 of *ESOL Illustrations.*

[Indicating the apple, say:
"What would you like? I'd like an apple. Please repeat. I'd like an apple."
Continue asking the question while indicating the items. Prompt only when necessary.]

## VOCABULARY: *would like* + Modified Non-count Nouns

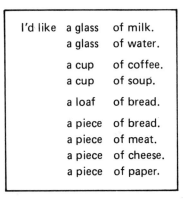

| I'd like | a glass | of milk. |
|---|---|---|
| | a glass | of water. |
| | a cup | of coffee. |
| | a cup | of soup. |
| | a loaf | of bread. |
| | a piece | of bread. |
| | a piece | of meat. |
| | a piece | of cheese. |
| | a piece | of paper. |

Teacher models the sentences several times, having the student repeat.

Use the pictures on p. 48 of *ESOL Illustrations* and a piece of paper.

**Note:** Since we cannot say *a milk*, we must indicate quantity by using modifiers like *a glass of* and *a cup of.*

Do not teach additional items at this point unless you have a more advanced student.

[Say: "Listen to *a glass of.*" Indicating the picture, say:
"I'd like a glass of milk. Repeat. I'd like a glass of milk."]

[Continue in the same way with the rest of the items.]

## DRILL: Substitution Drill with Visual Cues

Point to pictures on p. 48 of *ESOL Illustrations* as visual cues.

[Ask: "What would you like?"
Pointing to the picture of milk, answer:
"I'd like a glass of milk. Please repeat. I'd like a glass of milk."]

| Teacher | Student |
|---|---|
| water | I'd like a glass of water. |
| coffee | |
| soup | |
| bread | |
| meat | |
| cheese | |
| milk | |

## PRONUNCIATION: Vowel Sounds in *lock* and *luck*

See the Pronunciation section in Unit D for the steps to follow in teaching the vowel sounds in *lock* and *luck*.

**Note:** The tongue is lower in the mouth for *lock* than for *luck*. (The vowel sound in *luck* was taught in a different contrast in Lesson 10.)

| /o/ | /u/ | Sentences |
|-----|-----|-----------|
| lock | luck | Good luck. |
| not | nut | It's a nut. |
| hot | hut | He locked the hut. |
| rob | rub | I have peanut butter |
| doll | dull | for lunch. |
| sock | suck | It's a sub. |
|  |  | It's a sob. |

## ORAL EVALUATION

1. Review telling time on the hour, half hour, and quarter hour.

   [Using a cardboard clock, point the hands to these times.]

   | 3:15 | 4:45 | 7:15 | 10:30 |
   |------|------|------|-------|
   | 6:00 | 2:30 | 11:00 | 1:45 |

2. Review the names of the days of the week.

   Student should be able to name all seven since this is review.

   [Point to the days of the week on a calendar. Start by saying "Monday." Let the student continue, saying "It's Monday," and so on.]

3. Review contrast of simple present and present progressive tenses.

   Student should be able to make a difference between these two tenses fairly quickly. If not, be sure to review at the next session.

   [Do the Transformation Drill that follows Structure Focus: Contrast of Simple Present and Present Progressive Tenses.]

4. Review *in, on,* and *at* with place and time expressions.

   These are review items, so student should be able to do the drills fairly quickly.

   [Do Drills that follow Vocabulary: *in, on, at* with Place Expressions and with Time Expressions.]

5. Review food items in the sentence frame "I'd like _____."

   Student should know at least 10 of these items since most of this vocabulary is review. If he does not, review the items that cause difficulty at the next session.

   [Pointing to pictures of food items on pp. 26 and 48 of *ESOL Illustrations*, ask: "What would you like?"]

# II. Reading

Check your student's homework from Lesson 10. Encourage him to be neat.

## CHART 11: Page 62

Most of this chart is review for the student. Only a small part is new material. In Units B-F, the student learned to say, read, and write the numerals 1-50; in Lessons 1-5, he learned the numerals 51-100. Thus, the only new material is the word *Numbers* and the numerals 0 (zero) and 1,000.

| Do this: | Say this: |
|---|---|
| Point to headings. | Teacher: Please read.<br>Student: Lesson 11, Chart 11. |
| Point to *Numbers* at top of the chart. | Teacher: Numbers. Read: *Numbers.*<br>Student: Numbers. |
| Run your finger down the first column of numbers. | Teacher: These are numbers.<br>What are these?<br>Student: These are numbers. |
| Point to the number 0. | Teacher: This number is 0.<br>What is this number?<br>Student: 0.<br>Teacher: 0 means *not any*. |

Have the student read the numbers 1-29 in the top part of the chart. Have him point to each number as he reads it.

For the second part of the chart, if you think the student already knows the numbers to 99 fairly well, simply have him read 30-32 and 40-90. If you think he needs the review, have him read 30-32 and then write 30-39 on separate paper, saying the numbers as he writes them. Continue with 40-90 on the chart, having the student write and say all the numbers to 99.

For the last part of the chart, point to 100 and have the student read it and write it on his paper. Then write 200 on the board or on paper. Say: "This is 200." Have the student read it and write 200 on his own paper. Then say, "Write 300." Give help only if needed. Continue having the student write and say 400, 500, and so on to 900.

Write 1,000 on the board or on paper. Say, "This is one thousand. One thousand means ten hundred. Please repeat: one thousand." Have the student read 1,000 on the chart and write it on his paper.

## STORY: Numbers

Follow steps 1-7 in the Story section of Lesson 6. The new story words are: *live, their, telephone number, not, Ted's.* The numbers in the street addresses should be said as "nineteen," "nine," "four twenty-six," and "thirty-five seventy-four." In the telephone numbers, each digit is read individually. Use the questions below to check comprehension.

| | Teacher | Student |
|---|---|---|
| **Paragraph 1** | Do Mr. and Mrs. Hill live in Indian Valley?<br>Do the Hills live at 19 Valley Street?<br>What is their telephone number? | Yes, they do.<br>Yes, they do.<br>234-9169. |
| **Paragraph 2** | Do Mrs. Bird and Cal live in Indian Valley?<br>Do they live on Valley Street?<br>What is their telephone number? | Yes, they do.<br>Yes, they do.<br>234-8571. |
| **Paragraph 3** | Do the Olivers live at 426 River Street?<br>Is River Street in Indian Valley?<br>What is the Olivers' telephone number? | Yes, they do.<br>No, it isn't.<br>446-5541. |
| **Paragraph 4** | Where is Uncle Ted's pet shop?<br>Is his pet shop in Indian Valley?<br>What is Uncle Ted's telephone number? | It's at 3574 York Street.<br>No, it isn't.<br>745-4938. |

## SKILLS PRACTICE: Ending Sounds -p/f, -f/v, -m/n, -g/k

Do these exercises the same way you did those in Lesson 10. The pattern for what you are to say is given below.

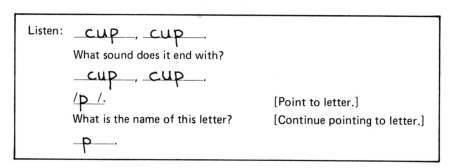

**Note:** Do not worry about words spelled with a final silent *e*, since the question is "What *sound* does it end with?" and the student will not *see* these words.

### 1. Ending sounds -p/f

| Write letters: | *p* and *f* | Minimal pairs: | -/p/ | -/f/ |
|---|---|---|---|---|
| Example pair 1: | cup/cuff | | pup | puff |
| Example pair 2: | wife/wipe | | tip | tiff |
| | | | lope | loaf |
| | | | cheap | chief |
| | | | leap | leaf |
| | | | beep | beef |
| | | | cup | cuff |
| | | | wipe | wife |

### 2. Ending sounds -f/v

| Write letters: | *f* and *v* | Minimal pairs: | -/f/ | -/v/ |
|---|---|---|---|---|
| Example pair 1: | have/half | | life | live (ī) |
| Example pair 2: | save/safe | | leaf | leave |
| | | | waif | wave |
| | | | proof | prove |
| | | | grief | grieve |
| | | | luff | love |
| | | | duff | dove |
| | | | strife | strive |
| | | | safe | save |
| | | | half | have |

## 3. Ending sounds -m/n

| Write letters: | m and n |
| Example pair 1: | Kim/kin |
| Example pair 2: | Dan/dam |

Minimal pairs:

| -/m/ | -/n/ |
|------|------|
| them | then |
| rum | run |
| bam | ban |
| cam | can |
| ram | ran |
| tam | tan |
| hem | hen |
| dim | din |
| Tim | tin |
| bum | bun |
| gum | gun |
| sum | sun |

## 4. Ending sounds -g/k

| Write letters: | g and k |
| Example pair 1: | pick/pig |
| Example pair 2: | bag/back |

Minimal pairs:

| -/g/ | -/k/ |
|------|------|
| peg | peck |
| tag | lack |
| rag | rack |
| sag | sack |
| tag | tack |
| wig | wick |
| bug | buck |
| dug | duck |
| lug | luck |
| dig | Dick |
| clog | clock |
| tug | tuck |

## SKILLS PRACTICE: Review -s and -'s

Write the following words in a column on the blackboard:

girl·
man
bird
Bob
Oliver
apple
pup
Glenn
egg
Dan
cup
Jill
zipper
Ted

Have your student read the words.

Now, write s and 's on separate index cards. Make the letters the same size as the letters on the board. Place the letter on the left edge of the card.

1. Point to *girl* in the column.

   Say:  The girls are in the shop.
   　　　The girls are in the shop.
   Place the *s* card after *girl* to form *girls,* and repeat the sentence.

2. Point to *man* in the column.

   Say:  This is the man's pup.
   　　　This is the man's pup.
   Place the *'s* card after *man* to form *man's*, and repeat the sentence.

3. Now give the *s* and *'s* cards to the student.

   Point to the word in the column that you want the student to work with. Then read the sentence below for that word. Beckon to the student to place the correct card after the word. Repeat the sentence once or twice, as necessary.

| | | | |
|---|---|---|---|
| girl | The girl's pup is jumping. | Glenn | Glenn's girls are in the tent. |
| man | Where is the man's shop? | egg | She is putting the eggs in the pan. |
| bird | Dan has two birds. | Dan | Where is Dan's cup? |
| Bob | She is Bob's wife. | cup | Mrs. Hill is buying six cups. |
| Oliver | The Olivers live on York Street. | Jill | Jill's pen is on the desk. |
| apple | Ann has ten apples. | zipper | Mrs. Oliver has two zippers. |
| pup | Where is the pup's dish? | Ted | The children are in Uncle Ted's shop. |

If the student forms the correct word, say "Good!"

If the student hesitates or makes a mistake, repeat the sentence and point to the correct card. Let him place the card after the word. Then repeat the sentence again.

# III. Writing

## CHECKUP: Page 64

Have your student write the alphabet in lowercase (small) letters, going across the page. Be sure he writes each letter to the far left in the allotted space so there will be room to write the capital letter next to it later. Check the student's work. If he has left out any letters, show him where and have him correct his work. Then have him write the capital letters.

## LISTEN AND WRITE: Page 65

Ask your student to write the letters that these words begin with:

| Bob | dish | Sam | girl | Van | kick | neck |
|------|--------|------|--------|------|------|------|
| Dan | Oliver | Ted | Indian | hand | Kim | Liz |
| Ed | Mrs. | fish | York | jump | leg | Ned |

## WRITING LESSON: Page 66

This writing lesson will be review for the student, since he has already learned to write the numerals 1-100.

Ask the student to read each number and then to write it. If he has trouble writing any number, trace the green dot-and-arrow figure.

## HOMEWORK: Page 67

Tell your student to copy on page 67 the numbers that appear on page 66.

## READING AND WRITING EVALUATION

Dictate the following numbers for the student to write. He is to write the numeral, not the word.

0, 1, 10; 2, 12, 20; 3, 13, 30; 4, 14, 40; 5, 15, 50; 100, 1,000.

Ask your student to read the numbers. Be sure he pronounces the final /n/ in the *-teen* numbers. Student should be able to write 12 out of 17 correctly.

# Lesson 12

## OBJECTIVES

When a student completes this unit, he should be able to:

1. Read the following new words:
   Chart words: *words*, number words from *one* to *five*
   Story words: *do, you, have, yes, no, my, snakes*.

   (In addition, the student has a brief introduction to all the number words from *zero* to *one hundred*, and *one thousand*. The chart showing the numbers and their number words can be used by the student as a reference for his personal use.)

2. Distinguish aurally between these ending sounds: unvoiced -th/t, -th/f, -th/s; -s/z, -s/sh; -sh/ch; and identify each sound with its symbol.

3. Choose between the period and the question mark to punctuate statements and questions he sees written out.

4. Write the plural form of nouns with *s* when given sentences that call for a plural subject in the blank.

## I. Conversation Skills

### REVIEW

Review any items that your student had difficulty with when doing the Oral Evaluation in Lesson 11.

Review also any other items that your student has had persistent difficulty with throughout the introductory units and the lessons. Refer to the notebook you have been keeping.

## II. Reading

Check your student's homework from Lesson 11.


### CHART 12: Page 68

Although the chart introduces briefly the number words from *zero* to *one hundred*, plus *one thousand*, only the words *one* to *five* are reinforced in the story, and those are the only number words the student is expected to learn at this time.

| Do this: | Say this: |
|---|---|
| Point to headings. | Teacher: Please read. |
| | Student: Lesson 12, Chart 12. |
| Point to *Number words* at the top of the chart. | Teacher: Number words. Read: *Number words*. |
| | Student: Number words. |
| Point to the numeral 0. | Teacher: What is this number? |
| | Student: 0. |
| Point to *zero.* | Teacher: This word is *zero*. Read. |
| | Student: Zero. |

Continue in the same way with 1-9. Ask the student, "What is this number?" Then tell him the word, and have him read the word. Review by having the student read just the number words from *zero* to *nine.*

Continue teaching the rest of the columns in the chart the same way. Follow this order: 10-19, 20-29, 30-32, 40-60, 70-90, 100 and 1,000.

Finally, ask your student to count from 1 to 100.

## STORY: Number Words

To teach the story, follow steps 1-7 in the Story section of Lesson 6. *But*, in teaching this story, teach two paragraphs at a time: paragraphs 1-2, 3-4, 5-6, 7-8. (Each set of paragraphs includes a question and its answer.)

The new story words are: *do, you, have, yes, I, my, no, snakes.* Use the questions below to check comprehension.

| | Teacher | Student |
|---|---|---|
| **Paragraphs 1-2** | Does Mrs. Hill have children? | Yes, she does. |
| | | (She has three children.) |
| | What are their names? | Ed, Kim, and Jill. |
| | Does Mrs. Hill have two girls? | Yes, she does. |
| | Does Mrs. Hill have one boy? | Yes, she does. |
| **Paragraphs 3-4** | Does Mr. Oliver have children? | Yes, he does. |
| | | (He has four children.) |
| | Does Mr. Oliver have four boys? | No, he doesn't. |
| | | (He has one girl and three boys.) |
| | What is the girl's name? | Pam. |
| | What are the boys' names? | Ned, Robert, and Will. |
| **Paragraphs 5-6** | Does Mrs. Bird have girls? | No, she has one boy. |
| | What is her boy's name? | Cal. |
| **Paragraphs 7-8** | Does Uncle Ted have children? | No, he doesn't. |
| | What does Uncle Ted have? | He has a pet shop. |
| | Does Uncle Ted have ten pups? | No, he doesn't. (He has five pups.) |

## SKILLS PRACTICE: Ending Sounds—Unvoiced -th/t, -th/f, -th/s; and -s/z, -s/sh, -sh/ch

Do these exercises the same way you did those in Lesson 10. The pattern for what you are to say is given below.

Listen: pat, pat .
What sound does it end with?
pat, pat .
/t/.  [Point to letter.]

What is the name of this letter?  [Continue pointing to letter.]
t .

**Note:** For the sounds /th/, /sh/, and /ch/, the last question should be: "What are the names of the letters?"

### 1. Unvoiced -th/t

Write letters: *th* and *t*

Example pair 1: pat/path

Example pair 2: bath/bat

Minimal pairs:

| -/t/ | -/th/ |
|------|-------|
| mat | math |
| pit | pith |
| boat | both |
| wit | with |
| toot | tooth |
| pat | path |
| bat | bath |
| tent | tenth |
| bet | Beth |

### 2. Unvoiced -th/f

Write letters: *th* and *f*

Example pair 1: roof/Ruth

Example pair 2: death/deaf

Minimal pairs:

| -/f/ | -/th/ |
|------|-------|
| half | hath |
| miff | myth |
| oaf | oath |
| reef | wreath |
| sheaf | sheath |
| roof | Ruth |
| deaf | death |

### 3. Unvoiced -th/s

Write letters: *th* and *s*

Example pair 1: pass/path

Example pair 2: math/mass

Minimal pairs:

| -/s/ | -/th/ |
|------|-------|
| Bess | Beth |
| mouse | mouth |
| tense | tenth |
| pass | path |
| mass | math |
| lass | lath |
| bass | bath |
| moss | moth |

## 4. Ending sounds -s/z

Write letters:    *s* and *z*

Example pair 1:  bus/buzz

Example pair 2:  fuzz/fuss

Minimal pairs:

| | -/s/ | -/z/ |
|---|---|---|
| | dose | doze |
| | bus | buzz |
| | fuss | fuzz |
| More words: | gas | jazz |
| | pass | fizz |
| | less | Liz |
| | miss | quiz |
| | kiss | size |
| | mess | prize |

**Note:** There are very few minimal pairs with -*s* and -*z* spellings for these two sounds, so continue the exercise with these other words.

## 5. Ending sounds -s/sh

Write letters:    *s* and *sh*

Example pair 1:  gas/gash

Example pair 2:  clash/class

Minimal pairs:

| -/s/ | -/sh/ |
|---|---|
| lass | lash |
| mass | mash |
| plus | plush |
| mess | mesh |
| Gus | gush |
| muss | mush |
| gas | gash |
| class | clash |

## 6. Ending sounds -sh/ch

Write letters:    *sh* and *ch*

Example pair 1:  dish/ditch

Example pair 2:  match/mash

Minimal pairs:    ✓

| -/sh/ | -/ch/ |
|---|---|
| hash | hatch |
| lash | latch |
| cash | catch |
| bash | batch |
| wish | witch |
| bush | Butch |
| hush | hutch |
| fish | Fitch |
| dish | ditch |
| mash | match |

# III. Writing

## CHECKUP: Page 70

1. Dictate these numbers for the student to write in the first column: 0, 1, 2, 3, 4, 5, 6, 7.

2. Dictate these numbers for the second column: 8, 9, 10, 11, 12, 13, 14, 15.

3. In the column at the far right, the student is to count the dots on each domino and write the numeral.

## LISTEN AND WRITE: Page 71

1. On the top half of the page, dictate these numbers for the student to write, going *down* the three columns:

   | | | |
   |----|----|----|
   | 16 | 20 | 60 |
   | 17 | 30 | 70 |
   | 18 | 40 | 80 |
   | 19 | 50 | 90 |

2. On the bottom half of the page, dictate these street addresses. The student is to write the street number in each blank. (These are the street addresses from the Lesson 11 story.)

   9 Valley Street
   19 Valley Street
   426 River Street   (Say: "four twenty-six")
   3574 York Street (Say: "thirty-five seventy-four")


## SKILLS PRACTICE: Using the Period and Question Mark

Before class, write the following sentences on paper or on the blackboard. Punctuate the first two sentences clearly with a period and question mark, but leave these punctuation marks *off* the other sentences.

> This is a quarter.
> Is this a quarter?
>
> Bob is in the shop
> Is Bob in the shop
>
> Are the girls fishing
> The girls are fishing
>
> Do you have children
> I live on York Street
> Are the cups in the box
> Do the boys have a pup
> Liz is looking at Glenn

Write a period and a question mark on separate index cards, placing each mark at the edge of the card.

1. First pair of sentences:

   Say the first sentence, and point to the period.
   Then place the period card at the end of the sentence.

   Say the second sentence, and point to the question mark.
   Then place the question mark card at the end of the sentence.

2. Second pair of sentences:

   Give the cards to the student. Say each sentence, and beckon to the student to place the correct card after it. Your intonation should help the student recognize the statement and the question.

3. Third pair of sentences:

   Point to each sentence; have the student read it and place the correct punctuation card after it. The student must now recognize a question or a statement through reading, without your intonation to help him.

   If the student read the sentence haltingly while he was trying to figure out which punctuation mark to use, have him repeat it again after you.

4. Continue in the same way with the remaining sentences.

## WRITING LESSON: Page 72

In each pair of sentences, a statement with a singular subject and verb is transformed to a statement with a plural subject and verb. The student is to write the missing noun plural with -s. The first blank has been filled in to show the student what to do.

Have the student read the first pair of sentences aloud. Have him read the next pair silently, fill in the missing word, and then read both sentences aloud.

Continue in the same way with the remaining sentence-pairs.

## HOMEWORK: Page 73

This is done in the same way as the Writing Lesson on page 72.

## READING AND WRITING EVALUATION

1. Write the following number words. Ask the student to read each word and write the number next to it.

   four        two        one        five        three

   Student should be able to do all these correctly.

2. Write the following words and ask the student to read them:

   I          yes        has        do
   you        no         have       my

   Student should be able to read at least five of these words.

# Lesson 13

In this lesson, the student begins reading the correlated reader *In the Valley*.

## OBJECTIVES

When a student completes this unit, he should be able to:

1. Answer written Yes/No questions about a short reading selection.
2. Choose the written singular or plural noun with -*s* to complete a sentence he hears.
3. Write the possessive form of nouns with -'*s* to complete a written sentence.
4. Write his name, address, and telephone number.

## VISUAL AIDS

1. Bring an envelope addressed to you.
2. Prepare the materials called for in the Writing Lesson sections.

# I. Conversation Skills

### REVIEW

Continue reviewing any items that the student is still having difficulty with.

# II. Reading

Begin reading *In the Valley* in class. In this lesson, you should complete at least the first story, or, if possible, the first two stories. Suggestions for teaching *In the Valley* follow this lesson.

# III. Writing

Check the student's homework from Lesson 12.

### CHECKUP: Page 74

Have the student read the short reading selection silently. The sample question, with its answer circled, shows the student what to do. Point to this question and read it aloud. Then point to the sentence in the reading selection that reveals the answer. Say: "Circle *no*," and trace the circle around the *no* answer.

Let the student do the rest of the questions silently.

## LISTEN AND WRITE: Page 75

Write the words *boy, boys* on paper. Have the student read the words.

Say: "Mrs. Oliver has three . . . ." and beckon for the student to complete the sentence with one of the words you wrote. After he says *boys*, say: "Circle *boys*," tracing a circle around the word with your finger. Let the student circle the word in pencil.

Give the following cues for items in the exercise. The student is to circle the word that completes the sentence correctly. You may repeat the cues as needed.

Say: "Number 1.    [Pause.]    Mrs. Hill buys two . . . ."
     "Number 2.    [Pause.]    Mrs. Hill has two . . . ."
     "Number 3.    [Pause.]    Mr. Oliver buys some . . . ."
     "Number 4.    [Pause.]    Uncle Ted picks up a. . . ."
     "Number 5.    [Pause.]    Queen is a . . . ."
     "Number 6.    [Pause.]    I have five . . . ."
     "Number 7.    [Pause.]    These are the. . . ."
     "Number 8.    [Pause.]    What is your telephone . . . ?"

## WRITING LESSON: Page 76

In each pair of sentences, the student is to fill in the possessive form of the noun with -'s. The first blank has been filled in to show the student what to do.

Have the student read the first pair of sentences aloud. Have him read the next pair silently, fill in the missing word, and then read both sentences aloud. Continue in the same way.

## WRITING LESSON: Page 77

Before class, prepare a sheet of paper for your student with the following sentences written on it. The student will use this as a model to copy from.

    My name is (student's name).
    I live at (student's street address).
    I live in (student's city).
    My telephone number is (student's phone number).

Have the student read each sentence aloud from the sheet. Then have him copy his name, street address, and telephone number in the appropriate spaces on p.77. Finally, have him read the completed sentences on p. 77 aloud.

## WRITING LESSON: Page 78

Before class, prepare another sheet with your student's address—including state and zip code—written on it. Space the address so the student can copy it in the three lines allowed on p. 78. (If the name of your state is long, you may use the postal abbreviation for it.)

Show the student the envelope addressed to you. Point to the appropriate items, and say: "This is my name. This is my address." (Showing the envelope will help the student understand the purpose of the address.)

Give the student the sheet with his address on it. Say: "This is your address."

| **Do this:** | **Say this:** |
| --- | --- |
| Point to student's street address. | Teacher: I live at (student's street address). Please repeat. |
| | Student: I live at (student's street address). |
| Point to city and state. | Teacher: I live in (city, state). Please repeat. |
| | Student: I live in (city, state). |
| Point to the zip code. | Teacher: My zip code is (student's zip code). Please repeat. |
| | Student: My zip code is (student's zip code). |
| Indicate entire address. | Teacher: This is my address. Please repeat. |
| | Student: This is my address. |
| | Teacher: My address is [say student's whole address]. Please repeat. |
| | Student: My address is [says own address]. |
| Point to *Address* on p. 78. | Teacher: This word is *Address*. Please read. |
| | Student: Address. |

Have the student write his name, address, and telephone number in the spaces marked for them on p. 78. The student may copy his address from the sheet you gave him.


## AFTER LESSON 13

There is no written homework for Lesson 13. You may ask the student to read again at home the story or stories from *In the Valley* that you read in class. You should finish reading *In the Valley* in class (see the suggestion that follows this lesson). Spend part of each class session reviewing conversation skills. When you have finished, do the two Evaluations for *Skill Book 1*.

# In the Valley

*In the Valley,* a small correlated reader containing related stories, should be used for additional reading practice after the student has completed *Skill Book 1* and before he begins *Skill Book 2.*

To teach each story, follow steps 1-7 in the Story section of Lesson 6. Before beginning a story, teach the meaning of any new vocabulary items. *In the Valley* actually contains three kinds of "new words."

**Variants.** Many of the new words are merely variants of words that the student has learned to read in *Skill Book 1* (for example, *thanks* is a variant of *thank*). These variants should not give the student any difficulty once you have pointed them out.

**New reading.** These are words the student has learned orally but has never read before. You need only to give help with reading these words.

**New vocabulary.** Some words and phrases are completely new to the student. You will need to explain their meanings as well as give help with reading these items. (Phrases made up of known words are new vocabulary if the way the words are combined gives a new meaning.)

The three kinds of new words that occur in each story in *In the Valley* are listed below, along with suggested ways of teaching the new vocabulary.

## PAGES 5-7: Uncle Ted Visits Indian Valley

**Page 5**   New reading: *visits*

**Page 6**   New reading: *visiting*

New vocabulary: *puts up a tent, picks apples*

1. Teach *put up a tent* by folding a piece of paper in half and standing it up like a small pup tent. Tell the student, "This is a tent."

   Then collapse the tent. As you put it up again, say: "I put up the tent."

2. Use the illustration on p. 6 to teach *picks apples.*

**Page 7**   Variant: *thanks*

New reading: *ten*

## PAGES 8-9: Ned Gets a Fish

There are no new words.

## PAGES 10-12: Uncle Ted and the Snake

**Page 10**   Variant: *bird's*

New vocabulary: *wings*

Use the illustration on p. 10 to teach *wings.* Say, "These are the bird's wings."

**Page 11**   Variants: *looks, run*

New vocabulary: *nest, under, look for*

1. Use the picture on p. 11 to teach *nest.*

2. Teach the word *under* by comparing *under* with *in* and *on.*
   Demonstrate as you say these sentences:

   The pen is on the book.
   The pen is in the book.
   The pen is under the book.

3. To teach *look for,* search through your purse, pockets, or desk drawer in a very exaggerated way, saying: "I look for my pen." Then, "find" your pen (which you hid beforehand) with a great show of pleasure and relief.

**Page 12**   Variants: *jump, yell*

## PAGES 13-15:  Mr. and Mrs. Hill Visit Sam's Shop

**Page 13**     Variants: *olives, zippers, cups, pans*

New reading: *visit* (a variant of *visits*, introduced on p. 5)

**Page 14**     Variant: *quarters*

**Page 15**     New vocabulary: *tells*

Say: "Glenn says to Sam," pointing to each man in the picture on p. 15 as you say his name.

Then say: "Glenn tells Sam," running your finger under the sentence. Continue with the first sentence of the direct quotation.

## PAGES  16-18:  The Pup Is Hurt

**Page 16**     New vocabulary: *hurt*

Demonstrate by pretending to bump into a piece of furniture, then saying: "I'm hurt. My leg is hurt!" while clutching dramatically at your "hurt" leg.

**Page 17**     Variants: *Robert's, give*

**Page 18**     There are no new words.

## PAGES 19-21:  Uncle Ted Visits Ann and Cal

**Page 19**     New reading: *am*

**Page 20**     Variants: *Hill's, sell, Cal's*

**Page 21**     There are no new words.

## PAGES 22-23:  Uncle Ted Packs Up

**Page 22**     New reading: *of*

New vocabulary: *packs up, is packing*

Use the illustration on p. 22 to show the meaning of the new vocabulary.

**Page 23**     There are no new words.

# Oral Evaluation for Skill Book 1

This Oral Evaluation covers the material introduced in Units A-F and the Conversation Skills sections of Lessons 1-13. The Oral Evaluation is divided into two parts. Part I is a review of 75 vocabulary items, grouped according to topic and presented in approximately the same order as they were introduced. Part II is a review of the basic structural patterns taught, grouped according to patterns.

## PART I. Vocabulary

**Procedure:** The 75 vocabulary items in this part appear on the Teacher's Evaluation Form which follows. To conduct this part of the Oral Evaluation, follow the directions below for each set of items.

**Items 1-7**  Use p. 10 of *ESOL Illustrations for Skill Book 1*.
Have the student name the colors. Ask: "What color is this?"

**Items 8-13**  Use pp. 11-13 of *ESOL Illustrations*.
Have the student name the occupations pictured.
Begin by saying: "Look at the man. What is he?"

**Items 14-23**  Use the map on pp. 16-17 of *ESOL Illustrations.*
Ask the student to name the countries and nationalities.
Say: "This is _____. He's (She's) _____."

**Items 24-30**  Use a calendar.
Ask the student to name the days of the week. Say: "It's _____."

**Items 31-35**  Use p. 24 of *ESOL Illustrations*.
Ask the student to name the parts of the body.
Use the sentence frame "This is the man's _____."

**Items 36-51**  Use pp. 26-28 and p. 48 of *ESOL Illustrations.*
Ask the student to name the foods pictured.
Point to the picture and ask: "What's this?"

**Items 52-57**  Use actual money: dollar bill, half dollar, quarter, dime, nickel, penny.
Ask the student to give the names of the money.
Say: "This is a _____."

**Items 58-65**  Use p. 33 of *ESOL Illustrations*.
Ask the student to name the family relationships pictured.
Begin by pointing and saying: "This is a family. This is the husband."
(Student gets a "free" answer for *husband*.)

**Items 66-69**  Use p. 39 of *ESOL Illustrations*.
Ask the student to name the animals pictured. Ask: "What's this?"

**Items 70-75**  Use pp. 46-47 of *ESOL Illustrations*.
Ask the student to name the recreations pictured.
Use the sentence frame "He/She (They) is (are)_____."

**Scoring**  Assess your student's performance and check the appropriate column on the Teacher's Evaluation Form that follows.

**Check column 1**  if the student identifies the item fairly quickly and with fairly understandable pronunciation.

**Check column 2**  if the student identifies the item with some hesitation but with fairly understandable pronunciation.

**Check column 3**  if, after a short wait, the student cannot identify the item at all, or if he identifies it incorrectly.

# PART I. VOCABULARY: Teacher's Evaluation Form

Student's Name _____

Student's Native Language _____

Date of Enrollment _____ Date Evaluation Given _____

| | 1 | 2 | 3 |
|---|---|---|---|
| 1. white | | | |
| 2. black | | | |
| 3. red | | | |
| 4. yellow | | | |
| 5. blue | | | |
| 6. green | | | |
| 7. brown | | | |
| 8. doctor | | | |
| 9. nurse | | | |
| 10. waiter | | | |
| 11. waitress | | | |
| 12. factory worker | | | |
| 13. taxi driver | | | |
| 14. Spain | | | |
| 15. Spanish | | | |
| 16. China | | | |
| 17. Chinese | | | |
| 18. Korea | | | |
| 19. Korean | | | |
| 20. Germany | | | |
| 21. German | | | |
| 22. the United States | | | |
| 23. American | | | |

| | 1 | 2 | 3 |
|---|---|---|---|
| 24. Monday | | | |
| 25. Tuesday | | | |
| 26. Wednesday | | | |
| 27. Thursday | | | |
| 28. Friday | | | |
| 29. Saturday | | | |
| 30. Sunday | | | |
| 31. man's neck | | | |
| 32. man's hand | | | |
| 33. man's leg | | | |
| 34. man's head | | | |
| 35. man's finger | | | |
| 36. apple | | | |
| 37. orange | | | |
| 38. banana | | | |
| 39. egg | | | |
| 40. olive | | | |
| 41. lemon | | | |
| 42. milk | | | |
| 43. bread | | | |
| 44. sugar | | | |
| 45. butter | | | |
| 46. coffee | | | |
| 47. water | | | |
| 48. potato | | | |
| 49. sandwich | | | |
| 50. meat | | | |
| 51. cheese | | | |

| | 1 | 2 | 3 |
|---|---|---|---|
| 52. dollar | | | |
| 53. half dollar | | | |
| 54. quarter | | | |
| 55. dime | | | |
| 56. nickel | | | |
| 57. penny | | | |
| 58. husband | | | |
| 59. wife | | | |
| 60. son | | | |
| 61. daughter | | | |
| 62. father | | | |
| 63. mother | | | |
| 64. brother | | | |
| 65. sister | | | |
| 66. pup | | | |
| 67. dog | | | |
| 68. cat | | | |
| 69. fish | | | |
| 70. sailing | | | |
| 71. swimming | | | |
| 72. camping | | | |
| 73. hunting | | | |
| 74. hiking | | | |
| 75. fishing | | | |
| **PART I Totals** | | | |

The publisher hereby grants permission to reproduce this Teacher's Evaluation Form for the purpose of evaluating student performance.

## PART II. STRUCTURAL PATTERNS

**Procedure:** In this part, the student is asked to produce the major structural patterns that have been taught. The 75 items in this part are listed below. They are grouped in sets according to structural patterns.

In each set of items, there are two examples for you to use to show the student what is expected of him. Say both the teacher's cue and the expected student response. Have the student repeat the response after you.

For the remaining (numbered) items in the set, give only the cue. Do not prompt the student or help him. If he seems confused, simply repeat the two examples given, having him repeat the response after you.

### Set A. Questions with *be*

| Teacher's cue | Student response |
|---|---|
| This is a book. | Is this a book? |
| I am going home. | Am I going home? |

1. They are students.
2. She is looking at the green book.
3. These are chairs.
4. We are going downtown.
5. It's Monday.
6. You are buying an apple.

### Set B. Questions with *do/does*

| Teacher's cue | Student response |
|---|---|
| You read the book. | Do you read the book? |
| He speaks English. | Does he speak English? |

7. Glenn goes fishing in the river.
8. Glenn and Liz have two daughters.
9. Ann has a brother.
10. We go shopping on Saturday.
11. You study every day.

### Set C. Questions with *be/do/does*

| Teacher's cue | Student response |
|---|---|
| You are Spanish. | Are you Spanish? |
| We speak English. | Do we speak English? |

12. He is Chinese.
13. They have two children.
14. Kim and Jill are jumping rope.
15. They go shopping every Saturday.
16. We go to church on Sunday.
17. Ann has a sister.

### Set D. Short Answers

(Either a *yes* or a *no* answer is correct, so long as the verb in the answer is correct.)

| Teacher's cue | Student response |
|---|---|
| Do you have a sandwich? | Yes, I do. |
| Are you Chinese? | No, I'm not. |

18. Does Glenn live in Indian Valley?
19. Are you going home?
20. Is Liz Glenn's wife?
21. Do you have any children?
22. Does the teacher have a dog?
23. Am I American?

## Set E. Negative Statements

| Teacher's cue | Student response |
|---|---|
| She buys an orange. | She doesn't buy an orange. |
| They are going to bed. | They aren't going to bed. |

24. The girl sells pens and pencils.
25. Liz and Glenn are going fishing.
26. They live in Indian Valley.
27. Queen is a cat.
28. The children play ball.

## Set F. Information Questions with *where, when, what, whose*

| Teacher's cue | Student response |
|---|---|
| Jill lives in Indian Valley. *Where?* | Where does Jill live? |
| This is Ann's book. *Whose?* | Whose book is this? |

29. They have lunch at noon. *When?*
30. He is going home. *Where?*
31. Ann has a red book. *What?*
32. This is my pen. *Whose?*
33. The children are buying a ball. *What?*
34. We live in Syracuse. *Where?*
35. He goes to church on Sunday. *When?*
36. You have Jill's ball. *Whose?*

## Set G. Object Pronouns

| Teacher's cue | Student response |
|---|---|
| I look at Mary. | I look at her. |
| I look at John. | I look at him. |

37. I look at the cat.
38. I look at Ann and Bob.
39. He looks at Ann and me.
40. I look at the children.

## Set H. Possessive Pronouns

| Teacher's cue | Student response |
|---|---|
| I have my ball. | I have my ball. |
| | |
| You have . . . [Pause] | |
| You have your ball. | You have your ball. |

41. He has
42. She has
43. The dog has
44. We have
45. I have
46. You have
47. The children have

## Set I. Plural Form of Nouns

| Teacher's cue | Student response |
|---|---|
| This is a child. | These are children. |
| This is a boy. | These are boys. |

48. This is a dime.
49. This is a cat.
50. This is a man.
51. This is a nurse.
52. This is a housewife.
53. This is a woman.

## Set J. *some/any*

| Teacher's cue | Student response |
|---|---|
| I don't have any sugar. | I have some sugar. |
| She's buying some apples. | She isn't buying any apples. |

54. They are buying some bread.
55. They don't have any nickels.
56. They have some dimes.
57. Mary has some paper.
58. The waiter doesn't have any coffee.
59. The teacher has some pencils.

## Set K. Place Expressions with *in, on, at*

| Teacher's cue | Student response |
|---|---|
| Main Street  I live on Main Street. | I live on Main Street. |
| Syracuse    I live in Syracuse. | I live in Syracuse. |

60. Indian Valley
61. 920 Main Street
62. Beacon Street
63. the United States

## Set L. Time Expressions with *in, on, at*

| Teacher's cue | Student response |
|---|---|
| night    I go home at night. | I go home at night. |
| afternoon I go home in the afternoon. | I go home in the afternoon. |

64. five o'clock
65. Monday
66. January
67. noon

## Set M. Simple Present/Present Progressive

| Teacher's cue | Student response |
|---|---|
| I go home every day. | I'm going home now. |
| I'm speaking English now. | I speak English every day. |

68. I'm looking at the teacher now.
69. I go downtown every Saturday.
70. She is reading a book now.
71. They go fishing every July.

## Set N.  Indirect Object with *to*

| Teacher's cue | | Student response |
|---|---|---|
| boy | I give the book. | I give the book to the boy. |
| girl | The teacher is speaking English. | The teacher is speaking English to the girl. |

72. the waiter     I'm giving fifty cents.
73. the woman     He's passing the butter.
74. them     She's reading the book.
75. Glenn     Jill is repeating the numbers.

**Scoring:**

Assess your student's performance and check the appropriate column on the Teacher's Evaluation Form that follows.

Evaluate the student's performance on a scale of 1 to 3, using the same criteria as for the vocabulary.

**Check column 1** if the student gives the correct structure, responding fairly quickly and with fairly understandable pronunciation.

**Check column 2** if the student gives the correct structure with some hesitation but with fairly understandable pronunciation.

**Check column 3** if, after a short wait, the student cannot respond at all, or if he does not form the structure correctly.

*Evaluate only the structure in question.* For example, suppose the student is asked to transform a statement into a question. After the cue "She is looking at a red book," he says: "Is she looking at a book?" responding fairly quickly and with good pronunciation. In such a case, check column 1 even though the student has omitted the word *red*. He *has* transformed a statement into a question, and that is the structure in question.

## PART II. STRUCTURAL PATTERNS: Teacher's Evaluation Form

Student's Name _____

Student's Native Language _____

Date of Enrollment _____ Date Evaluation Given _____

| | 1 | 2 | 3 |
|---|---|---|---|
| Set A: 1. | | | |
| 2. | | | |
| 3. | | | |
| 4. | | | |
| 5. | | | |
| 6. | | | |
| Set B: 7. | | | |
| 8. | | | |
| 9. | | | |
| 10. | | | |
| 11. | | | |
| Set C: 12. | | | |
| 13. | | | |
| 14. | | | |
| 15. | | | |
| 16. | | | |
| 17. | | | |
| Set D: 18. | | | |
| 19. | | | |
| 20. | | | |
| 21. | | | |
| 22. | | | |
| 23. | | | |
| Set E: 24. | | | |
| 25. | | | |
| 26. | | | |
| 27. | | | |
| 28. | | | |

| | 1 | 2 | 3 |
|---|---|---|---|
| Set F: 29. | | | |
| 30. | | | |
| 31. | | | |
| 32. | | | |
| 33. | | | |
| 34. | | | |
| 35. | | | |
| 36. | | | |
| Set G: 37. | | | |
| 38. | | | |
| 39. | | | |
| 40. | | | |
| Set H: 41. | | | |
| 42. | | | |
| 43. | | | |
| 44. | | | |
| 45. | | | |
| 46. | | | |
| 47. | | | |
| Set I: 48. | | | |
| 49. | | | |
| 50. | | | |
| 51. | | | |
| 52. | | | |
| 53. | | | |

| | 1 | 2 | 3 |
|---|---|---|---|
| Set J: 54. | | | |
| 55. | | | |
| 56. | | | |
| 57. | | | |
| 58. | | | |
| 59. | | | |
| Set K: 60. | | | |
| 61. | | | |
| 62. | | | |
| 63. | | | |
| Set L: 64. | | | |
| 65. | | | |
| 66. | | | |
| 67. | | | |
| Set M: 68. | | | |
| 69. | | | |
| 70. | | | |
| 71. | | | |
| Set N: 72. | | | |
| 73. | | | |
| 74. | | | |
| 75. | | | |

| | 1 | 2 | 3 |
|---|---|---|---|
| Part II Totals | | | |

The publisher hereby grants permission to reproduce this Teacher's Evaluation Form for the purpose of evaluating student performance.

# EVALUATING THE STUDENT'S PERFORMANCE

## Part I.    Vocabulary

If your student gets a total of 60 or more checks in columns 1 and 2, he is ready to begin *Skill Book 2*.

You should, however, look over the vocabulary items he missed and review them, a few at a time, in subsequent lessons.

If your student gets a total of 45-59 checks in columns 1 and 2, you must spend some time reviewing the vocabulary items he missed before beginning *Skill Book 2*.

Anything less than 44 checks in columns 1 and 2 indicates need for extensive review before beginning *Skill Book 2*.

Always combine review of vocabulary with review of structural patterns. For example, if a student was unable to name any of the countries and nationalities, combine a review of those items with a review of question and answer patterns.

## Part II.    Structural Patterns

If your student gets a total of 60 or more checks in columns 1 and 2, he is ready to begin *Skill Book 2*.

It is important, however, that you analyze the items he missed. If he missed most or all of the items in a section, be sure to review that structural pattern again before beginning *Skill Book 2*.

If your student gets less than 60 in columns 1 and 2, it is especially important to review any basic structures he is having difficulty with before beginning *Skill Book 2*.

Review only those structures that caused the most difficulty. If a student missed only one item in a section, review would generally not be necessary. Watch for sections in which the student missed most or all of the items, and review those structures in particular. In general, the more checks in column 3 in a particular section, the more time you will need to spend reviewing that structure.

# Reading and Writing Evaluation for Skill Book 1

To evaluate the student's progress in reading and writing skills, use the separate publication *Checkups for Skill Book 1*, available from New Readers Press.

## OBJECTIVES

The objectives of the evaluation are:

1. to measure the student's progress in relation to the learning objectives.
2. to diagnose the student's strengths and weaknesses in phonics, reading comprehension, and writing.
3. to help the student learn how to take a simple test.

## ADMINISTERING THE CHECKUPS

*Checkups for Skill Book 1* consists of six parts. There are no written instructions for the student to read, but each part begins with at least one sample question. Use the sample questions to show the student what he is expected to do. Correct the student if he makes a mistake in a sample question, but do not correct any errors he may make in the actual test items.

Begin by having the student write his name on page 1.

### Checkup 1: Sound-Symbol Relationships (Pages 1-3)

This checkup covers the 21 consonants in the alphabet, the five short vowels, and the consonant digraphs *ch, sh,* and *th*.

The student fills in the letter or letters for the beginning sound of 28 chart words and the ending sound of the chart word *box*. Each word, with a blank for the missing letter, is printed next to the illustration for the chart word.

**What to do**

The first two items (*apple* and *shop*) are sample questions.

Point to the picture of the apple and say, "Apple."
Point to the blank and say, "Apple. Write the letter."
Let the student write the missing letter *a* in the blank.
Correct him if he makes a mistake.

Point to the picture of the shop and then to the blanks.
Say, "Write the letters."
Let the student write the missing letters *sh*.
Correct him if he makes a mistake.

Now, let the student do the rest of Checkup 1 by himself.

### Checkup 2: Letter Recognition (Page 4)

The teacher says the name of a letter. The student circles that letter in a row of four letters.

**What to do**

Point to the sample item containing the letters *c, b, x, t*.
Say, "Listen: *b*. Circle the letter *b*."
Let the student circle the letter *b*. Correct him if he makes a mistake.

For the rest of Checkup 2, say the number (e.g. "Number 1"), then pause, then say the name of the letter. You may repeat the name of the letter.

| | | | | |
|---|---|---|---|---|
| 1. m | 6. p | 11. h | 16. r | 21. z |
| 2. g | 7. a | 12. l | 17. i | 22. q |
| 3. k | 8. j | 13. d | 18. v | 23. x |
| 4. c | 9. s | 14. n | 19. y | 24. u |
| 5. f | 10. t | 15. e | 20. w | 25. o |

## Checkup 3: Word Recognition (Page 5)

The teacher says a chart word. The student circles that word in a row of three words.

**What to do**

Point to the sample item containing the words *girl, bird, shop.*
Say, "Listen: *bird*. Circle the word."
Let the student circle the word *bird*. Correct him if he makes a mistake.

For the rest of Checkup 3, say the number, then pause, then say the word. You may repeat the word.

| | | | | |
|---|---|---|---|---|
| 1. egg | 6. pan | 11. shop | 16. apple | 21. Van |
| 2. neck | 7. zipper | 12. leg | 17. girl | 22. Mrs. |
| 3. fish | 8. woman | 13. jumping | 18. Ted | 23. Fran |
| 4. snake | 9. children | 14. in | 19. Sam | 24. Hill |
| 5. yells | 10. dish | 15. hand | 20. Ann | 25. Indian |

## Checkup 4: Listen and Write (Page 6)

The student writes the following items from dictation.

Row 1:      The letter for the beginning sound of six words from the skill book
Row 2:      The letter for the ending sound of six words from the skill book
Rows 3-4:  Twelve numerals
Rows 5-7:  Six chart words

**What to do**

Row 1:      Use the first dictation item (*fish*) as a sample.

Say, "Number 1," indicate the whole row, and then point to the first space.
Say, "Listen: *fish*. What letter does *fish* begin with?"
Let the student give the answer *f* if he can. If not, tell him.
Then say, "Write the letter." Let the student write the letter *f*.

To complete row 1, follow this pattern:
Say, " (word).  What letter does  (word)  begin with? Write the letter."

Dictate these words: *apple, woman, runs, has, jump.*

Row 2:      Use the first dictation item (*Ed*) as a sample.

Say, "Number 2," indicate the whole row, and then point to the first space.
Say, "Listen: *Ed*. What letter does *Ed* end with?"
Let the student give the answer *d* if he can. If not, tell him.
Then say, "Write the letter." Let the student write the letter *d*.

To complete row 2, follow this pattern:
Say, " (word) . What letter does  (word)  end with? Write the letter."

Dictate these words: *not, leg, run, him, look.*

Row 3:     Use the first dictation item (the number 6) as the sample for rows 3-4.

Say, "Number 3," indicate the whole row, and then point to the first space.
Say, "Listen: 6. Write the number." Let the student write the number 6.

To complete row 3, dictate these numbers: 9, 5, 7, 2, 8.

Row 4:     Say, "Number 4," and indicate the whole row.
Say, "Write these numbers."

For row 4, dictate these numbers: 16, 11, 14, 12, 20, 50.

Row 5:     There is no sample question for rows 5-7.

Say, "Number 5," indicate the whole row, and then point to the first space.
Say, "Listen: *up*. Write the word."

For the second item, dictate the word *man*.

Rows 6-7:  Do these the same way you did row 5.

For row 6, dictate: *leg, Bob.*
For row 7, dictate: *Pam, Liz.*

In doing Checkup 4, repeat the dictation items or the directions as needed. Watch to be sure the student is writing in the correct space at all times.

## Checkup 5:  Writing Capital Letters  (Page 7)

The 26 lowercase letters of the alphabet are shown on the page in mixed order. The student writes the capital letter for each lowercase letter.

### What to do

The first capital letter (*B*) is filled in to show the student what to do.

Point to *b* and say, "*b*." Point to *B* and say, "*capital B*."
Point to *c* and say, "*c*." Point to the space next to *c* and say, "Write *capital C*."

Let the student complete Checkup 5 by himself.

## Checkup 6:  Reading Comprehension  (Page 8)

The student reads a short paragraph of three or four sentences, then answers three questions by circling *Yes* or *No*.

### What to do

The first paragraph and its three questions are a sample exercise.

Ask the student to read the sample paragraph aloud.
Indicate the paragraph, and say: "Please read."

Point to the first question (*Do the girls have three eggs?*) and say, "Please read."
Then say, "Yes? No?" pointing to each of these answers.
Let the student answer *no* if he can.
(If he doesn't give the right answer, help him find the place in the paragraph that tells how many eggs the girls have.)
When the student says "No," tell him: "Circle *No*," and let him do it.

Have the student read the second question aloud and circle *Yes* or *No*.
If he doesn't circle *Yes*, have him read the last sentence of the paragraph again.

Have the student read the third question silently and circle the answer.
If he doesn't circle *No*, have him read the second sentence of the paragraph again.

Now, let the student complete Checkup 6 by himself.

# CHECKUPS FOR SKILL BOOK 1: Teacher's Evaluation Form

Student's Name _____ Native Language _____

Date of Enrollment _____ Date Checkups Given _____

| | Perfect Score | Satisfactory Score | Student's Score |
|---|---|---|---|
| **1. Sound-Symbol Relationships**<br><br>Each word completed correctly counts 1 point.<br>(Do not count the sample items *apple* and *shop*.) | 29 | 23 | |
| **2. Letter Recognition**<br><br>The following letters, if circled, count 1 point each.<br><br>1. m  6. p  11. h  16. r  21. z<br>2. g  7. a  12. l  17. i  22. q<br>3. k  8. j  13. d  18. v  23. x<br>4. c  9. s  14. n  19. y  24. u<br>5. f  10. t  15. e  20. w  25. o | 25 | 20 | |
| **3. Word Recognition**<br><br>The following words, if circled, count 1 point each.<br><br>1. egg  6. pan  11. shop  16. apple  21. Van<br>2. neck  7. zipper  12. leg  17. girl  22. Mrs.<br>3. fish  8. woman  13. jumping  18. Ted  23. Fran<br>4. snake  9. children  14. in  19. Sam  24. Hill<br>5. yells  10. dish  15. hand  20. Ann  25. Indian | 25 | 20 | |
| **4. Listen and Write**<br><br>Each item written correctly counts 1 point.<br><br>1. ----  a  w  r  h  j     5. up   man<br>2. ----  t  g  n  m  k     6. leg  Bob<br>3. ----  9  5  7  2  8     7. Pam  Liz<br>4. 16  11  14  12  20  50 | 27 | 21 | |
| **5. Writing Capital Letters**<br><br>Each capital letter written correctly counts 1 point.<br>(Do not count the sample letter *B*.) | 25 | 20 | |
| **6. Reading Comprehension**<br><br>Each correct answer counts 3 points.<br><br>**Sample set**  **First set**  **Second set**  **Third set**<br>Do      1. Yes    1. No    1. Yes<br>not     2. No    2. Yes   2. No<br>count.   3. Yes   3. Yes   3. Yes | 27 | 21 | |
| **Total Scores** | 158 | 125 | |

The publisher hereby grants permission to reproduce this Teacher's Evaluation Form for the purpose of evaluating student performance.

## SCORING THE CHECKUPS

Use the Teacher's Evaluation Form on the preceding page to record the student's scores. Do not count the answers to sample questions. In Checkups 1-5, each correct answer counts one point. The answers in Checkup 6: Reading Comprehension have been weighted; they count three points each.

The suggested satisfactory score is about 80% of the perfect score for each part. If you wish to translate the student's total score into a percentage, divide his score by the perfect score and multiply by 100.

## EVALUATING THE STUDENT'S PERFORMANCE

If the student does well in comprehension, even though he may have shown some weakness in word attack skills, he is learning to read.

If he does poorly in comprehension, even though he scores well in word attack skills, look for reasons why he is not transferring meaning and understanding to the words and sentences he is reading.

A look at the scores of the individual parts of the *Checkups* will give an informal diagnosis of the student's strengths and weaknesses in the various skills.

If your student obviously needs strengthening in particular skills in *Skill Book 1*, do not go back to that book for review. Rather, move on to *Skill Book 2*, but supplement the lessons with special exercises to reinforce the skills which need attention. The bibliography below suggests some prepared materials and some resources for preparing your own. You may need to devise some exercises yourself.

## BIBLIOGRAPHY

Avery, Bea. *Fun Learning*. Alhambra, Calif.: California Literacy, Inc., 1976. (May be ordered from California Literacy, Inc. at 317 W. Main St., Alhambra, California 91801.)

A collection of games and learning activities for reinforcement and enrichment in both reading and oral skills, with indications of their appropriateness for various skill book levels.

Eagle, Gertrude. ed. *More Stories 1*. Syracuse, N.Y.: New Readers Press, 1975.

This reader provides three stories correlated to the skills level of each of the lessons in *Skill Book 1*. It is useful for the student who needs intensive practice in reading comprehension. It may also be used as a change of pace with students who need a great deal of review in conversation skills before moving on to *Skill Book 2*.

Pope, Lillie. *Guidelines to Teaching Remedial Reading*. 2nd ed., rev. Brooklyn, N.Y.: Book-Lab, Inc., 1975. (May be ordered from New Readers Press.)

A good source of special aids for reading skills development, this revised edition includes special sections for ESOL students.

Rice, Gail. *Focus on Phonics-1*. Syracuse, N.Y.: New Readers Press, 1976. Accompanying teacher's edition.

This student workbook, correlated to *Skill Book 1*, gives additional practice in discriminating between sounds and identifying each sound with its symbol (letter). Both beginning and ending sounds are treated. Some practice in visual discrimination between similar letters and similar words (including reversals) is provided.

# Conversation Skills Word List

Words that appear in the list below are items introduced in the Vocabulary and Structure Focus sections. Items are listed only when the student himself is asked to produce them. Items that occur only in the Dialogs are not included.

The main entries are the normal dictionary-entry forms. Variants are listed under the main entries; for example, *children* is listed under *child*, and *going*, under *go*.

Additional listings show the structures in which the main entry word or variant is introduced. Both variants and structures are listed in the order in which they are introduced.

Listings in boldface refer to certain categories of words or expressions that have been introduced as a group. (The boldface words themselves, however, are not part of the student's vocabulary.)

| Unit or Lesson | Main Entries, with Variants and Structures | | | | |
|---|---|---|---|---|---|
| A | a | A | are | 2 | arm |
| 9 | afternoon | | You are (name). | 9 | at |
| | in the afternoon | | You're (name). | | at home |
| A | am | | You're a teacher. | | at work |
| | I am (name). | C | These are books. | | at church |
| | I'm (name). | D | We are students. | | at the river |
| | I'm a student. | | You are students. | | at the pet shop |
| F | Am I a teacher? | | They are students. | 9 | at noon |
| | Yes, I am. | F | Are you a student? | | at six o'clock |
| | No, I'm not. | | Are we students? | | at night |
| 2 | I'm walking. | | Are you students? | 11 | at (street address) |
| 7 | Am I going home? | | Are they students? | 11 | at 5:30 |
| 8 | I'm not going home. | | Yes, we are. | 3 | August |
| F | American | | Yes, you are. | 4 | banana |
| | I'm American. | | Yes, they are. | — | be |
| 2 | and | | No, we aren't. | | *See* am, are, is |
| | I have a book and a pen. | | No, you aren't. | 7 | bed |
| 5 | Bob looks at Ann and me. | | No, they aren't. | | going to bed |
| 10 | Glenn and Ann are camping. | 2 | You're walking. | 4 | big |
| 8 | **Animals (Pets)** | 7 | We are going home. | 1 | bird |
| 1 | Ann | | You are going home. | B | black |
| 10 | any | | They are going home. | B | blackboard |
| | I don't have any apples. | | Are we going home? | B | blue |
| | I don't have any bread. | | Are you going home? | E | Bob |
| 4 | apple | | Are they going home? | 2 | **Body, Parts of** |
| 3 | April | 8 | We aren't going home. | A | book |
| | | | You aren't going home. | 5 | box |
| | | | They aren't going home. | B | boy |

| | | | | | |
|---|---|---|---|---|---|
| **4** | bread | **3** | December | **2** | eye |
| **9** | breakfast | **A** | desk | **D** | factory worker |
| | have breakfast | **5** | dime | **6** | family |
| **6** | brother | **9** | dinner | **6** | **Family Relationships** |
| **B** | brown | **1** | dish | **6** | father |
| **4** | butter | **6** | do | **3** | February |
| **5** | buy . . . for | | Do I have a book? | **2** | finger |
| | I buy the book for a quarter. | | Do we have a book? | **1** | fish (noun) |
| **5** | buys for | | Do you have a book? | **—** | fish (verb) |
| **—** | camp (verb) | | Do they have a book? | **7** | fishing |
| **10** | camping | | Yes, I do. | **11** | go fishing |
| **11** | go camping | | Yes, you do. | **4** | **Food Items** |
| **8** | cat | | No, I don't. | **2** | foot |
| **5** | cent | | No, you don't. | **1** | Friday |
| | ten cents | | Does he have a brother? | **F** | from |
| **A** | chair | | Does she have a sister? | | I'm from Spain. |
| **11** | cheese | | Yes, he does. | **F** | German |
| **D** | child | | Yes, she does. | **F** | Germany |
| | child | | No, he doesn't. | **—** | get |
| | children | | No, she doesn't. | **4** | gets . . . for |
| **F** | China | **8** | I don't have a dog. | | Bob gets an apple |
| **F** | Chinese | | We don't have a dog. | | for the boy. |
| **7** | church | | You don't have a dog. | **9** | get up |
| | going to church | | They don't have a dog. | **9** | get dressed |
| **7** | class | | He doesn't have a dog. | **B** | girl |
| | going to class | | She doesn't have a dog. | **—** | give |
| **11** | I'm having a class now. | | It doesn't open. | **4** | gives . . . to |
| **B** | clock | **D** | doctor | | Bob gives an apple |
| **—** | close | **8** | dog | | to the boy. |
| **2** | closing | **5** | dollar | **6** | give . . . to |
| **4** | coffee | **C** | door | **10** | giving . . . to |
| **4** | cold | **7** | downtown | **11** | glass of |
| **B** | **Colors** | | going downtown | | glass of milk |
| | This is red. | **—** | drink | | glass of water |
| | This is a red pen. | **4** | drinking | **7** | Glenn |
| **F** | **Countries** | **2** | ear | **—** | go |
| | I'm from Spain. | **—** | eat | **7** | going to bed |
| **1** | cup | **4** | eating | | going to class |
| **11** | cup of | **4** | egg | | going to church |
| | cup of coffee | **10** | English | | going to work |
| | cup of soup | | speaking English | **9** | go |
| **6** | daughter | | teaching English | | go shopping |
| **11** | day | **C** | eraser | **11** | go camping |
| | every day | **11** | every | | go fishing |
| **1** | **Days of the Week** | | every day | | go swimming |
| | It's Sunday. | | every morning | **11** | goes |
| | | | every Sunday | **B** | green |
| | | | every August | **5** | half dollar |

| Unit or Lesson | Main Entries with Variants and Structures | | | | |
|---|---|---|---|---|---|
| 1 | hand | | | | |
| 1 | have | | | | |
| | I have a cup. | | | | |
| | You have a cup. | | | | |
| | They have cups. | | | | |
| | The men have cups. | | | | |
| | He has a cup. | | | | |
| | She has a cup. | | | | |
| 6 | We have a son. | | | | |
| | Do I have a book? | | | | |
| | Do we have a book? | | | | |
| | Do you have a book? | | | | |
| | Do they have a book? | | | | |
| | Does he have a book? | | | | |
| | Does she have a book? | | | | |
| | I don't have a dog. | | | | |
| | We don't have a dog. | | | | |
| | You don't have a dog. | | | | |
| | They don't have a dog. | | | | |
| | He doesn't have a dog. | | | | |
| | She doesn't have a dog. | | | | |
| | It doesn't open. | | | | |
| 11 | having | | | | |
| | having breakfast | | | | |
| | having lunch | | | | |
| | having dinner | | | | |
| | having a class | | | | |
| B | he | | | | |
| | He is a boy. | | | | |
| | He's a boy. | | | | |
| E | Is he a doctor? | | | | |
| | Yes, he is. | | | | |
| 1 | He has a cup. | | | | |
| 2 | He's walking. | | | | |
| 3 | He looks at the book. | | | | |
| 6 | Does he have a brother? | | | | |
| 7 | Is he going home? | | | | |
| 8 | He isn't going home. | | | | |
| | He doesn't have a dog. | | | | |
| 11 | He'd like an egg. | | | | |
| 2 | head | | | | |
| 1 | her | | | | |
| | She has her book. | | | | |
| 10 | He's passing the butter to her. | | | | |

| | | | | |
|---|---|---|---|---|
| — | hike (verb) | | | |
| 10 | hiking | | | |
| 7 | Hill (family name) | | | |
| 5 | him | | | |
| | Bob looks at him. | | | |
| 10 | Kim's speaking English to him. | | | |
| 1 | his | | | |
| | He has his book. | | | |
| 7 | home | | | |
| | going home | | | |
| 4 | hot | | | |
| D | housewife | | | |
| | housewife | | | |
| | housewives | | | |
| — | hunt (verb) | | | |
| 10 | hunting | | | |
| 6 | husband | | | |
| A | I | | | |
| | I am (name). | | | |
| | I'm (name). | | | |
| | I'm a student. | | | |
| F | Am I a teacher? | | | |
| | Yes, I am. | | | |
| | No, I'm not. | | | |
| 1 | I have a cup. | | | |
| 2 | I'm walking. | | | |
| 3 | I look at the book. | | | |
| 6 | Do I have a pen? | | | |
| | Yes, I do. | | | |
| | No, I don't. | | | |
| 7 | Am I going home? | | | |
| 8 | I'm not going home. | | | |
| | I don't have a dog. | | | |
| 11 | I'd like an apple. | | | |
| 1 | in | | | |
| | I have a book in my hand. | | | |
| 4 | I put the apple in the dish. | | | |
| 7 | in the river | | | |
| 9 | in (city) | | | |
| | in the morning | | | |
| | in the afternoon | | | |
| 11 | in New York (state) | | | |
| | in the United States | | | |
| | in (country) | | | |
| | in July (month) | | | |

| | | |
|---|---|---|
| 7 | Indian Valley | |
| A | is | |
| | This is a book. | |
| | It is a book. | |
| | It's a book. | |
| B | He is a boy. | |
| | He's a boy. | |
| | She is a girl. | |
| | She's a girl. | |
| E | Is he a student? | |
| | Is she a student? | |
| | Is this a book? | |
| | Yes, he is. | |
| | Yes, she is. | |
| | Yes, it is. | |
| | No, he isn't. | |
| | No, she isn't. | |
| | No, it isn't. | |
| 2 | He's walking. | |
| | She's walking. | |
| 7 | Is he going home? | |
| | Is she going home? | |
| 8 | He isn't going home. | |
| | She isn't going home. | |
| A, B | it | |
| | It is a book. | |
| | It's a book. | |
| E | Yes, it is. | |
| | No, it isn't. | |
| 1 | It's Sunday. | |
| 3 | It's January. | |
| 5 | Bob looks at it. | |
| 8 | It doesn't open. | |
| 9 | It's one o'clock. | |
| 11 | It's 1:15. | |
| | It's 1:30. | |
| 10 | its | |
| | The dog has its ball. | |
| 3 | January | |
| 7 | Jill | |
| 3 | July | |
| — | jump (verb) | |
| 2 | jumping | |
| 7 | jumping rope | |
| 11 | jumps rope | |
| 3 | June | |

| Unit or Lesson | Main Entries with Variants and Structures |
|---|---|

**11** piece of
    piece of bread
    piece of cheese
    piece of meat
    piece of paper

**9, 11** **Place Expressions**

**—** play
**7**     playing ball
**9**     play ball
**11**     plays ball
**F** Poland
**F** Polish
**11** potato
**—** **Pronouns**
**A**     I, you (s.), it
**B**     he, she
**D**     we, you (pl.), they
**1**     my, your (s.), his, her
**5**     me, you (s.), him, her, it; us, you (pl.), them
**10**     its; our, your (pl.), their
**8** pup
**4** put
    I put the apple on the table.
    put down
        I put down the pencil.
**8**     puts
**5** quarter
    This is a quarter.
    The book is a quarter.
**8** Queen (dog's name)
**—** read
**3**     reading
**9**     read
**B** red
**—** repeat
**10**     repeating
**3** river
**8** Robert
**—** run (verb)
**8**     runs
**9**     run
**—** sail (verb)
**10**     sailing

**9** Sam
**11** sandwich
**1** Saturday
**—** sell
**5**     sell . . . for
        I sell the book
        for a quarter.
    sells . . . for
**10**     selling . . . to
        The man is selling the book
        to the girl.
**3** September
**B** she
    She is a girl.
    She's a girl.
**E**     Is she a nurse?
**1**     She has a cup.
**2**     She's walking.
**3**     She looks at the book.
**6**     Does she have a sister?
        Yes, she does.
        No, she doesn't.
**7**     Is she going home?
**8**     She isn't going home.
        She doesn't have a dog.
**11**     She'd like a banana.
**5** shop (noun)
**10** show (verb)
**7** sister
**—** sit
**2**     sitting down
**3** snake
**10** some
    I have some apples.
    I have some bread.
**6** son
**11** soup
**4** sour
**F** Spain
**F** Spanish
**—** speak
**3**     speaking
**10**     speaking English
**11**     speaks
**—** stand
**2**     standing up
**9** street
    (with name of street)
    on York Street

**A** student
**9** study
**4** sugar
**1** Sunday
**4** sweet
**—** swim
**7**     swimming
**11**     go swimming
**A** table
**D** taxi driver
**A** teacher
**—** teach
**10**     teaching English
**Telling Time**
    **On the Hour**
**9**         It's one o'clock.
**11**     **On the Quarter and Half Hour**
        It's 1:15.
        It's 1:30.
        It's 1:45.
**3** tent
**—** thank
**4**     thanks . . . for
        The boy thanks Bob
        for the apple.
**8** that
**10** their
    They have their books.
**5** them
    Bob looks at them.
**10**     The teacher's reading
    the book to them.
**C** these
    These are books.
**D** they
    They are students.
    They're students.
**F**     Are they students?
    Yes, they are.
    No, they aren't.
**1**     They have cups.
**6**     Do they have a son?
**7**     They are going home.
    Are they going home?
**8**     They aren't going home.
    They don't have a dog.
**11**     They'd like a sandwich.

**A**   this
     This is a book.

**8**   those
**1**   Thursday
**9, 11**   **Time Expressions**
**7**   to (with *going*)

     She is going to work.
     She is going to class.
     She is going to church.
     She is going to bed.

**—**   to (with indirect object)

**4**   Bob gives an apple to the boy.

**10**   She is giving the book
       to the student.
   She is selling the book
       to the student.
   She is showing the book
       to the student.
   She is speaking English
       to the student.
   She is teaching English
       to the student.
   She is repeating the numbers
       to the student.

**1**   Tuesday
**9**   Uncle Ted
**F**   (the) United States
**5**   us
     Bob looks at us.

**3**   valley
**9**   Van
**D**   waiter
**D**   waitress
**—**   walk (verb)
**2**     walking
**4**   water
**D**   we
     We are students.
     We're students.

**F**    Are we students?
     Yes, we are.
     No, we aren't.

**6**    We have a son.
     Do we have a book?

**7**    We are going home.
     Are we going home?

**8**    We aren't going home.
     We don't have a dog.

**11**   We'd like a potato.

**1**   Wednesday
**10**   what
     What does Jill have?
     What does _____ mean?
     What is Sam doing?

**9**   when
     When do you study?

**9**   where
     Where is Sam?
     Where do you live?

**B**   white
**10**   who
     Who is she giving the pen to?

**10**   whose
     Whose book is this?
     Whose book do you have?

**6**   wife
**9**   Will (man's name)
**C**   window
**3**   wing
**D**   woman
     woman
     women

**11**   would like
     I'd like a glass of milk.
     I'd like an apple.
     You'd like
     He'd like
     She'd like
     We'd like
     They'd like

**7**   work
     going to work

**—**   write
**2**     writing
**3**   yell
     yells
     yelling

**B**   yellow

**E**   yes
     Yes, it is.

**F**     Yes, I am.
     Yes, you are.
     Yes, we are.
     Yes, they are.

**5**     Yes, he's looking at me.

**6**     Yes, I do.
     Yes, you do.
     Yes, she does.

**6, 7**   Yes, he is.
     Yes, she is.

**9**   York
     on York Street

**A**   you
     you (s.)
       You are (name).
       You're (name).
       You're a teacher.

**D**    you (pl.)
       You are students.

**F**    Are you a student?
     Are you students?
     Yes, you are.
     No, you aren't.

**1**    You have a cup.

**2**    You're walking.

**3**    You look at the book.

**5**    Bob looks at you. (s., pl.)

**6**    Do you have a book?
     Yes, you do.
     No, you don't.

**7**    You are going home.
     Are you going home?

**8**    You aren't going home.
     You don't have a dog.

**1**    your
     your (s.)
       You have your book.

**10**   your (pl.)
       You have your books.

**5**    zipper

Also see the Addendum to the Conversation
Skills Word List on the following page.

## Addendum to Conversation Skills Word List

| Unit or Lesson | Main Entries with Variants and Structures |
|---|---|
| 13 | address |
| 6 | Cal |
| 6 | Dan |
| 6 | Ed |
| 6 | Fran |
| | **Numbers** |
| 11 | 0 |
| 11 | 1,000 |
| 11 | of |
| |     cup of coffee |
| 4 | says |
| |     He says thank you. |
| — | show |
| 10 |     showing |
| |         She is showing the book |
| |         to the student. |
| 11 | telephone number |
| 13 | zip code |
| — | visit |
| 9 |     visiting |
| |         The boys are visiting |
| |         Uncle Ted |

## Vocabulary from *In the Valley*

The following vocabulary items are introduced in connection with the correlated reader *In the Valley.*

    hurt
        My leg is hurt.

    look for
        They look for the egg.

    nest

    pack
        pack up
        is packing

    pick apples
    put up a tent
    tells
    under
    wings

# Recognition Items

These recognition items are questions or requests. In the places where they are first used, only the teacher says them. The student is expected to understand and respond to them. The first time you use a recognition item, you should model the response.

Some of the recognition items listed here are taught to the student for production later in this manual; see the Conversation Skills Word List.

The recognition items are listed below in the order in which they occur.

| Lesson | Page | |
|---|---|---|
| A | 16 (40) | Listen. (Please listen.) |
| A | 18 | What's this? |
| A | 20 (22) | Repeat. (Please repeat.) |
| A | 21 | Listen to _____ . |
| A | 23 | Write _____ . |
| B | 32 | Listen. Are these the Same or Different? |
| C | 38 | What are these? |
| 1 | 67 | What do/does _(you/Ann)_ have? |
| 1 | 67 | What do/does _(you/Ann)_ have in _(your/her)_ hand? |
| 1 | 70 | Say _____ . |
| 1 | 70 (80) | Read. _____ . (Read. / Please read.) |
| 1 | 71 (79) | What's the name (of this letter)? |
| 1 | 71 (79) | What's the sound (of this letter)? |
| 2 | 86 | What are you doing? |
| 2 | 87 | What is _(the man)_ doing? |
| 2 | 90 | Whose _(book)_ is this? |
| 3 | 98 | What month is this? |
| 3 | 103 | _(Jumping)_ begins with what sound? |
| 4 | 107 | What's sweet/sour/big/little/hot/cold? |
| 4 | 108 | What does _(Bob)_ get for _(the boy)_ ? |
| | | What does _(Bob)_ give to _(the boy)_ ? |
| | | What does _(the boy)_ say? |
| | | What does _(the boy)_ thank _(Bob)_ for? |
| 4 | 109 | Pick up _(the pencil)_ . |
| | | Put down _(the pencil)_ . |
| 5 | 120 | What does _(the man)_ do? |
| 5 | 124 | How much is _(the pencil)_ ? |
| 5 | 126 | What are the names of the letters? |
| 5 | 127 | What is the sound of this vowel? |
| | | Please write the vowel. |
| 6 | 138 | What sound does it begin with? |
| 7 | 145 | Where is _(the woman)_ going? |
| 9 | 169 | Who is this? |
| 9 | 170 | What time is it? |
| 9 | 171 | When do you _____ ? |
| | | Where do/does _____ live? |
| | | What street do/does _____ live on? |
| 10 | 189 | What sound does it end with? |
| 11 | 199 | What would you like? |
| 11 | 201 | What is this number? |
| 13 | 213 | Circle _____ . |

# Reading Word List

*Skill Book 1* and its correlated reader *In the Valley* introduce the 163 words listed below, including 122 different words and 41 variants of those words.

Root words are listed as main entries, and variants are listed under them. (If only a variant is introduced, it is listed as a main entry.) Words used only in titles and directions are starred.

The number indicates the lesson in which the word is introduced; the abbreviation *cr* stands for correlated reader.

| | | | | | | | |
|---|---|---|---|---|---|---|---|
| 1 | a | cr | give | 2 | neck | 5 | shop |
| 13 | *Address | 4 | — gives | 8 | Ned | 3 | snake |
| cr | am | 7 | Glenn | cr | nest | 12 | — snakes |
| 4 | an | 9 | going | 12 | no | 9 | street |
| 2 | and | 1 | hand | 13 | not | 9 | Ted |
| 6 | Ann | 1 | has | 11 | number | 11 | — Ted's |
| 4 | apple | 12 | have | 11 | — numbers | 11 | telephone |
| cr | — apples | 4 | he | cr | of | cr | tells |
| 7 | are | 1 | her | 4 | olive | cr | ten |
| 3 | at | 7 | Hill | cr | — olives | 3 | tent |
| 1 | bird | 10 | — Hills | 8 | Oliver | 5 | thank |
| 9 | — birds | cr | — Hill's | 8 | — Oliver's | cr | — thanks |
| cr | — bird's | 5 | him | 9 | on | 1 | the |
| 6 | Bob | 4 | his | 12 | one | 11 | their |
| 5 | box | 1 | *Homework | 8 | Pam | 5 | they |
| 6 | boy | cr | hurt | cr | packs | 1 | this |
| 9 | — boys | 12 | I | cr | — packing | 12 | three |
| 6 | Cal | 1 | in | 2 | pan | 4 | to |
| cr | — Cal's | 7 | Indian | cr | — pans | 12 | two |
| 1 | *Chart | 1 | is | 9 | pet | 9 | Uncle |
| 2 | *Checkup | 7 | Jill | 8 | — pets | cr | under |
| 5 | children | cr | jump | cr | pick | 4 | up |
| 1 | cup | 9 | — jumps | 4 | — picks | 3 | valley |
| cr | — cups | 2 | — jumping | 8 | pup | 9 | Van |
| 6 | Dan | 2 | kicking | 9 | — pups | cr | visit |
| 1 | dish | 7 | Kim | 8 | — pup's | cr | — visits |
| 12 | do | 2 | leg | 4 | puts | cr | — visiting |
| 6 | Ed | 1 | *Lesson | 5 | quarter | 9 | Will |
| 4 | egg | 2 | *Listen | cr | — quarters | cr | wings |
| 12 | — eggs | 11 | live | 8 | Queen | 3 | woman |
| 1 | fish | 7 | — lives | 3 | river | 12 | *words |
| 7 | — fishing | 7 | Liz | 8 | Robert | 2 | *Write |
| 12 | five | 3 | look | cr | — Robert's | 1 | *Writing |
| 5 | for | cr | — looks | cr | run | cr | yell |
| 12 | four | 7 | — looking | 8 | — runs | 3 | — yells |
| 6 | Fran | 2 | man | 9 | Sam | 12 | yes |
| 5 | get | 2 | — man's | 13 | — Sam's | 9 | York |
| 10 | — gets | 8 | Mr. | 6 | says | 6 | you |
| 1 | girl | 8 | Mrs. | cr | sell | 5 | zipper |
| 7 | — girls | 12 | my | 5 | — sells | cr | — zippers |
| 2 | — girl's | 13 | name | 4 | she | | |